DAVOR ROSTUHAR

LOVE

AROUND THE WORLD

KEK

Klub za ekspedicionizam i kulturu

IMPRESUM

Davor Rostuhar: LOVE AROUND THE WORLD
Project by The Club for Expedition and Culture, Zagreb, 2018-2021

Project authors, managers, and creative directors:
Anđela Rostuhar and Davor Rostuhar
Project assistants: Valerija Povalec and Paula Brečak

Text and photographs: Davor Rostuhar
Translator: Ellen Elias-Bursać
Translation proofreader: Eric Bergman

Art and design director: Stjepan Drmić
Graphics and layout editor: Mirjana Mandić
Text editor: Kruno Lokotar
Researcher and fact-checker: Paula Brečak
Consultant: Ivona Lerman
Line editors: Anđela Rostuhar, Paula Brečak, and Ksenija Vujčić
Fixers and interview translators: Zrinka Radić, Abdelrahim Abuwarda,
Amir Kaboli, Baktygul Chockconova, Enrico Michelotto, Anoushka Sharma,
Mehak Saini, Pawan Ranta, Ramdayal Yadav, Sadama Rada, Reiko Naka,
Carlos Cordero, Mezei Dragos Andrei, Barbara Kiere, Goran Mihajlović,
Baritsica Matis, Enrico Callado, Aline Scaglione Dantas, Robert Kaunatjike,
Peter Marampei Nkurrunah, John Paul Kiwanuka, Kennedy Gomma,
Eric Baringo Lemungesi, Chouaib Bubba, Djimrangar Tousde, Michail Kollewijn,
Elleonora Gottardo, Kirsten Marieke, Gustavo Adolfo B, Mary Louise W.
Print: Kerschoffset

Translated from the Croatian edition, Ljubav oko svijeta, 2021
Publisher: The Club for Expedition and Culture, Zagreb, 2021

Printed in Zagreb, May 2021
© Davor Rostuhar, The Club for Expedition and Culture, 2021

A CIP catalogue record for this book is in the Online Catalogue of
the National and University Library in Zagreb as 001100740.
ISBN 978-953-49350-1-9

ACKNOWLEDGMENTS

Our warm thanks to the hundreds of wonderful people around the world who helped us locate engaging collocutors and helped us in so many ways to overcome the various challenges posed by this ambitious project and journey; members of KEK who were the wind in our sails; assistants Valerija and Paula as well as Štef, Mirjana, Kruno, Ivona, and Ksenija, our collaborators on the book, because we know we can always count on them; our dear parents who are always our greatest support; our close friends Miljenka Čogelja and Đuro Gavran who spent hundreds of hours listening patiently to our creative, business, and private issues, diagnosing them accurately and addressing them wisely.

Special thanks to all who agreed to be interviewed, opened their hearts and spoke candidly about their relationships and views on life, giving all of us a chance to better understand the world, life, and love.

NOTE

Because of the large number of people whose names appear in the book, we printed all those whom we interviewed in bold the first time their name appears in each chapter. When a page number appears next to their name, this refers you to the page where they will find the person's photograph. The names of other people who appear in the book, whom we did not interview, are not given in bold. All the people described here are authentic. All the names are their real names, except in two cases, where they chose to use pseudonyms. The Bushman names of !ui and !ao are spelled with an exclamation point to indicate the click sound that is found in their ancient language.

All the photographs in the book were taken by Davor Rostuhar, except those for the last four interviews, which were not possible to record in person because of the coronavirus pandemic. These photographs, at Davor Rostuhar's behest, were taken by:

p. 144: Photograph of Davecat – taken by Davecat

p. 144: Photograph of Chris – taken by Cristoph Kumpa

p. 145: Photograph of Carolina and Thomas – taken by Thomas Boulvin

p. 145: Photograph of Lori and Shawn – taken by Shelby McClain

"What is love?
Is love
universal?"

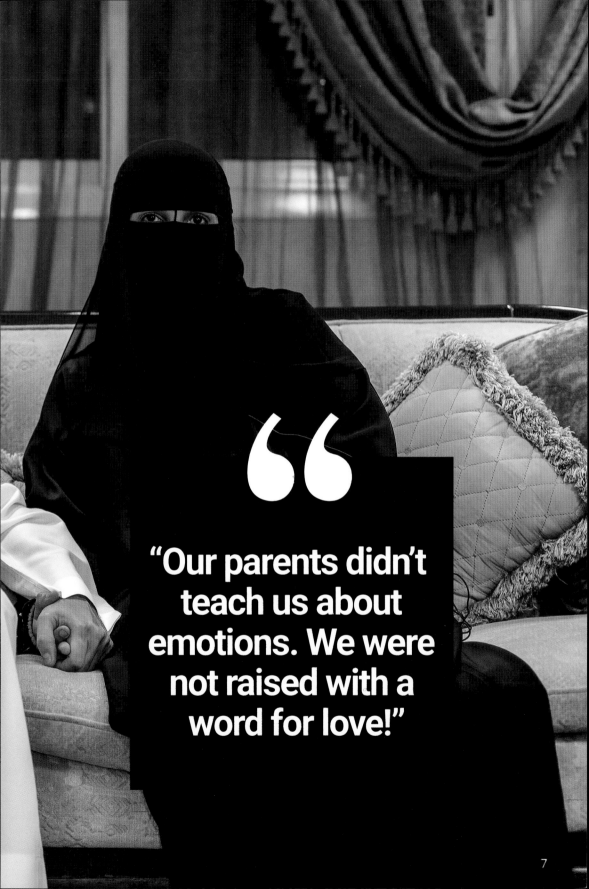

"Our parents didn't teach us about emotions. We were not raised with a word for love!"

"Love is when
we stand,
sit, sleep...
together."

"Love is complicated. But this is the first thing between people. It is what keeps them together."

P. 4

Davor (37) and Anđela (33) from Croatia became engaged in the Antarctic and decided to spend a year after their wedding on their honeymoon traveling around the world, exploring what love is and whether it is universal. "We wondered if the two of us would have come to love each other as much as we do if we'd been born into a different culture, in some other time and space?" says Anđela. "Would our love have been the same or different? Is love what keeps us together and creates the illusion that we too will overcome all the problems that will inevitably arise along the way? Is our relationship simply the outcome of a decision, practical affinities, and the sharing of similar values? Or is something more going on here?"

P. 6

Fahad (60) and Tamadur (55) from Saudi Arabia say they only recently began talking about emotions, when their country began to open slowly toward the rest of the world. "Our parents weren't educated, they taught us nothing about emotions. We grew up without ever knowing the word 'love,'" says Fahad. "The times are changing now. And that's as it should be. Our children are already living a modern life, and we, too, are changing." Women are no longer required to wear a niqab in Saudi Arabia, but Tamadur decided she would continue with that tradition and she is grateful to Fahad for respecting her decision. "Love is respect. Without respect there can be no love," says Tamadur.

P. 8

Ghasiram (60) and Kamla (50) from India are members of the Bopa nomadic people who wander with their camels around the Rajasthan deserts and practice one of the most extreme forms of forced arranged marriages. The marriages are arranged by the parents, most often when the couple are still children, and sometimes even before they're born. Ghasiram was fifteen when he married Kamla, who was only five, so she can hardly remember the wedding. "We didn't start living together right away!" says Ghasiram. "We had to wait to grow up, so everything could be ready for the *muklawa* ceremony. Only after the *muklawa* could we begin to live together and build a family. Now we have nine children and many, many grandchildren. And all is good."

P. 10

Uatongota (32), Kauarende (56) and Uazeupara (52) from Namibia are members of the Himba people who live from livestock husbandry and allow polygyny. "Why do I have two wives? Because with only one I would be very lonely. When one of them leaves the village to visit her parents, for instance, how can I then take care of both the children and the animals on my own? I would have to go to the well for water for them, to cook for them…. That is very difficult. That is why one needs to have two wives!"

1

WHAT IS LOVE?

I stood alone on the deck of an icebreaker, making its way through the frozen ocean waters along the Antarctic coast. The beauty of the ice-bound landscape on all sides and a fear of the unknown overwhelmed me.

Steep, black mountains loomed over the shore and blocked my view of where I was headed, so I could only imagine what mainland Antarctica— that endless barren ice-bound plain— might look like. In a few days' time I'd be setting out on my own across those untamed expanses without any support—except Anđela's encouragement—and proceed to walk across the 1,200 kilometers from the shores of the Antarctic to the South Pole. Only 23 people had done this before me. I was thrilled, as I have been whenever I've embarked on one of my expeditions, when I've braved the unknown. But *that* is not what scared me.

The ship maneuvered its way into the bay and slowed, seeking a place to drop anchor among the ice floes where it would spend the sunlit night. I felt the perfect moment was upon us for what I'd been dreaming of my whole life and had been planning for over a year: I'd found my safe haven and was ready to harbor.

PREVIOUS PAGE
BAY OF LOVE, ANTARCTICA

I went looking for Anđela and asked her to come up onto the deck with me to witness the grandeur of nature. We'd been together by then for three years. From the very beginning, both of us had felt this was it. She and I were a perfect fit. We both felt sure we'd commit to each other, marry, start a family. We'd brave the unknown together for the rest of our lives. In my pocket, I grasped the ring in sweaty fingers, hoping I wouldn't drop it into the icy water of the bay when I took it from my pocket and welcomed her to join me at the railing.

I was in love. I'd found everything in Anđela I'd ever hoped for in a partner. But I felt compelled to weigh the objective chances we had for a relationship that would last for the rest of our lives. She and I had both been through several failed relationships. The time had come for us to build one that would last. What horrified me was the very possibility of a negative response to a question I'd always found troubling: can the vast chasm that lies between us ever be bridged?

As far as what is and what isn't possible, my track record is clear. Most of what I have undertaken on my own has prospered. My projects that have relied on others have not. It would be naïve to believe that other people are to blame for this. I am more inclined to think the problem lies with me or with the times and world we live in. My fear, while I fingered the sweaty engagement ring in my pocket, was whether we'd be able to preserve our love once the infatuation had run its course, once we'd allowed the similarities that bind us to lose their hold and let the differences between us push us to the verge of madness.

This is the real unknown, I thought, and I felt I was ready to embark on the greatest adventure of my life. I took Anđela by the hand, drew the ring from my pocket, and knelt before her....

— — —

We went down to the icebreaker's dining room and ordered a bottle of their finest wine to celebrate. In less than ten minutes from the moment Anđela had agreed for us to spend our lives together, we were already busy making plans for our honeymoon.

A passion for travel has been our most powerful bond. I have dedicated my life to travel and expeditions and over two decades, starting from when I was sixteen, I have traveled through a hundred countries, led expeditions to the most remote jungles of Papua New Guinea and the Amazon, cycled from Croatia to Egypt, ridden a motorcycle across half of Africa, and reported from war zones in Palestine and Afghanistan, I've covered locations from the Himalayas to the Sahara for *National Geographic*, climbed icy mountains, rafted down wild rivers, kayaked across oceans, mapped the last realms of virgin wilderness, and recently I've been on polar expeditions that have taken me to the far north of Siberia, Scandinavia, and Greenland, and now, finally, to the Antarctic.

I'd met Anđela three years before when she responded to a job offer I'd posted. She hadn't been working with me long when the sparks began to fly between us. After work, we'd spend hours in long conversations and bit by bit discovered that we have surprisingly similar views of the world. From the very start, travel was what most compelled us.

Anđela has also traveled widely. She hitchhiked on her own around Iran, backpacked through Southeast Asia, volunteered for a year in Kenya…. I was most impressed by her perception of the world and the ways she found to reconcile its irreconcilable contradictions. She is what I have always wanted to be—a master of all worlds. She is able to enjoy sheer luxury or sleep rough on the pavement. She knows how to use all the perquisites of freedom and leisure, but she also relishes work, feeling useful, creative. She'd built her own autonomy and integrity, yet at the same time, she loves helping and serving other people and higher goals. She'd developed a skillful balance between the traditional and the modern, taking only the best from both worlds. She loves bringing joy to the people around her, but, at the same time, she doesn't feel that love needs to be unconditional. She knows the measure of her worth and demands what she deserves without compromise, but on her balance sheet of gains and losses, she sees no problems that could invalidate the viability of love. Right there, all that I'd ever been looking for in a single person.

Intoxicated by all of this, on our first morning when we woke up together, I said:

"I love you. You'll be the mother of my children."

How many times before had she and I woken up next to someone else for the first time, and all we had wished for was to slip instantly into acute amnesia. How pretentious and pathetic it is to utter a sentiment like this, even to a person you're head over heels in love with and even if you're feeling that no morning will ever dawn in which you'll long to escape them. But it was as if Anđela and I had instantly taken hold of the very wheel of life, we could see the matrix, see life as it truly is—and see ourselves, together, in that life. We were not inclined to play games.

"I know," she said, looking me straight in the eyes, "I do know."

We spent the next two and a half years learning how to work and live together. To tease out the thin, blurred line between work and private life and strike a balance between them. Anđela came into my life just as I was beginning my *Polar Dream* project, and the help she provided went far beyond anything I could have hoped for. Had she not pushed me through the rigorous preparations full of challenges and setbacks, had she not been there by my side when I staggered under the weight of my dreams, chances are I would have never made it to the Antarctic.

When I uncorked the bottle of wine at the restaurant on the icebreaker, I felt a welling of gratitude for all she'd done for me and, at the same time, an obligation to give her something in return.

"Maybe our honeymoon can last for a whole year and we can go wherever we like!" I said, and that inspired us to list all the parts of the world we'd like to visit together.

"I want to give you a whole year," I said, feeling the weight of my words. All my life I'd been working on my own story, I'd been at the center of my own universe, and I knew that sooner or later I'd want to put another person ahead of myself. To serve a person I loved. Nobody deserved this more than Anđela. But would I be able to? I wondered. Was this even possible?

"If what you'd like is for us to go to a desert island and spend the year there—we'll do it. If you'd like us to backpack our way around the world—let's. Anything is possible! But I do have an idea…" I said, aware I might disrupt the always delicate balance between our working and private lives. I didn't want to ruin the magic with a business proposition, but I was already more confident, because I'd gotten to know her. I'd learned that she prefers to not work on weekends or evenings, she doesn't take work with her on vacations and is far better at keeping the two parts of her life separate than I am, but, like me, after a few days of resting she is eager for work, action, creativity….

"I have always wanted to explore the nature of love around the world," I went on. "To choose 10, 20, 30 of the most varied cultures and talk with people who live there about love, relationships. What is love? Is it universal? These are the questions I would like to explore. I've been holding off on this until I found the person to spend my life with. Until now, I haven't been ready, but now I am. So, if you'd rather not work while we're on our honeymoon I will completely understand. Like I said, we can spend the year on a desert island. Say the word."

"Sure!" she answered after giving it some thought. "Love around the world! I like that idea, why we could…."

And we were off and running, exploring ideas: when we come home from the Antarctic we'll give ourselves a year, put together and publish the *Polar Dream* book and movie, we'll tour Croatia and neighboring countries, hold a million lectures, sell books and pull together the funds we need for the new project; we'll plan and hold our wedding and get everything lined up for a grand trip around the grand world. And right there and then, we threw our-selves into the planning: as much as we possibly could, we'd work to approach a cross section of humanity, country to country, in all its fullness. We'd look at a wide range of cultures representing different stages of human society: hunt-er-gatherers, agriculturalists and pastoralists, nomads, and an array of tradi-tional cultures, but also modern, technologically progressive communities, the whole spectrum. We'd visit each of the continents, we enthused, survey all the major regions, the deserts and jungles, the mountains and the islands scattered across the oceans, the big cities and the villages off the beaten track, and we would try to find people who belonged to all possible strata of society, all the major world religions, the rich and the poor, the healthy and the ill, the known and the unknown, people who are happily in love and those who suffer from serial broken hearts, everyone, everyone….

We'll put the same questions, more or less, to all of them, we agreed: how they met, what they hope from each other and their relationship, their chal-lenges and how they address them, where their ideas about love come from, what love means to them…. And we'll record their answers, of course, col-lect material and impressions for a book and lecture and documentary film. Meanwhile, we'll pore over the academic literature: psychology, sociology, anthropology, philosophy, history.... We'll reach out to leading scientists and scholars in each of these disciplines and ask them to talk with us about recent insights in the scientific study of love.

Anđela and I love learning things. Guided by the ancient imperative 'know thyself,' both of us seek knowledge through working on ourselves and through world travel. I tend to look to books for insight, while Anđela has an ear and feel for people, so we thought our different strengths would mean we'd complement each other well and make a strong team for this project. In the cultures where the lives of men and women are more segregated, she'd have easier access to the women's point of view, while I'd be able to approach the men. Both of us had met people on our earlier travels who were living in a variety of relationships, and both of us had already been wondering whether they, too, felt bound by love. More generally, is love the central connective tissue of humankind? Would the two of us have come to love each other as much as we do if we'd been born into a different culture?

So, what is love anyway? An emotion? A construct? A decision? Is it something natural, inborn in all of us, or is it something learned through nurture? I had come across literature that describes romantic love as a product of modern Western culture, hence not universal. And I had already come to know people whose marriages had been arranged for them by their parents, and others who'd entered into relationships for reasons of convenience and practicality. Yet when I visited indigenous communities whose way of life is profoundly different from ours, I had seen sparks flying between couples who looked as in love as Anđela and I are.

For both Anđela and me, love is one of our key values. Neither of us can imagine a fulfilling life without a happy, loving relationship. And both she and I felt that our lives would only be worthwhile once we'd entered into a meaningful bond with a partner whose qualities we admire and who shares and reciprocates our love. We find ourselves wondering where this attitude comes from. Why do people differ in how they think about love in different parts of the world? Is love one of the most important values for everyone or is it not?

What we now feel for one another—passion, respect, understanding, care— will these evaporate or will they last and grow? What lies ahead of *us* on the life path we have just agreed to follow? Surely there will be bumps in the road ahead. We'll be faced with challenges. Will we be able to overcome them? Will love help us? Is love the meaning of life? What is love?

— — —

We effused at the restaurant below decks on board the icebreaker, and the conversation continued over the next days while we were navigating in small craft among the colossal ice floes, walking among huge colonies of penguins, perched on the very edge of the ice-bound continent and watching the sun that never drops below the horizon during summer. Then we said our good-byes. Off I went on my trek, and for 47 days I made my way from the Antarctic coast to the South Pole. Every evening when I put up my tent and crawled into my snug sleeping bag, I'd call Anđela on my satellite phone. Then we'd pick up our conversation, planning, dreaming, brainstorming…. When we returned home to Zagreb, we embarked on exhaustive research into the phenomenon of love, laying the groundwork for our long trip. We resolved to spend all of 2019 traveling, from the first day to the last.

Our trip began, symbolically, in Paris, and then we went on to Oman, Saudi Arabia, Iran. From there we went to Kyrgyzstan, India, the Maldives, China, Japan. After five months in Asia, we went on to Oceania and traveled to Palau, the Solomon Islands, and New Zealand. Then we flew across the Pacific to South America where we visited Chile, Bolivia, Columbia, and Brazil, then off to Africa where we explored love-related customs in Namibia, Botswana, Zambia, Kenya, and Chad. From Africa we crossed over to Costa Rica and spent the last two months of our trip in the United States. We left Europe for the end, thinking the European interviews would be easy to conduct from our home base. For a time, we were slowed by the coronavirus pandemic, which paralyzed the entire world in 2020. When the dangers from the COVID situation lessened, we were able to hop over to Germany and Italy. We also carried out several interviews at home in Croatia. We conducted the last four interviews remotely, because the second wave of the pandemic prevented us from holding them in person. In total, we conducted 120 interviews in 30 languages.

Both Anđela and I circled the Earth for the first time. Our research was not limited to interviews with couples. It also included a study of the academic literature, conversations with leading scientists and scholars, and, probably most importantly, an analysis of our own relationship. Since our theme is vast and complex and touches on almost every facet of life, I will lend no credence to the seductive notion that our trip's chronology should govern the logic of the narrative. Instead, I'll jump from country to country, from example to example, as the story dictates.

In the end, the story is what matters most. And this, in any case, is not just any old story. This is the story of love.

2

THE LANGUAGE OF LOVE

Does love exist when a language
has no word for it?

"What is love?" asked 57-year-old Fahad with a quizzical look, repeating the question we'd just asked. We were interviewing him with his slightly younger wife Tamadur [p. 6] at their home in Riyadh, the capital city of Saudi Arabia.

We were very interested to hear what he'd have to say, because they were the first traditional couple that agreed to be filmed. **Fahad** sat on the sofa in front of the camera, his long white *thobe*[1] covering his whole body from his shoulders to the floor. **Tamadur** sat almost motionless next to him, her head and face covered by a black niqab[2] and her neck to the soles of her feet covered by a black *abaya*[3]. All we could see of her were her eyes. "To be frank, that word, love, was never spoken. We never used that word, even when talking about wedlock. Our parents were not educated, they didn't teach us about emotions. We were not raised with a thing called love."

At the very beginning of our journey, we realized that one of the greatest challenges was going to be communicating with the couples we interviewed. We chose to speak with all of them in their own language, through an interpreter, because we

PREVIOUS PAGE
TOURISTS AT LUGU LAKE, CHINA

felt this would be the best way for them to express themselves with candor. Even in cases in which they were able to speak one of the world languages we spoke, we insisted on professional interpreters. Still, right from the start there were problems.

"Love… that can't be expressed in words," said **Alex** in Paris [p. 111].

"Love doesn't come from words but from the heart," said **Nabila** in Oman [p. 110].

"Whatever I say, it isn't complete," said **Fariba** in Iran [p. 286].

Love is an emotion, love is not an emotion; love is the fireworks at the beginning of a relationship, love is the serenity that comes later.… One after another, there were different answers, and they did not just show us that people have different opinions concerning love, but that the word used for love means different things to different people.

Sometimes, the problem turned out to be one of translation. Or so it seemed to us, when, for instance, we interviewed **Ghasiram** and **Khamla** [p. 8], Bopa nomads who wander the deserts of India's Rajasthan on camels and sometimes arrange for the marriages of their children before they're even born. Whiskered Ghasiram started enumerating what love is with confidence: "It's when we are together, when we stand, sit, sleep…" Submissive Khamla, seated below him, chimed in and continued the series: "…eat, drink, sleep, stand.…"

Sometimes, the problem was perhaps not in the translation but in us and our preconceived notion of what love should be.

"Love starts with a good relationship grounded in respect," said **Elmira** from a small village in the heart of Kyrgyzstan, loosely clasping her husband **Melis**'s [p. 124] hand. They seemed to be a harmonious, peaceful couple, but I did wonder what she was talking about, since a little earlier she'd told us that her relationship with Melis began when he kidnapped her. With a group of friends, he'd snatched her from her student life in the capital city and kept her with him in the village until she agreed to stay.

Young **Shabnam** [p. 259] from Agra in India, the city famed for the Taj Mahal, the magnificent monument to love, told us she knows nothing about love and can't imagine loving anyone ever, because when she was 15 a man tried to take advantage of her, and when she rebuffed him—he splashed her with acid, which permanently disfigured her face.

During the first months of our journey we came to see that the notion of love and what it entails are experienced in extremely different ways. If Elmira says she loves a man who kidnapped her, but Shabnam cannot imagine what love is after the trauma she endured, could these conversations be about the same thing? Since Fahad and Tamadur never heard the word when they were children, and they'd never spoken about emotions, could they even love? Some philosophers and linguists[4] claim that there is nothing beyond language. Language is a tool that organizes our thoughts. Without it, we cannot make sense of the world around us. We cut nature up and organize it into concepts, to which we have attached words so that we can communicate about them. The invention of language is the greatest human accomplishment of all time. Our mastery of language sets us apart among the five million species that live on Earth, and this special position has allowed us an advantage over all other species and the planet we share with them.

But if this is so, if nothing exists outside language, what happens with people who have no word for love? Are they even able to love?

— — —

The Mosuo people live around Lake Lugu on the border between Tibet and Sichuan. We ventured to this distant province of China drawn by rumors that Mosuo culture is currently the closest system in the world to a matriarchate, and that among them, women have the first and last word in choosing their partners. Most scientists agree that there has never been a matriarchate in the full sense of the word, but matrilineal[5] and matrilocal[6] cultures have existed, and the Mosuo are certainly such a culture. In practice, this means that every child who is born remains in its mother's home and inherits its mother's property and status.

A young Mosuo woman lives in a large family home with her parents and brothers and may choose the partner she likes and whom she wishes to spend time with. The man she chooses is allowed to spend the night with her in her room, but in the morning he goes home. This sort of relationship between men and women is called *tiesese*, and it is the closest thing to marriage in Mosuo culture. Mosuo is one of the rare cultures that has not formalized the institution of marriage. If a woman becomes pregnant and bears a child, the father of the child is not fully responsible for the child or the woman. The child is raised by the mother's brother. The biological father may visit his children and continue his relationship with the woman if that is to her liking, but the latter is still limited to nocturnal visits. In the morning, he must return to his home and raise his sister's children. He has no formal or moral obligations—to his wife or his biological children.

Since these outer provinces of China and their unique minority cultures are rapidly being integrated into the dominant Chinese culture, Mosuo customs are changing. Nevertheless, still only a small percentage of Mosuo speak Mandarin, and most older people and some who are younger practice *tiesese*-type relationships. Sadama, our interpreter between the Mosuo language and English, took us to the exotic mountainous area and introduced us to traditional couples who were still practicing *tiesese*. They invited us into their richly carved wooden houses with large central hearths, many of them dressed in ornate traditional attire. They received us into their homes as warmly as only humble people who live from tilling the soil by hand can do. Although they were so shy that they blushed and their gaze dropped to the floor, they readily agreed to be interviewed.

The first interview was with an older couple in one of the typical wooden houses on the shore of Lake Lugu. Seventy-eight-year-old **Daba** told us how she began spending time with **Tsao** [p. 102], a man a little older than she, during the long-ago period when Mao Zedong was in power. At that point there were no Han Chinese near the lake; instead, this was a region inhabited only by ethnic minorities[7] of whom the Mosuo were the most numerous. People were poor and lived off the land, but Daba and Tsao lived well. He always came to her at night and went home in the morning. Their children were raised by her brothers. Daba and Tsao lived for decades in separate households, but in their old age they decided to live together as their world began to change.

We spoke candidly and fluidly, and I was proud that we were managing to communicate so well with members of a culture that is so different from ours. Until the moment when the question of love was raised.

"We have no word for this," said Sadama, the interpreter.

"Well, but do you have anything similar?" asked Anđela. "Do you have a word that describes the good feelings a man and woman have for each other?"

"No, we have nothing like that," was the firm answer.

For us this was a first. What crossed my mind was that perhaps the nomads from Rajasthan also had no word for love. This new information fell into place and helped several other things to make sense. Our interpreter in Rajasthan had seemed inclined to improvise and muddy the waters. Maybe she'd been trying to explain things to the interviewees, but she hadn't succeeded, because they responded by saying that loving was what they were doing when they slept, ate, sat, and stood….

"Do you have a word for 'emotions,' for 'to feel'?" Anđela was looking for another point of access to the subject.

"We do!"

"Can you then ask the lady what she feels for her partner?"

Daba was seated facing the camera inside their roomy wooden house, while Tsao was a little further back, behind her left shoulder. Both of them were sitting on chairs, but their body language was completely different. He was all twisted, sitting at a tilt as if at any moment he'd vanish from the viewer. His spine was bent under the weight of age, while she sat upright, calmly dominating the scene, radiating an invisible strength. She held a prayer wheel on her lap and slowly rotated it in her hands, ever serene. So I was startled when she laughed at Sadama's question.

"I have no feelings for him at all."

— — —

Can peoples who have no word for love even grasp the concept? We wanted to speak about this with someone who has considered the question seriously. Although some philosophers and linguists do assert that there is nothing outside of language, this is not, currently, the prevailing view. Today, most who are informed about the issue agree that language does not define the limits of what we can conceptualize and know. We sought help with understanding this from one of the world's leading linguists, Dr. **Anna Wierzbicka**, an 82-year-old Pole who has been living for half a century in Australia.

"Not everything comes to us through language. We are born with some concepts, which are hardwired. Of course, the child has to learn the word to connect to the concept, but the concepts are there. If they were not there, you couldn't teach them. For example, concepts such as *you* and *I*. These can be found in all languages. You have to know them before you can learn a language; or concepts like: *I know, I think, I want, I feel….* These don't come from language; we are born with them."

Anna Wierzbicka's greatest contribution to science has been her work compiling a *natural semantic metalanguage*. This is a universal language consisting of 64 words or concepts, which Wierzbicka, working with collaborators, has found in all known languages. Using this metalanguage one can communicate almost everything, even difficult abstract concepts.

"How does the word 'love' fit into this metalanguage?" I asked her.

"First of all, love is an abstract noun. It is far better to talk about the verb— to love. When I say, 'I love you,' I am actually saying several things: *I often think about you. When I think about you, I feel something, I often feel something. Because of this, I want to do many things. I want to do good things for you.* That can be translated into all the languages of the world."

"Good, but why then do many languages have a word for love, while others, like the Mosuo language, don't?"

"*Most* languages don't have a word for love. You should not be asking why people don't have a word for love. You should ask why do *we* have it? Just because a language hasn't encoded a word that explains a certain emotion, this doesn't mean that their speakers are unable to perceive this as an emotion or talk about it. This only means that their culture hasn't ascribed *meaning* to this emotion, and hence has not produced a word for it."

"Does this mean that love is not universal?"

"Whatever one thinks about the significance of love, it is an illusion to think that it is a universal, natural, or basic human concept. In many cultures around the world a mother feels something very good towards her child. I think this is probably universal. But love between a man and a woman varies far more from one culture to the next. Even in Ancient Greek they didn't have a word like love. They didn't think about this the way we think about it today."

The ancient Greeks had many more words for love than most modern languages do today, but none of them are about the kind of love we are researching. *Philia* was the most valued kind of love, love for the members of one's family and the state, more a love between friends than romantic love. *Eros* refers to sexual passion, lust, love for the external, for the physical. The Greeks valued beauty, but they didn't always consider *eros* to be something positive—they even thought that it could be dangerous, because it can strip away a person's self-control. Aristotle said that we outgrow *eros* in youth, while in adulthood we base our relationships, and marriage, on *philia*, and Plato said that *eros* and *philia* complement each other, that one grows from the other. *Agape* is something like unconditional love, a love that requires nothing in return, but it applies more to love of the gods or the love of the gods for humankind. *Pragma* is pragmatic, mature love founded on compromises, on effort and shared interests. *Ludus* is playful, immature love, flirtatious, youthful. *Storge* is a kind of empathy, most often the love shared by parents and their children. *Philautia* is love for oneself, *xenia* is love for a guest, *philantropia* is love toward humankind, humanity....

In our project, we are not exploring love for parents, friends, the community, homeland, God, kin, humankind.... But what should we call the love we are investigating? I wondered. If we say it is a love between a man and a woman, then are we to exclude love between same-sex couples? If we claim to be researching love between two people, are we excluding polygamous or polyamorous communities involving more than two people? If we say we're researching romantic or passionate love, are we excluding all those people in serious relationships that include no romance or passion? If we say we're studying love between partners, it sounds as if we're talking about a business relationship. If we say we're looking at sexual love, then what about those who are in asexual relationships or are sexually dysfunctional or they love each other but haven't been intimate for years...?

"Is it even possible to communicate, in language, what it is that we're researching here?" I asked Wierzbicka.

"When there is no other word, you can always try explaining it descriptively," she said.

"But I'm surprised that our languages have not created a word for this kind of love, even though it is one of the highest values in Western cultures."

"Sometimes, a single word can have more than one meaning," she explained. "Perhaps in your case, this is a little confusing and inadequately precise, but what you're describing to me is perhaps one of many meanings of the word *love*."

True. The people we spoke to sometimes understood love to mean only the on-fire phase of intensive infatuation, the falling in love part; at times they used the term to describe the erotic, sexual dimension of love, while at other times, it was used to indicate the more profound attachment that comes in a later stage of a relationship. Sometimes, they considered love to be a relationship full of respect; at other times, they mystified it as a divine power, and yet again, they sometimes denied love as an abstract concept that, they claimed, we'd invented....

As far as concrete concepts are concerned, such as *dog, knife, tree,* or *water,* misunderstandings or dramatically divergent interpretations are less likely. But when we're talking about abstract concepts such as *God, homeland, normal, natural, justice,* or *love,* people can often diverge in their understandings because different people attribute different meanings to these abstract concepts. Even in scientific literature there is a lack of a consensus. The love we're researching is called 'love' by some, 'romantic love' by others, some call it 'passionate love'.... This is why I think that at the beginning of this book we need to clarify at least a little of the terminology so we can more easily work our way through the linguistic chaos.

I like the division of love into three basic components or phases, as proposed by US anthropologist Dr. **Helen Fisher**, one of the leading authorities in the field of the scientific study of love. These three components are rooted in our biology. Fisher says that humankind developed three primary brain systems that guide mating and reproduction:

1) sex drive

2) attraction or romantic love

3) profound attachment

Unlike Wierbicka, Fisher claims that love is, indeed, universal, that it is innate to all people and originated several million years ago as an evolutionary strategy for the better survival of our species. She says that our sex drive motivates us to seek a certain range of possible partners. The romantic side of love or attraction channels our energy towards a single person. And the feelings of profound attachment allow us to stay with that person at least as long as we need to raise a child, until the child makes it through their vulnerable infancy. But if we are to better understand how and why evolution developed such mechanisms, it's worthwhile to look at what happened to love while our species undertook the great trek from the African savannahs to the urban metropolises.

3

THE HISTORY
OF LOVE

What path did love take from the African
savannahs to the urban metropolises?

New York felt like the most fitting place to end our trip. As we traveled around the world, we were, at the same time, traversing...

...a cross-section of the world's cultures in all their diversity, ending, aptly, in the iconic capital city of the West. The last evening in New York, we sat in a restaurant on the top floor of a Manhattan skyscraper, thinking back over all the places and people we'd visited over the year in 24 countries on all the continents. As I took in the spectacular nighttime panorama of New York City, it was as if I'd seen the whole world, and by traveling, we'd embraced it in full. Remembering all the fascinating cultures we'd encountered, I felt as if I'd seen the entire history of humankind. Indeed, our trip didn't just encompass the world; it was also a passage through time, through various stages in the development of human society.

I mused on how to set out the historical overview of that development as simply as possible. Aware of the risks that come from oversimplification, I

PREVIOUS PAGE
KALAHARI DESERT, NAMIBIA

thought it wise to break down our history into three key periods—aboriginal, traditional, and modern—and two major transitions: the Agrarian and Industrial Revolutions.

1) The aboriginal age—prehistory—covers the period when all our ancestors were hunter-gatherers, from the very beginnings of our species to the earliest farmers, the domestication of plants and animals, and the transition to a sedentary way of life.

- **Transition:** Neolithic or Agrarian Revolution[1]

2) The traditional age is a period in which the vast majority of people around the world work in agriculture and animal husbandry, and their lives are almost entirely structured by religion.

- **Transition:** Industrial Revolution[2]

3) The modern age is a period in which the impact of religion in the structuring of human lives is weakened, and there is a sudden rise in science, technology, education, and attention to public health.

It is important to note that all human societies didn't develop at the same pace. The Agrarian Revolution occurred independently in several places: first, 11,000 years ago in Mesopotamia; then 9,000 years ago in China and New Guinea; then 5,000 years ago in Mexico, the Andes, and Sub-Saharan Africa; and 3,000 years ago in North America. From there, it spread in all directions, but, depending on the environment and culture, this happened more rapidly in some places than others, and some people embraced the new changes while others held on to their old ways, the hunter-gatherer way of life.

The same applies to the Industrial Revolution: it first took place in Europe in the 18th century and only reached some parts of the world in the 19th or 20th centuries. There are tribes of hunter-gatherers who only experienced their first contact with the rest of the world in the 20th century, so they leap-frogged the more gradual transition that other regions went through. What had taken Western culture 10,000 years, they went through in one or two generations. What has always fascinated me as a traveler, and particularly when Anđela and I were celebrating the end of our grand tour, is that we are now living at a time when the entire span of the diversity of human societies can still be found; meanwhile, travel to the farthest corners of the Earth where all these communities still exist has never been easier, less expensive, faster, and safer. In the future, people may find travel even easier, but soon they will no longer be able to witness the extraordinary range of the cultural diversity of our species as it irretrievably disappears as local cultures merge into the larger global culture.

In this day and age on our planet, there are still societies separated by hundreds and even thousands of years of history. I am astonished to think that in the 21st century several tribes of hunter-gatherers still walk the planet. A glimpse into their life is a glimpse into the lives of human beings as they were during the first and longest period of our prehistory—what I call the 'aboriginal age.' In two of the places we visited, we were able to view that ancient world. One such place was in the heart of the Amazon, the home of the hunters and gatherers of the Matis people, who had still been living in Stone-Age conditions until 40 years ago when they had their first contact with outsiders. Although the blessings and curses of the modern age have been encroaching with ever greater speed on their lives, many of them still live as hunter-gatherers even today. The men hunt for monkeys and other animals, shooting poisonous darts through long blowguns, while the women gather the fruits of the forest.

Our stay with the Matis was one of the high points of our trip, as well as our stay with Bushmen, the !Kung people in the Kalahari Desert between Namibia and Botswana. Listening to their click language as they talked to us around the fire about love had the ring of ancient times. Many of them lived as hunter-gatherers until only 10-20 years ago, but then their world began to change drastically. Today, they are the victims of one of the many paradoxes of the modern age. The laws of the states in which they live allow foreign hunters, who are able to pay the large fees, to hunt big game, while they—who had wandered the south of the African continent and lived from hunting in the wild for thousands of generations before foreigners arrived—are no longer allowed to hunt.

Observing the Matis and Bushmen and talking with them, I felt as though I were speaking with my ancestors. For similar reasons, anthropologists have studied indigenous peoples who have had no contact with the outside world—a glimpse into their life and culture is a glimpse into the history and nature of humankind. The older the ways of life in societies, the easier it is to study them scientifically. Modern society has become so complex that many scholars say it can no longer be studied scientifically.

— — —

In New York we had the good fortune, honor and privilege to meet with one of the world's preeminent anthropologists, Dr. **Helen Fisher** [p. 388] of the Kinsey Institute. A leading authority, she is one of the most frequently quoted experts on the study of love. We visited her in her apartment next to Central Park on the last working day of 2019. Within minutes, she impressed us with her cordial, receptive, and lively manner. Though 74 years old, she was youthful, full of energy, with a child's curiosity. Her long and illustrious career stood like a buttress behind her responses to our question—firm, concise, and eloquent. We asked her to set out for us her widely accepted theories on the anatomy of love and explain to us her vision of the development of humankind and the evolution of love.

"Roughly four million years ago in East Africa," the friendly scientist told us, "the climate changed and trees disappeared. Our ancestors, hominids, climbed down from the trees and stood upright on two legs. This afforded them additional height so they could more readily spot the predators that hunted them on the savannah. The women could no longer tote children on their backs but had to carry them in their arms, so they were also unable to handle the poles and rocks they'd need for finding sustenance and defending themselves. This meant they needed men to support them with the child-rearing. I don't see how a single male could've protected a whole harem of females, but he could protect one. And so, we began to evolve the human drive to form a pair bond and rear our children as a team. If chimpanzees could talk and take a look at humanity, one of the most remarkable things that they would find is that we bother to pair up at all, since 97 percent of mammals do not pair up to rear their young. But for humans, this became a key turning point. As soon as we began to form into child-rearing couples, the cerebral system for romantic love began to develop in our brains as well as the capacity for profound, long-term attachment."

"Wasn't the size of the brain, or head, part of the problem?" I asked. "Because, as I recall from one of your books, didn't people's heads develop to become disproportionately large in comparison to other species?"

"Yes. At one moment in the evolution of hominids, the brain became so large in proportion to the mother's pelvic birth canal that women began having difficult births. Because of this, they bore their children earlier—and these less-developed, helpless babies needed additional care to survive the first critical days and months. The newborns of other species begin walking, crawling, or flying very quickly. Humans literally bring their offspring into the world unfinished. As the decades turned into centuries and millennia, the first hominid couples stayed together at least as long as their child needed to go through the earliest childhood, the first three to four years, the most vulnerable period of its life."

Until the Agrarian Revolution and the transition from the hunter-gatherer way of life to farming, humans everywhere lived in small, egalitarian groups. This means that they were all more or less equal in terms of power. There were no leaders or an elite who had control over others, and men and women were equal. They had clearly assigned roles, men hunted while women gathered food, but no one was more important than anyone else. The central reason for this is that men and women made equal economic contributions to the household. Women brought the same amount of calories into the family as men did. And resources were not stockpiled, because they couldn't be carried. The hunter-gatherer way of life was not tied to any one place, because the prey would be depleted sooner or later or learn to move on to a place where there was no threat from hunters. This is why hunter-gatherers were most often nomads, and nomads cannot acquire property because they cannot take it with them.

We saw this for ourselves when we met several members of the Matis people and the Bushmen, whom we'll meet again later in the book. In the Matis group [pp. 270-271], there were three men, four women, and as many children. Their only property was a few pots, water skins, blowguns with darts, and hammocks woven from vines, which they strung up between two trees and used for resting or sleeping. All of this could easily be stowed onto a canoe hewn from a single block of wood, and even when they set up camp on a riverbank or went off into the forest to hunt or gather food, they could easily bring with them the children and all their belongings, wrapped in the hammocks that doubled as carrying sacks.

The Bushmen of the Kalahari lived as nomads until recently, so, when they transitioned to their newfound sedentary way of life, they brought with them their disdain for property. The couple we interviewed, **!ui** and **!ao** [p. 384], had the most modest home I have ever visited. Their little dwelling consisted of a few sticks stuck in the ground, a sheet of tin spread over them, a torn mosquito net, and several shabby bedspreads, which were hung as the walls and floor of the dwelling. !ui and !ao also owned a small assortment of ragged clothing, but nothing more. All together, they didn't possess more than ten items. They'd never owned a pair of shoes in their life, nor dishes or cell phones or the other things without which we cannot imagine life today.

— — —

The Agrarian Revolution may be the most significant event in human history after the invention of language. The domestication of plants and animals and animal husbandry allowed humans, for the first time in history, to create and store surplus food in order to mitigate future uncertainty, but this also forced them to live in one place and work harder than they had ever worked before. An outgrowth of this change was the emergence of private ownership for the first time. People began to distinguish what belonged to them from the property of others. They invented writing so that they could list their belongings. Larger-scale conflicts broke out because the stakes were now higher. Food surplus allowed for the formation of elites and leaders. For the first time, a class appeared that didn't need to spend its time producing food, but instead could manage others who did it for them. In order to compensate for and justify these differences in power and to rule people more easily, the elite began to use a powerful new tool—religion.

Power differences also appeared within the family. Children began to be treated as a readily available work force, so women spent all their fertile years pregnant and bearing children, while a man needed to exert control over women's sexuality in order to be sure that his land and livestock would be inherited by his biological children. This led to the emergence of the patriarchy[3].

"Before the Agrarian Revolution, women brought as much food to the table as men did, so they were economically, socially, and sexually as powerful as men," explained Helen Fisher. "But at the moment when we began adapting to a sedentary way of life and farming, and especially once we'd invented the plow, the dynamics between men and women dramatically changed. The role of the man became much more important: moving the rocks, felling the trees, plowing the land, going off to local markets and coming home with the equivalent of money. Women could no longer go off the farm to gather food in the wild, so they worked at less important tasks: they weeded, pruned, prepared evening meals, wove clothing, bore children and cared for them. They bore more and more children, because children were valued as a work force, and this tied women to the home even more."

On our travels, we visited many cultures that still follow this traditional way of life today, and all these cultures are more or less patriarchal, but when Helen Fisher told us this, I thought of the most patriarchal communities we'd met—the Masai and Samburu tribes of Kenya and the Himba of Namibia. All of them live from livestock husbandry—they amass vast herds of cattle and goats for which they need a sizable work force. I was surprised by how openly they spoke of women and children as their chattel, and about how they beat them or cast their wives out should they be deemed unsuitable for any reason.

"When I had one wife, I had only a few head of cattle, but the herd began to grow, so I was able to pay the bride price and take a second wife," said **Shuel** [p. 252] of the Masai tribe from southern Kenya as he laid out his calculations for us. "Both of them bore me children and will bear me more. When the children grow up, they'll be able to tend to the herd, so that means acquiring even more cattle. When I have more cattle, I'll be able to take yet another wife and have even more children. But children are worth more than cattle. Cows are just property but children are wealth. A person who has many children but not a single cow is worth more than a person who has many cows but no children."

Uahaama, an elderly Himba woman, told us about the culmination of the ritual in which she was married to **Kerimunu** [p. 282], who was sitting next to her in their mudbrick dwelling in northern Namibia. "They gave me a new name, Uahaama, anointed my belly with unguents, placed a bucket on my head and sent me to fill it with water, and when I stepped out of the dwelling, he began beating me with switches. This meant that from that day forward he could beat me whenever he chose to." Kerimunu laughed triumphantly at this, and Uahaama seemed to see nothing wrong with it.

Judiah [p. 118], a young girl of the Samburu people from the north of Kenya, ran away from her family and tribe when she was twelve, because they wanted to marry her to an old man who was known to be infected with HIV. We met her at the Umoja women's village that provided shelter for women who were victims of violent husbands or the cruel traditional social system. "When you're married, you never have a moment's peace, because if a goat is missing, your husband beats you," Judiah, then 24, told us, both a little angry and a little resigned. "He blames you even if it's not your fault, just so he can beat you. He doesn't lift a finger, sleeps all day, while you tend to the animals and the children. He doesn't allow the children to go to school so they can tend to the livestock."

The fact that Judiah ran away from that life and found shelter at the women's village shows that the tradition is gradually eroding as the modern age encroaches. Until recently, there was no place where a woman could hide from the violence of the patriarchy. Unlike men, women had few choices or freedoms. They were merely to do what they'd been taught by their elders. They were expected to accept whatever their culture required of them or they'd be outcasts. Any behavior that was anomalous for the community was punished, and conformity was encouraged and praised. The desires and demands of individuals were not as important as the welfare and harmony of the community in which they lived. Each generation worked to repeat everything the previous one had done. In this repetition of familiar patterns, in this renewal of the centuries-old order, people found a sense of security. Emotions weren't accorded much importance, sometimes they were even thought to be wrong. Several generations lived under the same roof, children cared about the stories their grandparents told them, and, through those stories, they learned what was acceptable and what was not. This was how the moral codex was handed down, governed by religion.

In the traditional age, religion interpreted the world and consequently supervised the family and society, the economy and the law.... The life of hunters and gatherers in the aboriginal age was also organized by a form of religion, but it was simpler and less demanding. They were animists—they believed in the spirits of the forest and their ancestors. They also handed myths down through the generations, and these myths explained the origin of the world, relations in the community, and defined both good and evil. They lived, however, in small egalitarian groups, seldom numbering more than ten members, and mythology, or religion, was less of a presence in everyday and social life.

But, when people began living sedentarily in the valleys along large rivers, when they began tilling the soil and creating and amassing stores of food and other products, the population suddenly expanded. Life and cooperation in larger societies required more complex organization, so religions became more complex and stricter in the way they governed people's lives.

"With the transition to farming, all around the world men became more powerful and women more oppressed," said Helen Fisher. "And along with that, all kinds of beliefs evolved—that the woman's place is in the home, that she must be a virgin at marriage, that the husband is the head of the household, and marriage must last until death. As we neared the end of the time during which most people were living from farming and livestock husbandry, as industrial society began, women had moved back into the job market and again acquired more economic, sexual, and social power. The concept of virginity at marriage was abandoned, at least here in the United States. We no longer expect a woman to spend her whole life as a housewife. We no longer expect people to remain in toxic relationships until death do us part. We're shedding 10,000 years of our agrarian background and moving forward to the kind of male-female relationship that we had a million years ago."

— — —

The traditional age lasted, approximately, until the Industrial Revolution, after which began the modern age. Traditional structures then started eroding, and religion began to lose its sway over all aspects of life. The ascent and flourishing of science, technology, education, and health care began…. Ideas about human rights and people's equality were disseminated…. Individuals obtained a wider range of choices and freedoms. A growing amount of attention was paid to emotions. People were no longer under so much pressure to repeat the order of the older generations and fit into society as they found it. Instead, they could seek and discover new possibilities for self-realization. Cities developed and more people moved to them. The notion of a community in which several generations lived under the same roof was on the wane. Grandparents lost their moral authority; their stories no longer guided their grandchildren. The desires and dreams of the individual became more important than the benefit and harmony of the community.

The idea of romantic love coincided with the transition from the traditional to the modern age. Since the priority in the traditional age was the collective, marriages served as unions among families who held the community together. The younger generations learned about what relations should be only from their parents, grandparents, and other community members. Other ways of thinking weren't available to them, because they seldom ventured beyond their community. As the traditional age was waning, books began to appear, which described couples in love who spoke of their emotions, but most of the farming population was illiterate.

With the development of education, literacy was embraced by more people, and as printing technology developed, books became less expensive and more accessible to the general population. The dawn of the Industrial Revolution was the dawn of the era of Romanticism in literature. Romantic novels were wildly popular among members of the middle class, and the protagonists of such novels were individuals who valued personal emotions over entrenched social norms. People began seeking the love these novels promised. With the advent of radio, television, Hollywood movies, and the Internet and social media, the demand for such bliss grew even more vocal. One of the main features of the modern age has been the growing gap between desires and possibilities, dreams and reality, ideas of what life should be and impressions of what life really is....

But just as the traditional age didn't dawn everywhere at the same time, so it was with modernity, even within Western civilization. And furthermore, the most modern societies today are threaded through with elements of tradition, just as the most traditional societies manifest elements of modernity. Traditional mechanisms still influence many of us. But at first glance, it becomes quite clear that the farther someone is from tradition, the more that person is tormented and confused by the paradoxes of the modern age. In New York City, we met with some of the most modern couples of our journey but also with some of the most traditional. In later chapters, we'll come back to them.

For this historical overview, all that remains to be said is that, until recently, science held that emotions and love are not viable subjects for study, because they date only to the modern European culture of Romanticism and were disseminated worldwide via imperialism, colonization, and globalization. Until only a few decades ago, most scientists held that romantic love was not universal and that hunter-gatherers as well as societies based on farming and animal husbandry were oblivious to love before they made contact with European culture.

This paradigm shifted in the 1990s with the work of anthropologist Dr. **William Jankowiak**, who has argued that romantic love has been present in more than 90 percent of cultures. Other disciplines in science also began to put forward evidence for this thesis. The most salient came from a new discipline—neuroscience. The technology needed to scan brains and locate the sources and mechanisms for various emotions has only emerged with the transition to the 21st century. It was Helen Fisher who made some of the key discoveries in the neuroscience of love.

"Romantic love is a primitive, primordial, ancient adaptation," we were told by the famous anthropologist. "My colleagues and I scanned the brains of over one hundred people who were madly in love and we found that this basic brain system for romantic love lies way below the cortex where you do your thinking, way below the limbic regions in the middle of the head that orchestrate the emotions—at the very bottom or heart of the brain, in its oldest part. The basic factory that generates dopamine, that gives us that feeling of intense romantic love, that little factory lies right next to factories that orchestrate thirst and hunger. Thirst and hunger keep us alive, romantic love enables us to fall madly in love with somebody, form a pair bond, and drive our DNA into tomorrow."

"Love is a powerful drive. A primordial drive!" she concluded with enthusiasm. "We are built for love!"

— — —

The new discoveries Helen Fisher and scholars in the field of neuroscience have made throw an entirely fresh light on this fundamental question, a question that has been debated since the very beginnings of anthropology as a discipline—what lies behind our behavior, nature or nurture? Is our behavior the result of a biological program inscribed in our genes with which we're born, or is it due to various influences learned through culture? In terms of love, what best explains our choices and our actions—chemistry and biology, or psychology and sociology?

We found an incredible example for this debate off the beaten path in the heart of Africa, in a country where travel is nearly impossible—Chad. Our visit there was by far the greatest challenge on our trip around the world.

4
THE SOURCE OF LOVE

Does love have its source
in nature or nurture?

We'd heard that the nomads of the Wodaabe tribe gather once a year at the end of the rainy season somewhere out in the bush not far from N'Djamena, Chad's capital city.

Apparently, something that would be unusual and interesting for our project took place at this gathering, and we decided we should try to find it but learning more proved to be difficult. So, we decided to go to N'Djamena in the late rainy season and dedicate three weeks to organizing an expedition to find the Wodaabe. We knew this would not be easy.

Chad is one of the poorest, most dysfunctional and unstable countries in the world. On our tour, we had already seen that it is possible to find traces of the modern world in traditional and underdeveloped countries such as the Solomon Islands or Zambia—but in Chad, we found only scant evidence. N'Djamena is perhaps one of the last cities with no hipster cafés, stores selling imported goods, a tourist infrastructure, streetlights, or closed sewers. We hoped we'd find a tour guide or fixer in N'Djamena who

PREVIOUS PAGE
GUÉREWOL, CHAD

50

could help us find the nomads, but there is no such professional there. And communication was a problem, because we couldn't find anyone who spoke English, so we conducted all our communication in my limited French.

Chad is roughly divided into the arid, desert north—the people living there are mainly Muslim and speak Arabic—and the somewhat more humid and greener south, where the people are largely Christian and speak French. After our first three or four days in N'Djamena we finally found a person who spoke English and was willing to help us, but this was when our problems began. Djim was a bear-like man with a child's whimsy; he was constantly effusing about how thrilled he was to help us, while at the same time secretly looking for ways to take us for all we were worth. Although we'd agreed at the outset on how much we'd pay him, he kept pressuring to squeeze out a little more. Djim took us around N'Djamena looking for people who might know something about the nomads and their gathering. But with each new piece of information, the precise answer seemed farther away. Most people had never heard of the Wodaabe, several were sure that the gathering was going to be held a month from then, had ended weeks before, or was ending now. Nobody knew exactly where it took place. The only thing we could ascertain was that the gathering occurred out in the bush, some 80 kilometers west of N'Djamena.

Djim succeeded in identifying the vast number of permissions we'd need to venture outside the capital city, so off we went to submit petition after petition in rundown administrative offices that had never seen a computer. Each little challenge that would have been a routine procedure in most other countries was a tedious Kafkaesque process here. We could not rent a car, we could not find an interpreter from the Fula language spoken by the Wodaabe, we could not collect all the permissions we needed, we were not allowed freedom of movement in the city, almost everyone we asked about anything demanded large sums of money from us. After nine days of wading through this logistical nightmare, we finally sat in a barely serviceable jeep and ventured with Djim into the bush. But our problems were far from over. In every village we passed through, the local sheriffs stopped us, invited us in for tea, and informed us that we would not be able to continue on our way before we'd agreed to their conditions.

Never once did we feel threatened, nobody behaved aggressively toward us, but almost everyone we met came up with fanciful stories so they could extract as much money from us as possible. Djim, whom we were paying to help us, often connived with them against us. Since our budget was very tight, but we didn't want to give up, we fended off the demands as the negotiations went on for hours and my French quickly improved. It took us a full three days to traverse the 80 kilometers between N'Djamena and the gathering. We lost our way in the bush, followed the tracks of large herds of cattle, met with new, contradictory advice, wrangled endlessly with local sheriffs, and finally hired their people who were, supposedly, going to help us reach the festival and provide security, but actually were using us to line their pockets and complicate our job even more. We had to rent a jeep from one of the sheriffs, because he was so concerned about helping us arrive at our destination safely. Our vehicle, he insisted, would not be up to the task. The jeep, like the previous vehicle, broke down every few kilometers, but there was always a local person nearby with the exact spare part we needed. It was three of us, Anđela, Djim and I, who set out from N'Djamena, but by the time we reached our destination we were a party of—ten. All of them were supposed to help us, for a considerable fee, of course, but not only did they not help, they complicated things and made the journey harder. They hadn't even brought water or food for the trip through the hot desert for themselves, so along with all the other challenges we were facing we had to look after them all, find sources of water and buy food from the people we met along the way.

On the last evening of that crazy ride across the bush, we were still driving late at night when we heard the voices of people singing. Could we possibly have found the gathering? We'd already lost all hope. But as we approached, the sounds grew louder, and it was starting to become clear that this must be it. Right around midnight, when through the dusty windshield we began discerning people, then more people, then so many people we could no longer pass through, we stopped, got out of the vehicle, and ran towards the center of the crowd. We could not believe our eyes! We succeeded in finding the Guérewol! In front of us, an outlandish, incredible scene was unfolding. Surrounded by a myriad of observers, hundreds of tall, painted men were dancing and singing, pressed shoulder to shoulder, and tattooed women were milling around them, making their selections….

The Wodaabe [pp. 114-115] are a subgroup of the Fula people who live in Sahel, the semi-arid belt that runs across Africa south of the Sahara from the Atlantic to the Red Sea. There are about 100,000 Wodaabe, and most of them are nomads.

They drive their herds from Niger and Nigeria to Cameroon and Chad, usually wandering across the bush in groups of ten to twelve people, and only once a year do they have the opportunity to assemble in a larger number, always at the end of the rainy season, because by then fresh grass is available in abundance so they are not compelled to daily drive their livestock to new grazing lands. The annual gathering is known as the Guérewol, and it takes place on sites across the Sahel. For the young people of the Wodaabe this is their only chance to meet other members of their group and perhaps find someone with whom they'll start a family, so that their treks under the hot African sun would be more bearable.

— — —

The next morning at the Guérewol, we were finally able to see, in the light of day, the very people we'd been looking for. They did not resemble the other peoples of Chad we'd met. Most of the people we'd seen before had been dressed in Muslim garbs—long monochrome robes in muted colors—and many of the women covered their faces. The Wodaabe women did not cover their extravagantly tattooed faces, nor did they care if their breasts were covered. The Wodaabe men wore bright colors and jewelry. From early morning, and all day long, they helped each other smear on generous amounts of make-up in the shade provided by the acacias, and in the evening, they gathered on a meadow out in the bush. Excited women crowded around them, and behind the women pressed all the other curious Wodaabe.

The men's dance was not intricate. They stood close together, held hands, and moved a few steps forward and back, rose onto their toes, raised their chins and brows to the sky, opened their eyes wide and moved them left and right, bared their teeth, and through them sang hypnotic melodies that both in sound and rhythm reminded us of birdsong. The women followed their every move and gesture and quietly shared among themselves their opinions, shooting discreet glances at the dancers who struck them as most appealing. There were moments when, under the spell of one particular dancer, a woman would step out into the empty space between the men and women, take up the dance, and place her hand on the shoulder of the man her heart had chosen. By so doing, she'd let him know that she liked him. If the man liked her, he could seek her out later and invite her for a stroll in the bush, as far away from people as they could go.

This custom is not widely known elsewhere, and visually it is so attractive that, if it took place in a country that enjoyed greater stability and had a tourist infrastructure, it would draw a great number of tourists. More fascinating for us, however, than this remarkable and rare custom we were allowed to see and had taken on such risk and trouble for, was the fact that we were witnessing the last living culture in the world in which the men are the ones to parade their finery and demonstrate their skill through dance, while the women are those who choose.

In the animal world, it is nearly always the males who use finery and skills to attract the females. Lions' manes, deer's antlers, a peacock's tail… all these are examples of male finery, and the ritual of courtship is when these attributes are paraded. Codfish swim around their mates and make a drumming sound, snakes and frogs swell, cats' hackles rise, pigeons strut, lobsters rear up and brandish their claws, gorillas pound their chests. Why do humans typically go about this the other way around? Why is it that women are the ones who display their finery and work to impress the males? This is a mystery that has yet to be fully explained. The Wodaabe are the only known culture that does not follow the conventional pattern. Is their custom perhaps a relic of an ancient time when it was the males of our species who displayed their finery to impress the female? Is this perhaps the best evidence available that the whole game of courtship is actually a result of a biological code that is programmed in our genes?

We were interested in what the Wodaabe thought about this. Do they know why they do it this way and where their customs come from? We interviewed 20-year-old **Ali** and **Fadtima** [p. 112], five years his junior, who had just met each other at the gathering and fallen in love. Ali tried to explain how things function here. "We men groom ourselves to show our beauty. The women aren't allowed to do the same. I don't know why. This is how it has always been, so that's how we do it. Then we dance, the girls look us over, and if we like one another we are allowed to go into the shrubs and have fun together."

Fadtima was a little shy in front of the camera, but when the camera was off, she told us what had drawn her to Ali. "I really liked how he danced. He showed so nicely how white his teeth and eyes were. I called him into the bush, and he followed. Since then, we've come together a few more times and it is nice, so we have asked our parents if we may marry."

"If we want to stay together, our parents must first give their blessing," explained Ali. "We cannot marry if they don't. If they do, then she will join me and travel on with me and my herd around the bush."

Over the days we spent with the Wodaabe we learned that at the Guérewol, married women are allowed to have a brief affair. Both men and women were permitted greater freedom here than they enjoyed the rest of the year. If a woman isn't happy with her husband, she can meet someone else and decide to travel on with him. Although the Wodaabe are undoubtedly a patriarchal society of herders, nomads, it was clear, as far as we could tell, that their wives were not as constrained as were women in other groups in Chad. For instance, divorce was not as accessible an option for women in Chad's Muslim ethnic groups.

We were surprised that so many Wodaabe introduced themselves using Muslim names. They explained that most of them had converted to Islam over the last ten years. We couldn't make sense of this because wherever we'd traveled in areas where Muslims lived, we had often seen people performing one of the five daily prayers prescribed by Islam. The whole time we were at the Guérewol we never saw any of the Wodaabe praying. They explained that they'd converted to Islam only formally, because Muslims held the water sources that were key for the survival of their herds.

Does that mean that the dominant Muslim culture has not succeeded in supplanting Wodaabe customs because these are so powerful and rooted in human nature? Or is this due to cultural, social causes, meaning that Wodaabe customs will sooner or later come under the sway of the Muslim and global cultures it encounters? Religion is the backbone of culture. Believers usually hold firmly to the values promoted by the religion they adhere to. But economic considerations and the imperative of survival are often stronger. This biological, evolutionary, economic calculation sometimes overshadows all else. Clearly, it surfaces even through the aesthetic spectacle of the courtship rituals of the Wodaabe.

"When we choose a man, it matters that he's handsome," Fadtima told us, "but it is even more important that he has many cattle."

All these attractive physical attributes are often only indicators of health, wealth, fertility, and strength. It comes as no surprise that anthropologists have shown that men around the world value women's youth, the beauty of their lips, their smooth, taut skin, bright eyes, attractively distributed body fat, a lithesome step, and energy[1]. Women are drawn to slightly older, affluent, powerful, healthy, and strong men. Various enhancements for women in modern societies, such as silicone implants, high-heeled shoes, and stylish dresses and hair-dos, or, for men, fancy suits, expensive watches, and powerful cars, play the same function as do the colored face paint, elaborate jewelry, and dance for the Wodaabe.

When I first saw Anđela, I must admit, I was also drawn by the gleam of her turquoise eyes, the fullness of her blonde hair, her smooth and taut skin, the symmetry of her face, the attractive ratio and distribution of muscle and fat tissue, and her appealing figure. But when we asked the people we spoke to around the world what had attracted them to their partner, seldom could they clearly and explicitly describe the physical traits. Except in Latin America! The passionate and romantic Latinos saw nothing strange about identifying precisely what had stoked the heat in their blood.

"Mutual friends thought we'd like each other so they organized a blind date, and that was when I first met Alfredo," **Melissa**, Melissa, a willowy and attractive 35-year-old woman from Colombia, told us. "I didn't like him at first, but I was impressed by the fancy car he drove!"

"I was impressed by how nicely dressed she was and the fluid way she moved in high-heeled shoes, and her choice of perfume drove me crazy," added her husband **Alfredo** [p. 104].

"We went to a dance," continued Melissa, "and already in the car he told me the car wasn't his but belonged to a friend of his, which put me off a little. But I liked it that he recognized my scent and said it was his favorite. He told me he wasn't used to dating women who were taller than he is. I also wasn't used to dating shorter men, it was all a little unusual for me, but on the dance floor he captured my heart."

"We are both good dancers," Alfredo agreed. "As the night advanced, we danced a lot, heady from a few drinks, the perfume, the beauty of the dance moves, the magic of the night…."

"I liked it when he kissed my neck, so after a lot of dancing and drinking we finally kissed. I decided to give him a chance. I liked it when I saw that he took the trouble to dress well when we started dating."

"I was always careful to be well-dressed, wear a nice scent, I'd fix my hair before I left the house, fingernails, pull any extraneous hairs…."

"I also fixed my hair, nails, eyebrows, and regularly went for a waxing…," said Melissa. "And it worked. Here we are, married, with two small children. It wasn't love at first sight, and I don't know what exactly happened that allowed us to succeed, but chemistry clearly played a part."

— — —

"I am a chemist, and I knew exactly what was happening when I felt the fireworks go off inside me every time I was near Richard. But the fact that I knew and understood the process did nothing to change my experience," we were told by **Kirstin** [p. 105], a 41-year-old chemistry professor at Arizona State University in the United States.

"The sparks, the fireworks going off inside my brain, that's dopamine, a big jolt of dopamine," she explained. "Dopamine is a neurotransmitter, a chemical the brain uses to communicate with itself. It's what is known as a 'reward' molecule. The brain produces it every time we do something that increases our chances of survival or promotes the potential for sexual behavior. We come into this world with no instruction manual. As animals evolve, they either behave in a way that promotes their survival and reproduction or in a way that doesn't. It helps in this process if we have a mechanism in place that can let us know whether we're doing the right thing. Whether we're doing something positive for the procreation of our species."

"So, dopamine is like a dog biscuit?" interjected **Richard**, who'd been listening to her, as had we, with rapt attention; intermingled with his attention were also a spark of his appreciation and pride.

"Ha ha, it's like a mechanism signaling, 'Atta boy, this will help you survive!' Every time you do something that advances survival or procreation, for example when we find sugar, the brain's favorite fuel, or fat, a very dense source of energy…. For most of our time evolving on this planet we have struggled to find sources with enough calories, so we are always on the look-out for them…. And this is why when we found and consumed sugar and animal fat, we were rewarded by that agreeable dopamine rush, which said to us, 'Good job, this will help you survive and multiply!' The same thing happens when someone attracts us. The brain thinks, 'Ah ha, maybe sex! Good!' and that's why we get that feeling of fireworks in the head."

"Isn't dopamine also a cause of addiction?" I asked.

"Yes, dopamine imparts a pleasant feeling, and we tend to want more and more of that. There are drugs that facilitate this pathway. People may become addicted to substances because the substances hijack the dopamine pathway to stimulate that pathway artificially, hence enabling the rush of dopamine for something that isn't behavior-related and doesn't advance either survival or reproduction. Some kinds of attraction to a person may be a form of addiction. In that phase of attraction, you only want that person, you desire *more* of that person. Then this shuts down the rational part of the brain in the frontal lobe, in the cortex. When you're dazed with dopamine, you can't think logically."

"But it's not just about dopamine, is it?"

"The second thing that happens in parallel is that the neurotransmitter serotonin gets downregulated. The brain uses serotonin for many things, such as for a feeling of contentment and satisfaction. Because of this downregulation of serotonin, instead of feeling calm, you feel desire, you long for something. You desire the person who has attracted you. This reduction of serotonin secretion is typical, for example, for people who have OCD. Some scientists equate the 'fireworks' phase of relations with OCD—you can think of nothing else, you don't want to eat, you don't want to sleep, the rational part of your brain has shut down. It doesn't last forever, even if the person continues to attract, because you can't walk around with the logical side of your brain shut down. Sooner or later, you have to begin to think logically about how suitable that person is for a more serious relationship."

Kirsten and Richard met each other through their children from their first marriages. Both of them had failed marriages behind them and were focused on their careers, but once their children became friends, they got to know each other and became closer. Little by little, they realized they liked each other, and their friendship turned into a bond that passed the test of time and became serious.

"This transition from the first fireworks phase to a more serious relationship happened seamlessly for us," Kirstin continued. "It's not that I woke up one morning and realized the fireworks were over. In fact, the fireworks still do happen from time to time, though briefly. But we gradually began to think logically, long-term…. That's when the oxytocin hormone comes into play. It kicks in during the transitional phase when people start to bond in a more serious relationship. Oxytocin is responsible for one's ability to assess what comes up in social situations and the resulting involvement. Oxytocin helps a couple bond and work together to achieve a common goal. But it also has its dark side. Anger, confrontation, those are also social approach behaviors in which oxytocin plays a part. So, let's say that we are now in that long phase when oxytocin has the upper edge, with occasional blasts of dopamine….."

"So, are you saying that love has several phases?"

"Yes, love develops, I think, through three phases. The initial phase is the phase of lust. Here the sexual hormone of testosterone is in play for both men and women. This is what is responsible for sexual desire. The second is the phase of powerful attraction, the fireworks. At this phase, you can think of nothing but each other, you don't need to eat or sleep, all you want is to be with the person. This is when the neurotransmitters of dopamine and serotonin are active and suppress the rational part of the brain. But since this phase is not possible to sustain for long, sooner or later we evolve into a third phase, the phase of a lasting bond. This is the oxytocin phase, and this is where our ability to exert rational reason and make decisions returns."

I was interested to see that though Kirsten may have been using slightly different terms, what she was talking about was the same three-phase system of the brain that Dr. **Helen Fisher**, the anthropologist, had established. What Kirsten called lust, Fisher termed the sex drive; the phase of attraction or fireworks is essentially the phase of attraction or romantic love; and what for Kirsten was a lasting bond, Fisher called attachment.

So, if our brain chemistry is so clear that it can be registered on brain scanners, then this would suggest that it is innate to all of us. The fact that Ali of the Wodaabe will, in order to impress Fadtima, spend his youth amassing a collection of jewelry and maintaining the whiteness of his teeth, using make-up to accentuate the whites of his eyes and the attractive contours of his face, and then, when the time comes, paint himself in bright colors and sing and dance in the bush, or that Melissa and Alfredo from Colombia will choose clothing to heighten their physical attributes, apply expensive scents, fix their hair and nails, and then harmonize their movements on the dance floor—these are the results of nurture, of culture.

Does Wodaabe culture call into question the stereotype that women pay more attention to their appearance and invest more effort in the seduction and conquest of their partner? we wondered. We talked about this with anthropologist Helen Fisher.

"When we look at the animal world it is mainly the males who adorn themselves in various ways and dance in order to impress the females, but when we look at human society, it's the women who are all very colorful and dressed up and doing the courting" confirmed Fisher. "In fact, men also engage in courtship behavior. Even in cultures where men do not show off or dance, they acquire knowledge and skills, work and earn money and, in so doing, show women they can look after their wife and potential offspring. Both men and women invest a great deal of effort in courtship, but they do so in their own way, and these ways differ from one culture to another."

"So what, then, is it? Is our romantic behavior inborn or learned? Is it due to nature or nurture, biology or psychology?" I asked.

"Our behavior is 100% biology and 100% culture!" she answered boldly. "There are two parts of our behavior, our human personality. There's our temperament, all of those characteristics that we express because they're part of our biology—some of us are better in math, some are better in music, some are stubborn, some more creative…. This all comes out of our biology. But the other half of who we are is based in psychology, and this encompasses everything we grew up to believe, do, say, and think. A good example is religion. We know there are genes that predispose you to be more or less inclined to believe in god. You're born with that. But if you're born in the United States, you're more likely to be a Christian, or if you're born in Iran, you're more likely to be a Muslim. That depends on culture. As far as love is concerned—our culture determines what our rituals of courtship or marriage will look like, but in every culture, we feel the same intense drive to love—and that comes from biology."

Kirsten, the Arizona-based chemistry professor, told us something similar.

"The fact that we understand the chemistry behind lust, attraction, and attachment, and that we know how an excess or shortage of certain chemical substances secreted in the brain can influence us doesn't mean that we can add or subtract these elements at will in order to fall into or out of love. In chemistry, I know that if I mix baking soda and vinegar, I'll get a volcano of bubbles.

That's easy, pure chemistry. But people are not beakers. I can't add something to a person who doesn't love me to make that person fall in love with me and feel the fireworks of emotion when they think of me. Nor can a person whose heart has been broken block certain chemicals and thereby make the loss of love less wrenching. Love is not only chemistry; it is also psychology."

"Why then do people talk about having a broken heart or that their heart is full of love, if everything is actually going on in their brain," asked her husband, Richard.

"Because when we see or imagine a person who attracts us, our heart starts racing, and people think that love comes from the heart. Also, when we experience powerful emotions, our breath often catches in our chest, so that's another reason. Yet another reason is because historically people thought that blood was created in the heart. The ancient Romans thought that everything that was human was contained in the heart. However, today we know that everything love-related happens in the brain."

"Oh, I love you with my whole brain!" exclaimed Richard, and she laughed, dropped her chin a little while keeping her eyes on him, and their faces both flushed with the same nuance of the reddish color that the Wodaabe dancers paint on their faces when, once a year at the end of the rainy season, they dance in the Sahel bush.

5

MARRIAGE

Why are arranged marriages more
resilient than love marriages?

Six years before our journey around the world, I traveled around Africa on a motorcycle. When I was on my way through the lands of the Maasai people, the proud...

📍 PREVIOUS PAGE
MAASAI MARA, KENYA

The moment before Nalotesha first sees her husband, with whom she'll leave forever the home where she grew up.

...young man **Shuel**—whom we met briefly in Chapter Three—announced that within a few days, he'd be going to fetch his second wife, **Nalotesha** [pp. 254-255]. He'd never seen her, nor had she seen him; their fathers had arranged the marriage. He boasted that he'd be going to fetch her with his best man and would bring her to his village. I had the feeling that this would be a unique opportunity for me to witness the rite of passage, so I asked if I might document the process. He agreed without hesitation, but asked me for a favor. Since we were in the middle of the rainy season and his village was a three-day walk from hers, he asked if I could find a vehicle in which all of us could bring her back, so his bride wouldn't have to wade through the mud in her wedding finery while crossing the rain-drenched muddy savannah of Maasai Mara. I was glad to and asked for directions for how to reach her village. I drove there and explained my intentions to Nalotesha's father, Ole Sankei. He readily agreed and warmly hosted me at his home. While we waited for Shuel, I got to know Nalotesha.

The day she was born, rain fell all day, so her parents gave her the name of Nalotesha—She Who Comes with the Rains. She spent every day of the next sixteen years of her life living in her family's manyatta[1] in the scattered village of Inkamurunya, on the edge of the Maasai Mara savannah. Each manyatta consists of several dwellings made of twigs, mud, and cow dung, laid out in a circle and surrounded by a fence woven of thorny shrubs that prevents lions and other wild animals from attacking the livestock that spend the nights inside the fence. They told me I had nothing to fear because the lions didn't come this far north, and since their manyatta was quite near the road, there were not too many other wild animals there.

Nalotesha's brothers and cousins took the livestock out to pasture every day, while she, carefree, waded through the mud around the house, drank cow's milk, slept in the smoky house, looked after her younger brothers and sisters, milked the cows and sheep, and helped the women with the chores. Some of the other girls her age attended school, but this privilege had not been extended to her. When she first menstruated, she was put through a brutal initiation ritual—circumcision[2]. This was the most painful day of her life, the day she became a woman and began wearing special jewelry that let everyone know she was of marriageable age.

Nalotesha's father, Ole Sankei, was not one of the rich elders of his people, he only had a hundred head of cattle, but that was enough for him to support his large family. Life was easy when the rains were plentiful, but in years of drought he'd had to send his sons with their cattle to the south to graze on the lands of other clans. Since this was risky, because he wasn't on good terms with all of them, he usually went along with his sons and the herd. Sometimes, he had to fight in order to save his own skin. During the last drought, lions decimated his herd, and the rest of the cattle were stricken by a disease that required medical treatment he couldn't afford. Luckily, he ran into a good man, Lentuala, who gave him the money he needed for the medicine. Grateful to Lentuala for helping him get out of a difficult situation, and glad that he had a new ally in the south, Ole Sankei offered him several cows or the hand of one of his daughters.

Lentuala said that he needed nothing, but his son Shuel was prepared to take a second wife. And so they agreed to the wedding.

Lentuala came back to Inkamurunya several months later and brought with him a cow, which he gave to Ole as his pledge for the bride price Shuel owed for his daughter, Nalotesha. They sat around the fire and negotiated the details of the wedding. Shuel was overjoyed when he heard that all had been arranged. He was proud that already by the age of 21 he had managed to raise enough cattle to afford a second wife and was well along the way to becoming a prominent member of his clan.

Shuel, along with his best man, arrived the evening before he would take Nalotesha away with him forever, and Nalotesha hid in a dark side room of one of the huts in the manyatta, because he mustn't see her. That evening, Shuel, his best man, and members of Nalotesha's close family sat together in the same dwelling. Shuel gave each of her family members one of the plaid blankets the Maasai wear, and he brought several sacks of sugar for the whole family. He promised to send the remaining five cows he owed as soon as the rains ended. Ole Sankei told Shuel he must protect and care for his daughter Nalotesha, respect her, give her her cows and provide protection, give her many children and care for them all. To Nalotesha, he said that the time had come for her to leave his household, the way all Maasai women, sooner or later, leave. He told her he had made the effort to find her a good husband and a good family with many cows and a good reputation and she should be grateful to him for that. Her obligation was to respect her husband and love him no matter what he was like, whether he was stupid, ugly, or pitiable. He told her that the next day, when she left his home, she mustn't look back, and she shouldn't return for five years or until her first child had reached the age of one.

No one dared interrupt her father, and those to whom he was speaking as well as the newlyweds had to voice their approval of his words. This was when Nalotesha and Shuel heard each other speak for the first time. They agreed to everything that was said. When the father's speech ended and everyone went off to their dwellings, Nalotesha and Shuel, sight unseen—were married.

Rain fell all night. It didn't stop in the morning, as if Nalotesha were also fated to depart in the rain. Ole Sankei's youngest sons took the cows out to graze that morning as always, but the acrid smell of the cattle still clung to the house, to the deep, wet mud around the hut, to the pores of the dry mudbricks of the manyatta walls, to the plaid blankets the people of Inkamurunya used to wrap themselves in. No rain could rinse that smell away. Along his best man and other inquisitive souls, Shuel waited outside in the rain for Nalotesha to emerge from the house and embark on her journey into her new life. From early morning, her mother and stepmother had been dressing her. They painted her skin with red ocher pigment, the sacred color of the Maasai. They festooned her with jewelry of many colors, and especially with sacred blue beads, because the color blue is divine: it reflects the hue of the heavens. They wrapped her in clean, new shawls of many colors but especially green, the color of God's greatest blessing—fresh grass after the rain.

When she was ready to step away from one part of her life and step into another, she stopped at the exit from the house as if she were hesitating. I was standing near her and I could see her eyes fill with tears. She stood there like that, without moving, her head bowed, frozen in the last moments of childhood. A tear or two slid down her face and dropped to the dusty floor. The rain stopped as Nalotesha stepped into her new life.

She walked on, head bowed, along a path marked by her father and uncle who had poured milk and beer fermented from honey, seeds, and grass along it. At the end of the path, Shuel waited for her with a broad smile. On they walked together, and she still didn't look at him, nor did she turn to look back at the house where she had spent every day of her life. All the things she owned, as well as the dowry she was bringing with her, fit into a single suitcase that her older brother and Shuel's best man brought to the jeep. The jeep set out for Shuel's village. Nalotesha and Shuel sat on the backseat side by side, but she stared ahead, melancholy and downcast.

The rain had stopped, but the Maasai Mara was soaked, the rivers swollen, and every so often we had to stop and push the jeep out of the mud. At the first river we had to cross, Shuel grabbed Nalotesha, raised her up in his arms and carried her over; this was the first time she smiled at him. Afterward, they began talking softly in the jeep. With curiosity, Nalotesha surveyed the countryside, which she was seeing for the first time, and she commented to Shuel how the grazing lands were greener, there were more zebras and antelope, and the water in the streams was clearer.

By the time we reached Shuel's village of Empopongi, the celebrations had already begun. Young men Shuel's age were singing throaty, multi-part songs and jumping in place. At the entrance to Shuel's manyatta, Nalotesha was greeted by his mother. She rubbed butter onto Nalotesha's head and poured milk and beer before her feet. Nalotesha entered the house and sat in a place that would remain hers; people brought her milk to drink and set a little child on her lap, believing this would ensure that she'd bear many children. Although the festivities celebrating her arrival had begun outside, she would remain inside until the next morning, when the elders of Shuel's clan entered the house and discussed what name they'd give her. A new name for a new life. They settled on **Noonkuta**—Fresh Rainwater.

Six years later, Anđela and I, on our journey around the world, went looking for Shuel and Noonkuta; we found them living in the same place. Noonkuta had meanwhile borne three children. Shuel's first wife, **Nashaa**, had become her dearest friend. Noonkuta had only left Empopongi once, when her first child reached the age of one. That is when she returned to Inkamurunya and visited her old family. She said she had no intention of ever going back, because now this was her home and she liked it better. The grasslands were lusher, there were more cattle, the people were better.

— — —

A century ago, French ethnographer Arnold Van Gennep observed that all cultures recognize rites of passage between various life cycles and these proceed along three stages: old status—liminal stage—new status[3]. Leaving behind the old status means a separation from the familiar and the metaphoric death of the old self. The liminal stage is a special moment of transition during which all earlier accepted forms and boundaries are left behind, while the new status is a return to the ordinary world but with an altered awareness, a new identity.

A half century later, anthropologist Victor Turner further elaborated on Van Gennep's concept of the rites of passage, focusing on the liminal stage of transition[4]. While in this phase, the person is no longer in their old status but not yet in their new one, either; they are in a sort of limbo, in-between. They are separated from their familiar world and therefore not the same as they were before they made the transition, but they have not yet gone through the transformation to a new stability. At this stage, the structures and traditional values they've known dissolve and sometimes are even overturned. The identity of the person who is participating in the rite then dissolves and the person becomes disoriented but open to new possibilities. Boundaries melt away and they stand on the threshold, prepared to cross over from what they were to what they will become.

The courtship period, the bachelor and hen parties, the wedding rituals, are all typical of the liminal stage of rites of passage. In the case of enduring traditional cultures such as the Maasai, these are rites of total transformation. Nalotesha literally left her whole life and all the people she'd ever known behind her and entered a life that was to her a different, entirely new and foreign world. The fact that she entered the liminal stage of the rite of passage as Nalotesha and came out of it as Noonkuta was the most precise symbolic manifestation of the death of the old and birth of the new self.

In modern societies, fewer people opt for a traditional marriage, and engagement and weddings are changing in character. But these are still rites of passage of a kind. In the society in which Anđela and I live, most people have two wedding ceremonies—the first in a church, and the second before a justice of the peace. We felt that marrying in a church would be hypocritical as we are not religious, and the ceremony with the justice of the peace was done without fuss, purely as a formality. Still, we wanted to mark this important rite of passage in our lives and celebrate it with a wedding, so we invented our own ritual. We found a charming venue in the woods on a mountain slope near Zagreb and invited a hundred of our closest family and friends. Instead of a registrar or priest, a friend of ours officiated, and we wrote our own vows. We did keep some of the traditional elements, such as rings, witnesses, and the first dance, and we didn't refuse presents from our guests, but there were small, original elements of our own, too. For instance, we set out an open, blank book on a table and asked our guests to write their advice to us on "how to avoid divorce."

Our marriage is also modern in that there was no financial exchange, no bride price paid for the bride by the groom, or dowry, which the bride brings with her into her new life in some cultures. Also, we entered into marriage of our own free will. Almost all marriages in the traditional age were arranged. Even today, in the 21st century, more than half of the marriages around the world are not the result of free will but are arranged either by parents or relatives[5].

There are four different kinds of marriage:

1) Forced arranged marriage, in which the bride and groom have no right to their choice or a veto;

2) Consensual arranged marriage, in which the parents propose partners, but the bride and groom are allowed the right to refuse the proposal;

3) Conditional free-choice marriage , in which the bride and groom choose each other themselves but must receive the blessing of their parents;

4) Autonomous marriage, in which the parents have no say in the matter.[6]

Shuel and Noonkuta's marriage was forced, because Nalotesha hadn't seen Shuel before she was married to him, nor could she refuse to marry. We found an even more extreme example of forced marriage in the nomadic Bopa people, in Rajasthan in India, at the home of the couple we encountered in Chapter Two, **Ghasiram** and **Kamla** [p. 8], who told us that love for them was when "we stand, sit, eat, drink, and sleep together." Kamla was only five when her parents married her to 15-year-old Ghasiram. Although they only began living together later, when they were ready to start their family and look after themselves, they went through the marriage ritual as children.

"I had no choice, I did as I was told," Ghasiram told us, and Kamla can barely remember the event.

Within their culture, there are even children married younger than this.[7] Bopa girls are sometimes married to much older men, and some children may even be married before they're born!

"It goes like this," Ghasiram explained to us with confidence, as if this were the most normal thing in the world: "my daughter is pregnant, your daughter is pregnant. You and I agree that if one is a boy and the other a girl, they'll marry. This is how a wedding takes place in utero."

The Bopa's neighbors in Rajasthan, the Kalbeliyas, who share ancestors with European Roma, and who engage in ritual dancing and snake charming, are also very traditional, but they practice conditional free-choice marriages.

"I met her at a wedding. I liked how she danced," we were told by 27-year-old **Naru**. "First, I asked my uncle whether she was one of my blood relatives. He said she was the daughter of his brother-in-law, so that meant we could marry. I went to her parents and asked for her hand. They agreed, but only accepted me for a probational period."

His wife **Sharda** [p. 135] explained how the liminal stage of engagement looks in their culture and how long it lasts.

"Each Kalbeliya who wishes to get married must spend two years in a probational marriage here, and during that time they will prove that they are serious and mature enough for wedlock. Naru had to live with us, do everything we do, fetch water, gather firewood on a nearby mountain, cook, and do everything he was asked to do. This is our tradition, this is what our parents did, and their parents before them. If there were no probational period, how would I know that I hadn't married someone who has problems with alcohol or gambling, or someone who will cause trouble for me later?"

Nowhere is there as vast a variety of cultures as there is in India. Here, one can probably find any and all forms of relationships and marriages—polygynous and polyandrous communities, wives who throw themselves onto their husband's funeral pyre, the kidnapping of brides and kidnapping of grooms, hunter-gatherer peoples and the most modern of individuals…. All these co-exist in incredible India side by side. But the most prevalent type of wedlock is the arranged marriage. Even young people who have experienced romantic affairs with partners they chose themselves often break these off and prefer to enter into wedlock with a partner chosen for them by their parents.

In a modern Mumbai neighborhood, full of recently built residential high-rises, green parks, sports fields, urban cafés, and promenades without a single sacred cow or crippled beggar in sight, we interviewed **Satinder**, a 45-year-old manager, and his slightly younger wife **Richa** [p. 116].

"They prepare us throughout our childhood for arranged marriage, so this is nothing out of the ordinary for us," Satinder told us. "We also teach our daughters from their early childhood that they cannot return home once they've married. They may come as guests, but this is no longer their home, because their husband's home is now their home. You already know you'll be building a family with this person and getting along, so you see only their virtues, not their faults."

Satinder was Richa's first partner, but unlike her, he had been in a romantic relationship before and he'd experienced what it was like to fall in love and embark on a relationship without the mediation of parents. When relationships like this end in wedlock, Indians refer to them as 'love marriages.' I was always surprised when I heard them using this phrase, because implicit was the suggestion that there is no love in arranged marriages.

"I loved a woman, I was with her when we were students, but I knew I couldn't marry her, so bit by bit I convinced myself that I'd be better off entering into an arranged marriage than a love marriage," Satinder continued. "I knew a love marriage could never be as good as an arranged marriage. Arranged marriages function better, because people enter into love marriages out of passion, so they aren't able to think clearly about practical matters and all they care about is their opinion, while in arranged marriages whole families negotiate and support the success of the relationship. Parents know their children better than their children know themselves and they know better what will have a good chance of success and what will not. This is why arranged marriages fail less often."

"When a couple is faced with problems," said Richa, "then these are not just their problems, but both families work together to solve the problems, while in a love marriage, the couple has to deal with everything on their own, and that is why those relationships founder more easily."

"When you're young and in love, your emotions run strong," said Satinder. "You miss the person, you think about them all the time, you write to each other, but this lasts a few years and then it fades. An arranged marriage is more mature, because here you are starting a family, you have to understand your spouse, build your relationship."

Satinder spent the whole interview talking about the advantages of an arranged marriage and he praised Richa, who was sitting next to him, as an excellent wife, mother, and housewife. This made his mention of his romantic student affair all the more surprising for us.

"That was love," he said with a long sigh. "But what can you do.... You don't always get what you want in life."

— — —

Arranged marriages needn't exclude love. Widespread is the thinking, which we heard from many people in India, but also from others around the world who live in arranged marriages, that in autonomous marriages there is love at first, but over time it fades, while in arranged marriages love is born gradually and endures. That's what we were told by **Zeinab** and **Davood** [p. 277] who live in a large village in southern Iran near the Persian Gulf. One could almost see the sparks flying between them. Their chests swelled when they spoke of their feelings, they sometimes dropped their eyes when they honored each other with long, pointed gazes, and they spoke with confidence, firmly, in a way that showed that they were in love and weren't afraid of anything and had nothing to lose.

"Although we're from the same town, I didn't know him before we were married," 23-year-old Zeinab told us. We interviewed her with Davood at their home. "Maybe I'd seen him once or twice in passing. I was 17 then and I didn't know anything about intimate relations or love. I just did what my parents told me to do. But as soon as we began spending time together, bit by bit we cultivated feelings for one another. Today, we love each other so much that we find it hard to be apart. When he goes to work he sends me nice texts now and then, and I prepare food for him and can hardly wait for him to come home. Every day we love each other more. Our love is nothing less than the love we see in the movies when people fall in love at first sight! If I were to be reborn a hundred times and if I could choose, I'd always choose Davood!"

Zeinab, exactly like Kamla or Noonkuta, had no choice. But in many of the cultures in which arranged marriages are the norm, the newlyweds are allowed to refuse a proposal from their parents—in some cases only once, in others, two or three times, in some, countless times. This is a limited choice, but better than none at all. Of the 120 interviews we conducted on this project, 20 of them were couples who lived in arranged marriages with the option of refusal, which meant that the young people could turn down the partner who'd been arranged for them by their parents. We noticed that the more traditional a society was, the less there existed a right to choose. We found the largest number of arranged marriages in Asia and Africa. Throughout the Middle East and urban Africa, the institution of arranged marriages is weakening, but it still dominates in India and the other countries of South Asia, as well as in rural Africa.

One can also find arranged marriages in the modern world. Some of the most traditional people we found were right in the middle of New York City. In Brooklyn, we interviewed **Yoni** and **Rivky** [p. 143], Orthodox Hasidic Jews. They had met each other through a rabbi who was serving as a matchmaker. They had a half-hour meeting at Starbucks, after which Rivky had to decide whether to enter into a lifelong relationship with Yoni or not. On the other hand, the hunter-gatherers whom we interviewed chose their partners themselves. This doesn't mean that hunter-gatherer societies never arrange marriages. During earlier expeditions around New Guinea I stayed with tribes of hunters and gatherers who chose their wives from other clans and paid a pre-arranged bride price for them. But the hunter-gatherers with whom we spoke on this trip, the Matis from the Amazon and the Bushmen in the Kalahari, had the freedom to choose whom they'd share their life with and whether they'd leave that relationship.

The possibility of divorce is one more indicator of how traditional a society is and how free the women are. Many young women all over the world, like Zeinab, Kamla, and Noonkuta—who had entered into arranged marriages— not only don't have the right to choose their partner, but most often have no way of leaving these marriages. Traditional societies across the world do not offer women many social niches where they can hide if they wish to escape a bad marriage. Throughout history, if women in traditional societies didn't want to be married housewives and mothers, they had no other options but two—to be either prostitutes or nuns[8]. Married women were not economically independent, so if they wanted to leave their marriage, they seldom had options for survival. Statistics show that in certain modern Western societies, 50% of marriages end in divorce, while the average global rate of divorce among arranged marriages is only 6%; the rate in India is only 3%[9]. But that needn't serve as proof that arranged marriages are overall more successful. It can only indicate that women in modern societies have greater freedom to dissolve relationships with which they are dissatisfied.

In traditional societies, the only insurance of any kind for a woman who wishes to leave a marriage is her dowry. She can leave with the dowry she brought with her and the bride price the groom paid for her, and these can provide her with a new beginning. But few women choose to take that step, because the new beginning is not easy. And, in fact, it is seldom even an option.

Was there divorce in Maasai society? I asked Shuel. By then, he had become a prominent member of his clan, whose herd had grown over the six years since I'd last seen him and who soon hoped to take a third wife. We talked out in front of his manyatta while, out of the corner of my eye, I watched a large herd of giraffes pass by. The wild animals of Maasai Mara came close to people in their search for food, because the hot summer sun had already baked all the grass dry. Everything alive was waiting for the rains to come and the eternal cycle to be renewed. Shuel's first wife, Nashaa, sat to his left, and his second wife, Noonkuta, to his right, in the sparse shade of an acacia tree, now and then lazily brushing away the dozens of flies buzzing around them. Sweat dripped from their foreheads. They were all very pleased that we had brought them a photo album with the wedding pictures as a gift. Few of the Maasai can boast of such a thing. Shuel said he'd proudly show the pictures to all the Maasai and this would enhance his reputation even more. Noonkuta and Naasha didn't say much.

"It's not easy to dissolve a marriage between a husband and wife," Shuel said to the camera. "If there is a problem, first brothers and friends must try to help. If the woman has made a mistake and apologizes and pays the fine, she can be forgiven. But if she has done something egregious, then the entire clan gathers to discuss it. If the community concludes that divorce is the only solution, she may have her dowry returned to her and leave the manyatta. But she may not go far! She must build her own hut next to the manyatta and live there. She still belongs to the family and to her husband, but she receives no more benefits or support from the family."

I watched Noonkuta while he was speaking. She didn't blink; she showed no non-verbal reaction that I could see or register. She just sat there, motionless. It seemed as if she wasn't even bothered by the flies or the heat that radiated from the heat-baked savannah of the Maasai Mara.

6

POLYGAMY

Are we monogamous or
polygamous by nature?

Not far from the manyatta where Shuel, Naasha, and Noonkuta lived, we came across an older Maasai in the scattered village of Empopongi,...

...who was sitting in the meager shade of a thorny acacia and watching several women build a hut of twigs, mud, and dung, and he kept calling out to them. When he saw us coming, he stood and came over to welcome us, introducing himself as **Muterian**. We had heard that there were Maasai who had ten wives or more so we were on the lookout for the man with the largest number of wives in Empopongi. Our query led us to 56-year-old Muterian. His household numbered six wives and 22 children. When a family is this large, one seldom finds them all in one place. Two of Muterian's wives were off with the cattle, while the other four were there, building the hut. **Norkisaruni**, who was 45, **Normejoole**, 30, **Noosiamon**, 27, and **Nandungo Enkop** [p. 106], 23, were having a jovial time while they worked: every so often, one of them

PREVIOUS PAGE
WADI BANI KHALID OASIS, OMAN

78

would fire off a comment and the rest would burst out laughing. The laughter reached a peak when Muterian explained to them that we'd be interviewing them as a group. He didn't ask for their permission, he simply informed them of his decision.

"Why do we Maasai have numerous wives?" Muterian repeated our question. "There are several reasons—they can help one another build huts, they can help with work around the manyatta and with the children and cattle, and when the time comes for childbirth, the others can help the birthing mother. A man who has only one wife is poor. It's like having only one eye. If he loses it—what is left for him? It is prudent to have several wives. If you have three or four wives, only then is your life easier. If you have six wives, like I do, then you are almost problem-free."

"Is this true?" we laughed. "Is a problem-free life even possible?"

"The greatest trouble comes from having to look after all of them, provide enough food, clothing, shelter, money…. But the larger the family, the more of everything you have, and that's easier. I have six wives and 22 children," he said proudly, but he was not eager to say how many head of cattle he owned. Maasai love to acquire livestock, but they don't like to say how many cattle they have.

"How does such a large family manage? Are all the women equally dear and important to you, or do you prefer one over the others?" we asked.

"That depends on each one. If a wife serves you well, if she brings you food, speaks nicely to you, doesn't shout, is obedient, answers quickly to what you ask, if she shows she cares about you and loves and honors you, then there's no need to beat her. My love depends on her character. Some have wives they love more, some they love less, but that all depends on each woman. If a woman is rude or answers in an unseemly way—how can you love her? The more wives you have, the more they compete among themselves to treat you well and have you love them more. All my wives treat me well, I have no favorite, because they all obey me and I love them all the same. They all prepare my food, none of them has done anything unseemly, I have never seen them with another man, each of them comes to me in my hut when I tell her to."

"Do you have any rules about how much time you spend with which wife?"

"Every wife has her own hut where she lives with her children, and I have mine where I live alone. The women are not allowed to come to me whenever they feel like it, we have a set schedule for visits. One can stay for two or three days, but none may stay longer than a week. And when they're bleeding, or from when they become pregnant and until the baby is four to five months old, they may not come. While one or two wives are pregnant, the husband has more time for the others. But our wives aren't jealous the way wives are in some of the other tribes...."

We found traces of jealousy among women in polygamous marriages among the Himba people on the half-arid northern part of Namibia. Just as with the Maasai, the Himba are iconic African pastoralists. They are scantily clad and richly adorned from head to toe with pieces of leather and tails, bones, shells, metal, and the occasional scrap of cloth. Their skin and hair are red from ochre, and they add mud and ash to their hair to make thick dreadlocks. Because of this unique appearance and beauty, and because of the deeply traditional way they still live, they are often visited by tourists. Despite this, however, their lives haven't changed much.

"I chose my first wife, **Uazeupara**, myself. I liked her because she was very beautiful, so I asked for her hand in marriage from her parents," **Kauarende**, 56, told us while sitting between his two wives in their mudbrick dwelling that held no furniture or other belongings, just a hearth in the middle and the occasional gnawed bone stuck into the straw roof. "We were married about 30 years ago and she has borne me nine children, but later I began to feel lonely, so I desired another wife. That is when I married **Uatongota** [p. 10]. That was seven years ago."

"How did you feel when he told you he wanted another wife?" Anđela asked 45-year-old Uazeupara, Kauarende's first wife.

"I wasn't happy about it," she said. "At first I suffered. Later, I got used to it."

"And why did you need a second wife?" she asked Kauarende again.

"When you have only one wife and she goes off somewhere for several days, who will look after all the children and the livestock? Who will fetch the water? Who will make the food? You feel lonely. A man needs to have at least two wives. But this is not easy. You must see to it that they don't quarrel. You must be careful to share your time equally with them. If you spend more time with one, then the other will think you don't love her anymore. You need to watch out for that, it's not easy. This is a great struggle."

"We don't quarrel much!" interjected Uazeupara, nodding toward 32-year-old Uatongota, who was sitting by Kauarende's other side and wasn't saying very much, because she was nursing her youngest child. "Most of the time, we get along well, we cook together for everyone, we fetch water together and tend to the animals. But when Kauarende goes to be with her, I miss him terribly and I can hardly wait for him to come to me, and when he does come, I am happy."

"Can you explain what you feel for him? And what love is for you?" Andela asked, although we already knew that traditional people don't often speak about feelings and often have no word for love. The Himba themselves did volunteer information about their feelings, and we heard them using their word for love—*orusuvero*.

"When I think about him," said Uazeupara, "there is something that ripples through my body, from my head and down my back. Maybe that is love. I don't know. It is so complicated."

"Love is very complicated," confirmed Kauarende and concluded, "but this is the first thing between people. It is what keeps them together."

— — —

We found the most polygamy in Africa, among traditional, tribal peoples. A year earlier, when we were planning the trip, we assumed that we'd most often find polygamy among Arabs in the Middle East. Muslims are known to be allowed to take up to four wives, and while I traveled through various Muslim countries, I often made the acquaintance of people in rural areas throughout the Arab lands who boasted that they had several wives. On this trip, we visited Oman and Saudi Arabia during our first month, but we couldn't find a single community of a husband with several wives who'd agree to be interviewed together in front of our camera. We spoke with several dozen men who were in polygamous marriages, but they all gave us the same story—that both wives were hardly ever to be found in the same place at the same time, that each woman had her own house, far from the other, that the women never had any contact with each other, usually were very jealous, and furthermore did not get along, so the husband had to be careful to spend an equal amount of time with each of them, most often one day with each.

The reason for this may be that among the Muslims in the Middle East the tradition is now losing its hold, especially in the richer countries such as Saudi Arabia. Although revenue from the petroleum industry ends up in the hands of a small elite, we did have the impression that the average Saudi lives much better than the average Kenyan or Namibian. And wealth doesn't just bring financial prosperity but also social progress and acceptance of new values. Although Saudi Arabia is one of the more closed societies in terms of politics and values and women have few rights and freedoms and the law is not civilian but religious, Islamic, Sharia, the patriarchy there seems to have weakened far more than it has among the Maasai and Himba. This surprised us a little, because there has been the assumption in the West that women in Saudi Arabia are pushed aside and abused, while the Himba and Maasai are romanticized by many in the West, and they are seen as legendary, proud African icons. Maybe these stereotypes spring from the huge visual contrast between typical Himba and Saudi women. Himba women wear leather attire covering only their most private parts, leaving their breasts bare. Most Saudi women cover their entire bodies, including their faces, with a black niqab, some showing only their eyes and hands, and some—not even that. However, appearances may be deceptive. While the Maasai and Himba men spoke openly about how they beat their wives or do not beat them even though they could, Arabs in polygamous relationships seemed to fear their wives. In all the traditional, patriarchal societies I've come to know, women and men hold separate roles. Who does what is clear. In most of these cultures, men do the more physically demanding jobs, such as building a dwelling. Among the Maasai, however, they leave even that to the women. The only job for Maasai men is to rule over their kingdom.

Arabs, Maasai, and Himba are only a few of the cultures that allow polygamy, or more precisely—polygyny. Polygamy means 'several spouses' and includes both polygyny and polyandry. Polygyny, the custom by which one man has several wives, has been permitted in 85% of all the cultures ever studied, while polyandry, the custom by which a woman has several husbands, has appeared in fewer than 1% of all cultures[1]. Both polygyny and polyandry are disappearing across the world, influenced by globalization and the increasing impact of women's rights. Fewer people are embarking on polygamous marriages, and more and more countries are outlawing them.

When we planned our tour, we felt that for the sake of the breadth of our project we needed to find cultures in which polyandry was still practiced, but we knew this would be a tall order. Polyandry is most practiced in the Himalayas and Tibet, and I have traversed these regions several times over the last 15 years. I trekked through the most isolated parts of Tibet, Nepal, and Bhutan and documented the most traditional Himalayan cultures, but on my way, I encountered polyandry only once, in Upper Mustang, and the people involved were very elderly. I had the impression that this was dying out as a custom. But our research led us to believe that in the Kinnaur Valley in the Indian Himalayas people were still practicing polyandry, so we decided to go there and see for ourselves.

The road into the Kinnaur Valley is extremely rugged, so we rented a four-wheel drive jeep and hired a driver, a fixer, and an interpreter, and—off we went on our adventure. I had traveled along many dangerous roads by then, such as those through the Afghan ravines or the famous Bolivian 'death road,' but this drive was the worst, longest, and most harrowing of my life. The rocky, unpaved road often ran along a cliff edge, and there were places where erosion and landslides almost completely blocked our progress. Our driver performed miracles as he maneuvered through the debris or skirted along the very edge of a road that ran above a kilometer-deep drop. He was an excellent driver and saved our lives, but he was also a pain in the neck and bent on robbing us. In the two long days we traveled from the foothills of the Himalayas to the Kinnaur Valley, he threatened to leave us several times if we didn't give him a raise. But we deflected that challenge and arrived alive and well in the village of Pangi, nestled in the sky among the clouds.

The village spreads across the slopes of the Himalayas high above a river that flows along the valley floor. People live in stone dwellings surrounded by orchards. When we arrived, the apple trees were in bloom. In Pangi, we found and interviewed three families who live in polyandric marriages. They were all remarkably welcoming and heartfelt. Like the Himba and Maasai, and unlike the Arabs, they had no qualms about being filmed together. The most accessible for conversation were **Jitendra**, 40, and **Rattna** and **Sadnam**, both 38 [p. 242].

"Our parents arranged the marriage between Jitendra and me more than 20 years ago, and after two years of marriage they asked if we'd also accept Jitendra's younger brother, Sadnam, into the marriage," Rattna told us with a smile. She was very amused by the interview. "We agreed, because that is how we do things in our valley. Our parents also lived in a marriage like this and many other people do as well. Our children may live as we do, or maybe they won't. We have four children, three daughters and a son."

"Do you know who is the father of which child, or does that not matter?" asked Anđela.

"We do know but it doesn't matter, because both are equally fathers to all our children. The children call Jitendra *bode papa*—older father, and Sadnam *chotte papa*—younger father. We share everything and decide on everything together. Nobody is more or less important. I love each of them equally, and spend equal time with each of them, one week with one, the next week with the other."

"How would you feel if one of them was involved with another woman on the side?" asked Anđela. This was something we asked all the polygynous families. If a man has several wives, why can't a woman have several husbands? And vice versa. The Himba and Maasai were appalled at this possibility and explained that this would be out of the question.

"If that were to happen, what could I do about it?" answered Rattna. "I would be sorry, but what could I do? I'd go on living with the children, and he would go on living with his wife and children."

In this part of the Himalayas, where polyandry used to be very widespread and is now beginning to disappear, there is one even rarer form of polygamy, and that is polygynandry, or group marriage. This form describes the practice in which a woman marries two or three brothers, and then they bring her younger sister into their marriage. All along our way to the Kinnaur Valley and back we asked around to see if anyone knew of anybody living in such a marriage, but in vain. It is quite possible that this custom has died out altogether. Jitendra, Rattna, and Sadnam told us they remembered when they were little that there were such marriages, but nobody knew of such a case today. Anđela explained to them that their custom of polyandry is very rare, that few cultures practice it, and she asked them why it was that in their culture women took several men into wedlock.

"This is our way of keeping the property from being divided," Jitendra took the lead. "I inherited land from my parents and now I'd have to share it with my brother, and then each of us would have less. And then when our children divided it, again it would be fragmented. And so on until there was too little land to support a family. This way is better. The property is not divided. We help one another. In the morning we till the soil, in the afternoon we tend to the sheep and goats. Everything we earn stays in the family. And it is better for the children that they are raised by more people. If one of us is ill, the other will jump in and help. We are all one family. We get along well."

Although we'd hoped to find that women were in charge in polyandric families, the patriarchy prevailed here as well. Rattna may have come across as freer than the women of the Maasai and Himba, but their culture was, without a doubt, patriarchal. The institution of polyandry had taken root in order to preserve property from being divided and frittered away as it was passed down patrilineally. Western culture resolved this same problem by passing all property on to the eldest son or to one of the sons, while the other sons, and especially the daughters, were disinherited. We were given proof of the patriarchate in the Kinnaur Valley when Anđela asked Rattna whether she could divorce them, if they caused problems.

"Sometimes the two of them get drunk and brawl, and then I don't feel comfortable with them," she answered, still smiling. "But what can I do about it? Even if I wanted to leave, I have nowhere to go."

— — —

So, if polygamy is present in 85% of cultures while only 15% of cultures are exclusively monogamous, is this proof that we are naturally polygamous? We asked American anthropologist Dr. **William Jankowiak** at the University of Nevada, Las Vegas, about this when we visited him at his Las Vegas home. In Chapter Three, we already mentioned his groundbreaking research into the universality of love, and we will have more to say about it later. But he has also touched on other themes, with special attention for some time now on the study of polygamy in the United States.

"After several years of observing several polygynous Mormon families I saw that each man had a favorite wife," the 72-year-old social scientist told us. "People enter into polygamous marriages for a variety of cultural, social, or material reasons, but when we closely study their internal dynamic, we see that the husband is always emotionally attached to one person. Love is always a dyad, a relationship between two people. You can have one person who is primary for you for several years, and another after that, but I never found proof that someone can love two people at the same time. We people as a biological species are not sexually monogamous. We have to make a moral commitment that we'll be sexually faithful to our partner and we can keep that promise. But as far as love is concerned, here we're monogamous. If you are truly in love with one person, nobody else interests you. We are sexually polygamous—but emotionally monogamous!"

We posed the same question to anthropologist Dr. **Helen Fisher** who, in the earlier chapters, already took us through the history, biology, and neuroscience of love.

"Eighty-five percent of human cultures permit a man to build a harem, but within these societies only a few succeed in doing so," she said, and we had seen this ourselves. When we sought Maasai, Himba, and Arabs who had more than one wife, everyone knew to tell us where to look for them, but most of the men had only one wife or were not married at all. "This is very demanding, because you must have many goats, many head of cattle, many fruit trees, a great deal of land, you must be rich and prominent in society and you must constantly address discord among your jealous partners. In polygamous households, there is a very high stress level. This is why the great majority of men and women in all cultures world-wide form a pair bond and are monogamous. When we look at our primeval hunter-gatherer past, people formed a pair bond to raise their babies because they were constantly on the move, they couldn't accumulate cows and goats and money and land. Individual men could pull away from the others only through their charisma or if they were exceptionally skilled hunters. Maybe men such as these were able to have more than one wife, but all the rest were monogamous. Monogamy is our past, present, and future. Our brains have evolved in such a way that we form pair bonds, and we have developed a series of psychological mechanisms by which we fall in love, feel a profound attachment, and maintain this connection through jealousy and a heightened focus on one person."

"Does this mean that monogamy is our evolutionary strategy?" we asked.

"Yes, but not pure monogamy. I claim that our evolutionary strategy is serial monogamy with adultery!" she added with a flourish, and then explained.

"Our reproductive strategy has three parts. The first is that we form couples in order to raise our offspring, and the second is that we are unfaithful. I have studied adultery in 40 cultures and divorce in 80 societies and I have found that in all cultures people not only form a pair bonds in order to raise their children as a team, but they might also sleep with someone else in secret. Not everybody does this, but the number of people who embark on adultery is remarkable. The third part of the strategy is serial pair bonding, a series of partnerships one after another: marriage-divorce-remarriage. The demographic statistics of the United Nations from 1947 to 2011 show that the largest numbers of divorces occur around the fourth year of marriage. Why? Because this is the length of time a man and a woman need to raise one child through infancy. For millions of years of our past, men and women stayed with their child through the critical phase of the beginning of life, until the child had grown enough to play with its agemates, of which there were many in the community, and who were looked after by all the adults. The parents could then part ways and form new pair bonds with other partners with whom they'd have new children, thereby increasing the genetic variety of their offspring, which is definitely an adaptive evolutionary strategy."

If a glimpse into the lives of peoples who function today as hunter-gatherers is, in a sense, a glimpse into the long phase of the aboriginal period when our ancestors lived that way—ever since they evolved beyond the ape and up to the Agrarian Revolution when they moved on to farming and the sedentary way of life—then our stay with the Matis in the Amazon provides substantiation for Helen Fisher's statements.

— — —

The episode with the Matis was one of the most extraordinary moments of the project, and not only because we were in the heart of the legendary Amazon with members of an indigenous people whose first contact with white people happened only 40 years ago. Nor was this because they are some of the few remaining hunters and gatherers left in the world. Neither was it due to every aspect of their culture being interesting to us, from how they look to how they talk, what they do, what they believe, and how they look at the world. Rather, it was because nothing was odd, insulting, or awkward for them.

"You can ask them whatever you like," we were told by Goran, our fixer and interpreter, who was from Serbia but has lived most of his life in Leticia, on the border between Colombia, Peru, and Brazil. For a time, he lived with the Matis people, and since then he has visited them regularly over the last 20 years. The Matis love him so much that one of them named his son after Goran. "They speak about everything without a hint of restraint, they gossip about one another, discuss sex in great detail, and have no taboos or topics that are off limits."

This episode was also very amusing. As soon as we began to ask them for their basic biographical information, who is with whom, for how long and so forth, we began to feel as if we'd stumbled into the grand finale of a Mexican soap opera, and now we had to decipher all the links and ties among the few of them who were present and their past partners. This task was all the more challenging because of all the couples we interviewed in the course of our project, this was the only time we had to resort to relay interpretation. One of the Matis who lives in the village and speaks Portuguese was our interpeter from their language into Portuguese, and Goran interpreted from the Portuguese into Serbian, which is so similar to Croatian that we could communicate with Goran in our respective native tongues with no effort.

"My first wife was my brother's wife before," **Baritsica** told us while he rocked on a hammock strung between two trees with his wife **Shawa** [p. 272]. "With her I had two sons. But she decided to go back to my brother, so I found another wife with whom I also had a son. But she left me and went off with another man. Then, for a time, I was alone. Then I met Shawa. I knew her from when she was a little girl, and I'd always liked her, but she always had a man. Then when I saw her she told me she'd separated from her husband and was alone, so I told her I wanted to be with her. And so the two of us are now together and we have two children. One is named Benin, the other—Goran."

"At first I had a different husband," Shawa said, offering her side of the story. "I know Baritsica from before, but my mother wouldn't let me be with him. She took me to a man and told me to be with him. He was my first husband, but he wasn't a good man. He was always looking at other women and I didn't like that. I left him and married his brother. He was a good man and with him I have a son. But he was killed by the Korubo Indians. I don't know what happened, I only know that they killed him with a poison dart. He was young, and our son was just a baby, so I worried about how I'd manage on my own. Then another man appeared so I was with him. But when I learned that he too was chasing other women, I left him right away. I thought about how I'd like to have a good man who would give me food and shelter, so I went back to my mother so she could help me with the child, but she was with another man, so she wouldn't let me stay with her. Then I was alone again, until Baritsica appeared. Now he is my husband."

Other Matis we spoke to had been through similar dramas. From these stories, as well as from everything else they told us, including what they communicated non-verbally, it was clear that they were completely different from the Himba, Maasai, and other traditional, patriarchal societies. The women among the Matis were much freer, even equal to the men. They chose for themselves whom they'd be involved with and when to leave them. There were those who stayed with one partner for a long time, but mainly they were serially monogamous and were seldom longer than a few years with each partner, and then they'd move on to be with someone else. Nobody admitted to adultery while on camera, but they did mention the infidelity of others. Maybe infidelity was a taboo for them.

Perhaps in many other cultures it would be taboo to marry a girl whom you'd adopted and raised. The incest taboo is, after all, universal. All known cultures ban marriage between one's closest kin: brothers, sisters, parents, and children. The main reason for this is that offspring from people who are so closely related may be born with many deformations. Despite this, history has recorded rare cases when brothers and sisters have married, often in European cultures. To marry an adopted child who is not a blood relation is not quite as scandalous for natural reasons as it is for ethical reasons, and ethics and morals are cultural constructs. One of the Matis from our group married his adopted daughter, but others did not perceive this as problematic. This may be because he had a strong reason for such a drastic move.

"I was young when the white people came for the first time," **Iva**, the oldest man in the community, told us. The Matis don't count their years, but when they want to date an event they say how old they were, approximately, when it happened. Around 1980, a major turning point in their history took place:

for the first time, they encountered the world from outside their jungle. They'd had no idea there was such a thing.

"My father was the one who first met the white people," Iva told us. Of all the Matis we met he was the most elaborately adorned in precisely smoothed pieces of wood, bone, and thorns, which protruded from holes in his nose, face, chin, and ears.

"After this almost everyone died from disease. The whole tribe was wiped out. Only a few of us survived, and the three of us are the only ones of all the people here who experienced that," he said and pointed to **Tume**, to his left, and **Kana** [p. 268], to his right. All three of them were sitting on a hammock. Matis do not count in hundreds, but certain researchers have ascertained that before the first contact there were about 400 of them, and after the plague caused by the viruses introduced by the white people, less than 100 survived.

"All of our parents died. My wife Tume and I were old enough that we could look after ourselves, but Kana was a little girl and had no one. So we took her in and helped her survive. Later, when she grew up, I took her for my second wife. I asked Tume whether this would be okay, and she agreed. Too many people had died and I felt it would be good to have two wives, so they could bear me more children, and our tribe could pull through. Now we have 12 children together. But still there are too few of us. I think we should all have two wives and have more children so there will be many of us once again."

The Matis, who like most hunter-gatherer societies were serial monogamists, resorted to polygamy when they were faced with extinction. Might this be proof that nature is stronger than nurture? I wondered. But if behind our actions we have 100% nature and 100% nurture, as Helen Fisher explained to us in Chapter Four, is it possible that we are both 100% polygamous and 100% monogamous?

Or not….

"It's not easy to keep two wives," Iva told us, slightly out of sorts. "When I am with Tume, Kana is angry at me. And when I'm with Kana, Tume is angry at me. They are forever squabbling. Sometimes it's impossible to be with two women!"

INTERMEZZO 1

A PARADISE WITHIN

PALAU, MICRONESIA

The sea waves swell gradually after we've left the last island behind, but they are still low enough to be more playful than worrisome. The regular rhythm of the waves rolling toward us syncs with the rhythm of our paddles. The kayak slices in a straight line across the surface of the sea toward a little islet on the horizon where we'll be setting up camp for the night. I'm in the stern, and Anđela's in the bow. We paddle with an easy rhythm. In unison, we dip first our left paddle, then right, then left, then right. Inside the kayak I press pedals with my feet. With them I steer us and keep us pointed in the right direction. The dry chambers of the kayak are loaded with food, water, and everything we'll need for a week of active vacation.

This may be the first time since we set out on our trip that I feel as if we're on our honeymoon. The five months in Asia wore us down. If the classic honeymoon setting is a tropical paradise, the closest we had come to this was when we arrived on the Maldives, but we went there to recuperate from India, which had sapped our health and mental resilience. Both of us were plagued by diarrhea during our months in India. We ran high fevers. But in spite of it all we still hurried from distant Himalayan valleys to the Rajasthan desert, leaped onto overcrowded trains and buses, choked in the smog of Delhi and the humidity of Mumbai. For the five months we spent in Asia we ran in all directions seeking stories and people, neglecting ourselves. Even our last stop on the Asian tour—Japan— unexpectedly wore us down. It so happened that we'd scheduled our visit there with what turned out to be bad timing—just as the emperor abdicated and passed his role on to his son, inaugurating a new era. This colossal event just so happened to coincide with the Golden Week holiday, which meant that almost all the Japanese were off traveling around their country. For the length of our visit, we couldn't find accommodation, so we slept out on the streets or, for instance, in a bamboo grove in the middle of the temple complex in Kyoto center. We agreed that we'd take at least a week of vacation during our stay in the next country, leave behind our laptops, cameras and recording equipment, and everything having to do with work, log off the Internet, and venture off somewhere, on our own, into nature.

We couldn't have made a better choice. Palau is the most exotic tropical destination we could have chosen, and, at the same time, it also seems to be a secret known only to a select few. Anyone we told before the trip that we were planning for a stay on Palau looked at us with surprise. Few are aware of this country, demographically the world's second smallest, located in Oceania amid one of the most poorly visited parts of the Pacific—Micronesia. I had been dreaming for years of visiting this remarkable archipelago but was waiting for the right person with whom I could realize my dream. That day had finally come.

The smooth skin on Anđela's back catches the golden glow of the sun as it dips into the sea. I use her body as my compass as I steer us toward our destination on the horizon. My eyes are glued to the back of her neck and I stare at it with what might seem like absentmindedness, but I am very much alert. The steady rhythm of our paddle strokes root me to the moment and flood me with enchantment. We haven't spoken for a time. There is no need. We savor these moments of synchronicity—everything is crystal clear. That we've found each other overwhelms me with gratitude. I admire her fearlessness in venturing with me to the ends of the Earth. To follow me each step of the way, with each paddle stroke, into the craziest of dreams. I no longer dream alone.

We have been paddling through the most intricate section of the Palau archipelago for four days now, navigating a labyrinth of little islands strewn across the ocean like green tears. They loom steeply skyward, with lush vegetation hanging down to the water that seems more green than blue. In some places, this vertical world shifts by some miracle to the horizontal with beaches and their gentle white sands. We spend the night on a beach, and the next morning on we go. We know that a few small boats with divers pass through the archipelago every day, but we haven't seen any yet. Larger-scale tourism still hadn't discovered this miracle of nature.

During the day, we stop when the waters beneath us are red with coral; we leave the kayak afloat on the surface, and, while we're still tied to it, we don our masks and slip into the quiet, undersea world. Never have I seen such underwater magnificence. I don't know what is more astonishing here, the above-surface world or the below-surface realm. When I think back to the frozen wastelands of the Antarctic and then grasp where I am now, I'm consumed by a fascination for our so very agreeable and hospitable planet that cruises through the immensity of the universe at exactly the right distance from the sun, and I feel a boundless awe for the unbelievable sequence of random events that have allowed me to see what I'm now seeing. Hypnotized, I gaze at a birthmark between Anđela's shoulder blades, seemingly dancing as she paddles, and I'm plunged into a sense of mindfulness of the moment. We are in the middle of a vast ocean amid whose expanses, oasis-like, a little cluster of islands have formed. Between them lies an oceanic universe. We dance through this space as if we're soaring among the stars. We're together. What were the chances we'd find each other? What were the chances we'd fall in love? Is this not, within this tiniest of chances that such a thing could occur, the most reliable proof that none of this can be random? Or is that randomness precisely what makes it even more precious?

The wind dies down once the sun has dipped below the horizon. The ocean surface stills. We near the islet where we'll spend the night. As we pull into the bay, a calm settles over the water. We see no activity on shore, but we hear it. Small beings rustle on land and splash as they enter the sea. Each new place we come to leaves us with a more powerful impression; but this cove is perfect. The turquoise shallows, the Edenic garden of the beach, and the shelter of the powerful cliffs—the golden mean.

In we paddle and pull the kayak up onto the beach, strip off our wet clothes, and explore the beach and surroundings. We seem, here, to have all a weary seafarer might ever need: deep shade, dry firewood, the presence of turtles, and fish jumping in the shallows, but none of the Pacific rodents that have a way of usurping life in paradise.

And this truly is paradise. I can imagine nothing finer. Not in the heavens or on Earth. I watch Anđela walking naked under the lush treetops that will guarantee us perfect shade the next day. I watch as she, with the curiosity of *homo sapiens*, explores our new temporary home, how she goes for a dip in the sea at twilight and crouches in the white sand to poke around for tiny shells.

I feel myself arriving at a moment beyond which there is nothing further, nothing more to be pushed for. The goal is no longer to achieve something more but to hold on to what we have. Our plan for the next day was to explore a few more coral reefs and the barren beaches of a distant isle in the archipelago. But the allure of faraway shores suddenly dims. Here I have all I need, and we've already come far enough. I tell Anđela I'm thinking about us staying put, doing nothing at all for a day. I ask Anđela how she feels about that. She agrees without saying much. With her smile she shows she wants the same thing.

We settle in. Light a fire. Lie on the warm sand and watch the stars light up across the night sky above Oceania. We're quiet. Our toes wiggle in the shallows as we feel the tide slowly coming in.

The moon rises and with its soft blue glow it lights the steep slopes of the many islets around us.

in love with occupies your life, becomes your everything, you can't stop thinking about her, you don't care about her faults, beauty, wealth, status, nothing.... All you care about is her, just as she is."

Abdoulaye (42) and Suad (25) from Chad were not together before they married. When Suad came of age for wedlock, her parents began receiving proposals from suitors for her hand. The only condition imposed by Suad was that her future husband would allow her to complete her university studies. Abdoulaye was the only suitor who agreed to this.

Mathew (32) and Naomi (22) from Zambia say they fell in love at first sight, though at first Naomi was a little suspicious. "My mother taught me my whole life to be aware of people because all they want is to use me," says Naomi. Beyond the fact of marginalization of people with albinism in many African societies, their lives are also threatened because of the widespread belief that certain of their body parts can be used to treat serious illness or bring wealth into a household when used with black magic. "I gave him my trust and he has not betrayed me," says Naomi of Matthew. "Trust is the most important thing in every marriage."

Daba (78) and Tsao (82) from China belong to the Mosuo, a people who live on Lake Lugu on the border between Tibet and Sichuan. Members of this people traditionally practice one of the loosest forms of marriage, the *tiesese*, in which women are the head of the family and remain for their whole lives in the family home. The fathers of their children do not live with them: the children are raised by their maternal uncles. "We didn't live together. I never went to him. He visited me at night. When our children were born, I raised them with my brother," says Daba. "But now, we live together because we are old, and the times are changing." Although there are still young people who enter into *tiesese* marriages, the number is diminishing and more couples are opting to live together. In the Mosuo language, there is still no word for love, nor is there any similar concept.

Apo Zhedan (64) and Nongjin Zhima (51) from China live on the shore of Lake Lugu. "When we started out as a couple, we weren't living together," says Apo Zhedan. "But I had no sister, so I didn't have to raise her children, while Nongjin Zhima had three sisters, so the house was full of adults and children, and there wasn't enough food to go around. This is why I invited her to live with me, so we'd have an easier time of it."

Aqidu Zhima (47) from China is a member of the Mosuo people. "My husband and I didn't live together earlier, but ever since my mother died, he moved in with me," she says. "Now he is not here. When he saw you coming, he ran away. He doesn't want to have his picture taken."

Alfredo (41) and Melissa (35) from Colombia say that each of them exceeded their expectations for one another. "For me, love is the feeling when you think your heart will explode, when you know your man is here for you when you need him and when you're simply grateful for what you have. Alfredo exceeded my expectations as a husband and a father," says Melisa, and Alfredo adds: "My only remaining expectation is for us to grow old together."

Richard (46) and Kirstin (41) from the United States met through
the children from their previous marriages, and the better they got to
know each other, the more deeply they fell in love. "Attraction has all
the characteristics of addiction," says Kirstin. "Although as a chemist
I am well versed in what goes on in my brain when I fall in love, I am
not immune to these processes just because I understand them."

Nandungo Enkop (23), Nooslamon (27), Muterian (56), Normejoole (30) and Norkisaruni (45) from Kenya are members of the Maasai people, who practice polygyny. Some men have more than ten wives. Muterian has six wives and 22 children. "When you have six wives, as I do, it may happen that you prefer one over the others," he says, "but this depends entirely on them and their character. If a wife serves you well, if she brings you food, speaks nicely to you, doesn't shout, is obedient, answers quickly to what you ask, if she shows she cares about you and loves and honors you, then there's no need to beat her. If a woman is rude or answers in an unseemly way—how can you love her? The more wives you have, the more they compete among themselves to treat you well and have you love them more. All my wives treat me well, I have no favorite, because they all obey me, and I love them all equally. They all prepare my food, none of them has done anything unseemly, I have never seen them with another man, each of them comes to me in my hut when I tell her to."

Masao (76) and Hisae (71) from Japan say that in their country there was no talk of emotions and love at the time when they married. "Now we talk about everything and that is much better," says Hisae. "I'd say that this is why we love each other more now than we did before."

Fabrice (47) from France and Eva (45) from Palestine say they needed to do a lot of work on themselves to come to their current phase of peace and harmony in which they live now, together in Costa Rica. "Love is not enough! You need to work on yourself, rein in all your consciousness and your whole spirit, face all your illusions, endure the pain..." says Fabrice, and Eva adds: "Everyone must take responsibility for their projections and emotions! Nobody else can be responsible for my emotions. They are inside me, they are mine. Fabrice cannot hurt me if I don't allow him to. Once he cheated on me, but I didn't allow him to hurt me with that. It hurt him more than it hurt me. This is why it reinforced our relationship instead of destroying it."

Nabila (28) and Hilal (38) from Oman fell in love at first sight and decided to be together, though Hilal had already been married for 15 years. Instead of dissolving his first marriage, Hilal took Nabila as his second wife, because polygamy is permitted in Oman. "Neither my first wife nor Nabila are happy that they have to share a husband," says Hilal, "but the choice isn't up to them. Here, the choice is up to the man. This choice is something God has given us—and with it comes the duty and responsibility for us to take care of our wives."

Judith (34) and Alex (28) from France legalized their relationship with a PACS, a civil solidarity pact—the French alternative to marriage. "Fewer and fewer young people are choosing to marry," says Judith. "A PACS suffices to make life a little easier in terms of administration. There is no longer any need for a wedding; it's too official and too romantic."

"We men groom ourselves to show our beauty. Then we dance and the girls look us over. If we like one another, we are allowed to go into the bush and have fun together alone."

Ali (20) and Fadtima (15), Chad

Young men of the Wodaabe tribe parade their beauty for the women

Portable dwellings where the Wodaabe sleep when they travel across the Sahel with their livestock

Preening for the dance

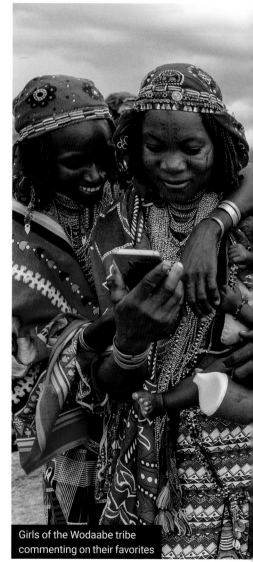
Girls of the Wodaabe tribe commenting on their favorites

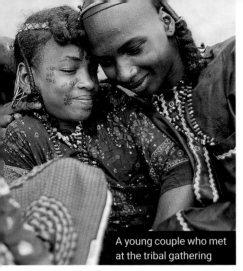
A young couple who met at the tribal gathering

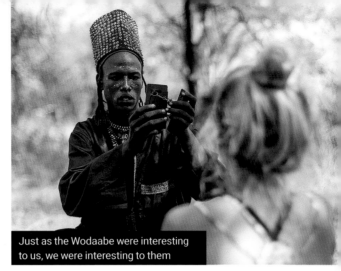
Just as the Wodaabe were interesting to us, we were interesting to them

Our team, who barely managed to locate the nomad gathering

The Wodaabe are a subgroup of the Fula people who live in Sahel, the semi-arid belt that runs south of the Sahara from the Atlantic to the Red Sea. There are about 100,000 Wodaabe, and most of them are nomads. They drive their herds from Niger and Nigeria to Cameroon and Chad. They usually wander across the bush in groups of ten to twenty people, and only once a year do they have the opportunity to assemble in a larger number, always at the end of the rainy season, because by then fresh grass is available in abundance so they are not compelled to drive their livestock to fresher grazing lands daily. The annual gathering is known as the Guérewol, and it takes place on sites across the Sahel. For the young people of the Wodaabe this is their only chance to meet other members of their group and perhaps find someone among them with whom they'll start their family and with whom their treks under the hot African sun would be more bearable. The Wodaabe are the only culture we know of where the men put on makeup in order to attract the women. When they watch them and evaluate their beauty, the women pay the most attention to the whiteness of their teeth and the whites of their eyes.

Richa (49) and Satinder (45) from India met through their parents, who arranged their marriage. "People enter into love marriages out of passion, so they aren't able to think clearly about practical matters," says Satinder. "Arranged marriages fall apart less, they are arranged by the parents who know their children better than their children know themselves and they know better what will have a good chance of success, and what will not."

Debora (38) and Alexander (46) from Brazil say that they haven't had an easy time of it, but love has guided them through all the challenges. "We had many difficult moments," says Debora. "When I was 14, on one of our first dates we had a serious traffic accident in which Alexander lost a leg. I was already pregnant at 16, his son from his first marriage died a few years ago.... But here we are, fighting day in and day out, realizing our dreams, we have two wonderful sons, we go to the beach, we dance.... I'd say we're winners!"

Tracy (42) from the United States and Natsumi (40) from Japan live and raise their child in Japan. "There is a large cultural difference between us," says Natsumi. "When we argue, I want to crawl into my cave and stay there, but he wants to talk. Americans always want to talk. They are constantly asking: 'How are you?' We Japanese don't talk about emotions. If you love me, shouldn't you already know how I am?"

do not intend to marry. When you are married you never have any peace of mind because your husband beats you if a goat is lost. You are blamed for everything, even when it's not your fault. You do everything, you work hard, and he doesn't work at all, just sleeps and beats you. I don't need the stress."

Jane (50) from Kenya has been living in the women's village of Umoja for more than 20 years. "I was married to a man much older than me when evil men with small eyes raped me. Because I was raped, my husband took my children from me and threw me out in the middle of the night. I do not wish to marry again. I can no longer love men. Because of how my husband treated me, my heart has learned to hate men."

Richard (64) and Cheryl (64) from the United States fought a serious
form of cancer that brought Richard to the brink of death. "There is a difference between knowledge and understanding," says Richard. "We all know that we'll die, but I experienced what it means to be counting the days. We tried to use every moment, we danced on the bed in the hospital, enjoyed every second of life because we knew they were our last seconds together. And when the diagnosis, thank goodness, changed and I pulled through, we went right on doing that... dancing and enjoying life."

Teodora (54) and Agustin (59) from Bolivia got to know each other in their village when they were children. After they were married, Agustin began working as a guide in the high mountains, and Teodora helped him by cooking for his clients at the base camp. In time she, too, responded to the call of the mountains, and with the *Cholitas Escaladoras* group she climbed the highest peaks of South America. Now Agustin is helping her prepare to climb Mount Everest. They spend every spare moment on glaciers, practicing climbing.... "Love is when you understand and support each other, when you are together and when you look after one another," says Teodora.

Ahmed (36) and Shaheema (32) from Maldives met over Facebook and decided that they'd use the money they would have spent on a wedding for their

Frank (64) and Aleth (62) from France have long been in a marriage rife with challenges, but also understanding. Frank fell in love with other women several times and was the most surprised of all when he fell in love with a man—a friend of their son's. But each time he did, Frank talked about it with Aleth, who at first found it difficult to accept that her husband was not emotionally monogamous. She learned to put up with this thanks to his candor and the fact that he'd never, actually, cheated on her. "Our relationship is like sailing on the ocean," says Aleth. "I hold the tiller, and he is the wind that propels the boat. A boat with no wind goes nowhere, and wind with no boat serves nothing."

Elmira (38) and Melis (40) from Kyrgyzstan began their relationship with a kidnapping. The custom of bride kidnapping used to be widespread throughout Europe, Asia and Africa, but today one seldom encounters it; in Kyrgyzstan, it has held on more than anywhere else. More than half of the current marriages there began that way. "I had completed my studies in Bishkek, the capital, and found a job there, but when I came to visit my family in Kyzart, where I'm from, Melis kidnapped me," says Elmira. "I protested, I had other plans for my life, but everyone persuaded me that he was a good man, so I stayed." Melis had long postponed this: he was shy and withdrawn, he didn't like the idea of the kidnapping, but he also didn't like being pressured by his community—all his agemates had already married. "I finally decided to take the step when my father gave me his ultimatum," says Melis. "He threatened that he wouldn't give me the money for the wedding if I didn't bring her home the very next day."

Marat (35) and Bubukairy (32) from Kyrgyzstan live in Bishkek, the capital city, where the centuries-old tradition of kidnapping brides is fast losing its grip, but the two of them used the tradition to their own advantage. They had been in a secret two-year relationship when Bubukairy came sobbing to Marat to say her parents had promised her hand to another suitor. "I had no choice but to kidnap her," says Marat. "But ours was a consensual kidnapping. We went out of town and didn't come back until her parents agreed to our marriage."

124

Meerim (25) from Kyrgyzstan succeeded in resisting a kidnapping attempt. "All the girls quake at the thought that someone might one day kidnap them and they all say they'd never stay in such a relationship. But when this happens to them, most of them accept it in the end," says Meerim. "I did not. An acquaintance kidnapped me, but I ran away. My father raised me to be independent. That I don't allow anyone to decide about my life instead of me!"

Cristina (55) from the Philippines and Henrik (65) from Denmark live in Los Angeles. "Romance is an aesthetic game, it can be entertaining, but one shouldn't identify with it because it is fragile, transitory, and has to do with unimportant appearance," says Henrik. "The essence is outside the game, outside all games—in the intellect, in the spirit."

Sonia (30) and Rohit (35) from India are followers of the Vaishnavism tradition in which a man and woman join in wedlock only for as long as they need to raise their offspring and then part ways and devote themselves to spirituality. "Romantic love requires reciprocity, but true love only desires to give," says Sonia. "True love is service. True love is when you genuinely recognize the desires and needs of another person and do all that is necessary to make them happen, unconditionally. Romantic love is in the material world, where everything is transitory and fades, while true love is in the spiritual world."

"A woman is the
source of life.
So, when we wish to
marry, we must pay
a steep price in shells."

Peter (53) and Maria (58), Solomon Islands

Fishing on the waves in hand-made crafts

Duddley and Juliane in front of their house

The village is nestled under the treetops, overlooking the shores of the Pacific

A celebration in the village

The largest number of people with blond hair outside of Europe live on the Solomon Islands

A waterfall not far from the village where the people go to bathe

A celebration in the village

This community, probably the most traditional in the Solomon Islands, is held together not by tribal membership or belief in the same gods, but by resistance to unfettered development and the colonization of the islands, and the desire to preserve the traditional way of life, *kastom*, the path of the ancestors. The community is almost entirely self-supporting, in harmony with nature. They cultivate gardens of taro root, yams, and bananas on the slopes of mountains in the island's interior, and, at sea, they catch fish using little seafaring crafts hollowed out of single logs. They wear traditional clothing, the women in grass skirts and the men in a loincloth fashioned of tree bark. Their monogamous marriages are arranged by parents, but the young people are allowed to spurn the proposal if they are not pleased with it. Once the marriages are official, however, only death will part them. The children are not raised by their parents alone, but by the entire community. Some young people go off to study in the capital or to temporary jobs, but most of them don't stay away from the community for long.

children. Sometimes she gets so angry at me and flies into a rage that I have to run away and leave her alone. I wait until she calms down and then I come home. Meanwhile, she has forgotten why she was so angry. And then everything is fine and on we go, living together happily."

moved forward, but he couldn't follow me." Marco says that his situation was similar. "In my first marriage I was lonely. As if I were the only one to propel things forward and make an effort. I had no support from my ex-wife. Everything is completely different with Adela. Life is now full of joy and laughter."

Sharda (25) and Naru (27) from India are members of the Kalbeliyas, a traditional people who are dancers and snake-charmers. "When we met, we were very much in love, but we hadn't yet married, so everyone told us we mustn't spend time together and speak in public because that was against the custom," says Sharda. "We told them: 'We don't care! If this bothers you—change the customs!'"

Jessica (18) and Ifene (20) from Zambia live under a railway bridge in the center of Lusaka, Zambia's capital. "Here on the street, where we live, many children are infected with HIV," says Jessica. "We are careful. Ifene protects me from others. If I were to learn that he's infected with HIV I'd stay with him no matter what, because I love him."

Andre (38) and Aline (37) from Brazil found themselves living on the streets at the beginning of their relationship because of financial problems. "Aline always makes sure I look good, she washes and irons my clothes, and then when I look good, she's jealous," laughs Andre. "Even when we were living on the streets and sleeping in cardboard boxes, she made sure I looked as good as I could, she enjoyed showing me off, she was boasting that I'm her husband, and then if someone took a liking to me, she was jealous."

Briseida (20) and Klinsman (22) from Bolivia are both traditional wrestlers and local celebrities. "I am ultra jealous," says Klinsman. "Our job is such that we have many fans, but when I see the fans flocking to her, this drives me crazy. Maybe that's because I don't like to lose. I don't like to think I could lose what I treasure most in my life."

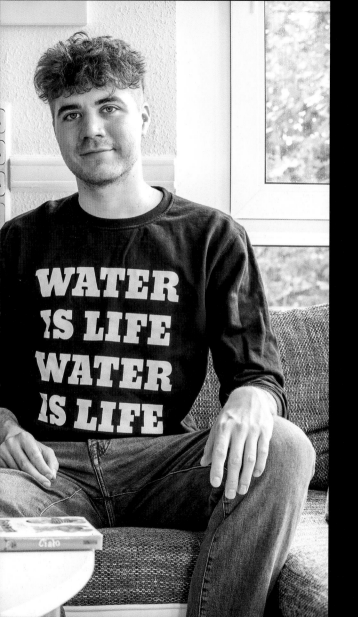

Christian (32), Nicole (33) and Fabian (29) from Germany have been living in a non-hierarchical polyamorous relationship for ten years. "At first, Christian and I were in an open relationship," says Nicole. "He had different partners, but I had only Fabian. Fabian began sleeping over at our place more often, and so it was that one day he moved from the sofa in the living room to our bedroom. When Christian and I married, everything was marvelous, like a fairy tale, but we realized we were missing Fabian in our union, so we decided to become a triad." Once they had a child, they decided to close their triad to other people, and today they are working together to legalize polyamorous marriages. "We know who the biological father is and we had to register him as such, but we don't tell this to anyone, and we raise our child with two fathers who have equal standing. In Germany, one can't register two fathers, which may become a problem in many situations in life, for instance if the child were to have to be hospitalized, or if something happens to the 'official' father," says Nicole.

Yi Hang (25) and Zhou Jie (26) from China say they were each other's first reciprocated love. "The very first time we went out on a date, we couldn't bear to part," says Yi Hang. "I walked her home. Then she walked me home. Then I her. Then she me.... We couldn't part."

Yoni (41) and Rivky (38) from the United States belong to a community of Orthodox Hassidic Jews who practice arranged marriages. "Love is a modern fabrication of the media and Hollywood that teach you that you are always needing something, and that love is everything you need," says Yoni. "In American culture, people honor love, love sells products, and culture teaches you that you need all of it. But in essence, people don't need anything. In our Hassidic community, we don't marry out of love, but because we need one another. Love comes later. I need *you*. I don't need *something* from you, I need *you*. What does love have to do with that?"

Davecat (49) from the United States describes himself as a robosexual because he is attracted to gynoids—robots and dolls in the shape of women. He has been married to Sidore, his doll, for almost two decades. For the 20th anniversary of their marriage he is planning on upgrading her with software that will allow him to speak with her. "Organic people don't fall in love with others as they actually are, but in their projection of what the other person is. With synthetic partners at least you know what you're dealing with, they accept you as you are. The only thing that's too bad is that you can't go out with them to concerts, to introduce them to other people.... But this too will become possible in the not-so-distant future. The technology is advancing with leaps and bounds."

Chris (56) from Germany turned to dolls and female robots after his ex-wife hurt him. "Life with dolls is becoming less unusual in society. There are ever more Hollywood movies exploring these themes. It is already normal in the world of science fiction. And in China, this is a big thing. The Chinese are at the forefront of production of dolls and of the number of people who choose a doll for their partner."

Carolina (38) from Spain and Thomas (42) from Belgium met through an online app for finding a long-term partner. "The matching applications are very convenient and useful," says Thomas, "especially for those of us who are very busy. It is neither easy nor comfortable for me to go out in search of someone. If I don't go out to bars and clubs, where will I be able to meet a potential partner? If I'd come across Carolina at a railway station, I would have had no way of knowing we are as compatible as we discovered ourselves to be over the web."

Lori (49) and Shawn (52) from the United States found out, via a matching app, that their compatibility is at 100%, so they decided to meet in person. "We clicked immediately," says Shawn. "Everything was perfect. She made me laugh and I made her laugh. It was love at first sight!"

Eduardo (5) and Valeria (6) from Colombia say they can't remember when they first met because they were still babies then. "Valeria can't have any other boyfriends but me, because that's how it is, because my mom has only one boyfriend," announces Eduardo and adds, "but I can have all the girlfriends in the world if I want!"

Teruo (92) and Michiko (88) from Japan were married before telephone lines had been installed in their village. Teruo had a friend deliver a letter to her, inviting her to go out to the movies in the next village. "He lived near me and was good-looking, so I agreed to his proposal of marriage," says Michiko. Both of them admit that in their 67 years of marriage they have never thought about what love is.

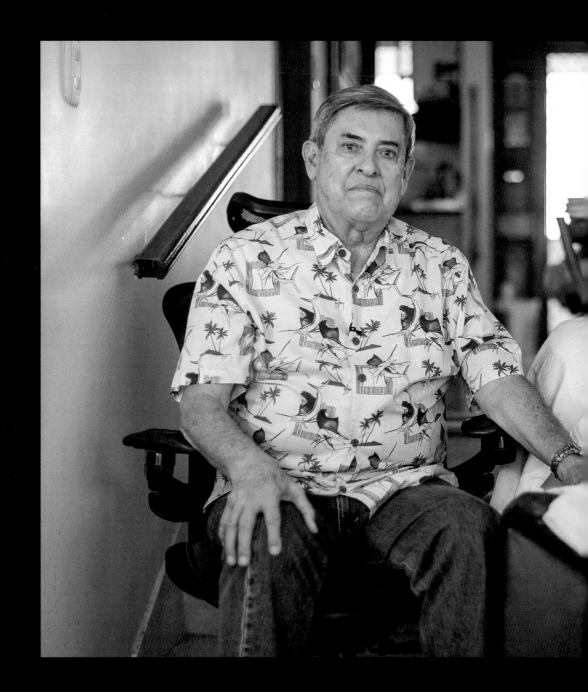

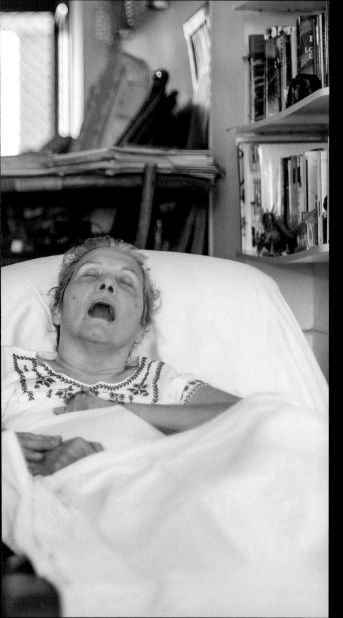

Jorge (75) and Amalia (70) from Colombia have been married for more than half a century. Fourteen years ago, she was diagnosed with a serious form of progressive and irreversible dementia. "Whoever knew Amalia before she got sick was completely enchanted by her personality," says Jorge. "She entranced people with the power of her spirit and goodness. She even accepted the horrible diagnosis bravely and calmly. My feeling of love for her is constant and unwavering. She fulfills my life. Just the fact that I can be next to her, as I am now, makes me absolutely happy."

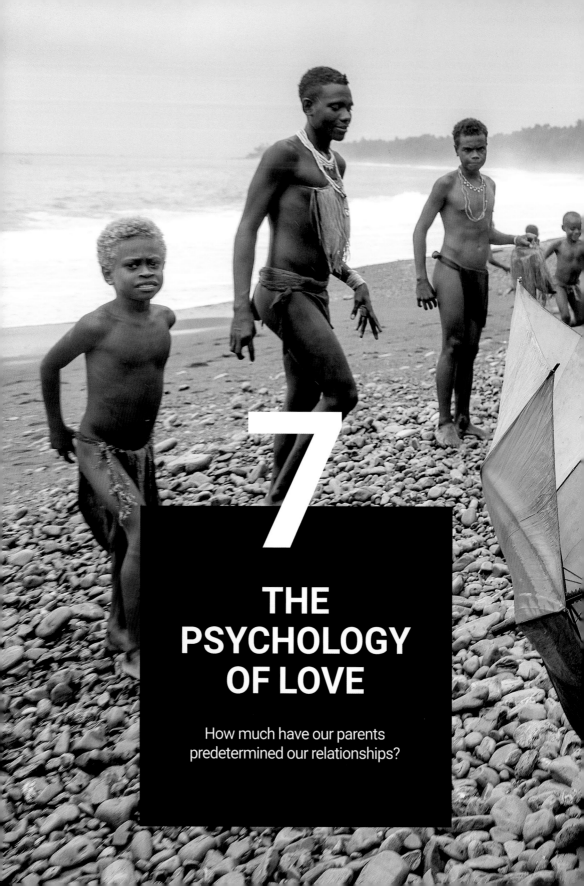

7

THE PSYCHOLOGY OF LOVE

How much have our parents predetermined our relationships?

What is paradise? Where is it? Does all this travel of mine revolve around my search to sense it, to find it? If paradise is perfect, where can that perfection be found on Earth?

Nature is not perfect, it is cruel and unjust, but within its complex balance perhaps it's the closest thing to perfection we'll find. The way I see it, nature is not complete without people—people who are attuned to nature. But since people are imperfect, they destroy paradise. Can a natural site be found that has been settled by a people who have not usurped it or imposed themselves upon it, but have embraced being a part of its complexities? I focused on this question obsessively for four years as part of my 'Jungle' project. The closest thing I found to my version of paradise was in New Guinea with a Papuan tribe who had, at the time, been living utterly cut off from the modern world. The Papuans are Melanesian, a broad cultural group that has had the briefest contact, historically, with modern civilization, and among them are the very last peoples who live in utter harmony with nature, or as close as possible in the 21st century.

I definitely wanted us to visit at least one Melanesian community on our

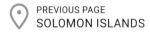
PREVIOUS PAGE
SOLOMON ISLANDS

world tour, but instead of New Guinea, where I'd already led four quite extreme expeditions, this time I chose the Solomon Islands. The reason for this was an image I once saw long ago, which made a huge impression on me. The image was one of the opening sequences in the Terrence Malick film *The Thin Red Line*. The plot takes place in the Pacific theater during World War Two. A few American soldiers have fled the horrors of war and they find peace on an idyllic beach, far from combat, where time has, apparently, stood still. The locals for whom the beach is home live an enchantingly easygoing life. The interaction between the soldiers and the local people, the ocean, the beach, the smiles, the carefree life in paradise... all this is in stark contrast to the horrors of war, to which they are later forced to return.

When I saw those scenes in the movie, something touched me deep inside, as only the finest works of art can do. At the same time, this moved me to go off to that part of the world and find a similar place. I could assume, of course, that what I'd seen was a stage set designed for the movie. I also realized that even if such a place had indeed existed, it probably no longer exists, because, after all, 75 years had passed. However, as I knew something about the history of the region and its current situation, I was hoping we might be able to discover a place like the one shown in the movie. Since the people on screen were dark-skinned but had blond curly hair, I thought it might have been filmed in the Solomon Islands where, for whatever reason, the largest number of people with blond hair outside of Europe live. I knew that beyond Melanesia we'd find it difficult, perhaps even impossible, to identify a people living as traditionally as some still live in New Guinea, but I felt it was worth a try. Our research before we set out produced no results, but the fact that something isn't on the Internet may, in fact, bode well. Sometimes the real exploration only begins when you set foot in a place.

We started making inquiries as soon as we flew from Palau to Honiara, the capital of Solomon Islands. For most of the 20th century, these islands were a colony of Australia, and today they are still under its influence, so most of the people there speak English, which was a boon for our research. We quickly learned that there were no tribes left anywhere on the islands who hadn't stepped into modernity. We did learn, however, that there was a group of people who'd decided to defy the harmful impact of development and had chosen to live traditionally and in harmony with nature. Here, as has been the case in so many places the world over, the great colonial powers and capitalist corporations had stolen or snatched up vast expanses of land for a pittance so they could exploit the resources as quickly as possible. Already on our flight above the islands we could see immense monoculture plantations producing cheap palm oil. Scenes like this always make me wonder whether we human beings as a species are anything better than the most ordinary pests and parasites, more drawn to devastation than to harmony.

The recipe for destruction was very simple. Foreign powermongers from the political and business worlds bribed tribal elders to sell them their land for a pittance, and then they cleared it and exploited its resources above and below ground. The pattern repeated from one tribe to the next. People everywhere are susceptible to corruption, but there are also incorruptible people who oppose injustices. Rebels from tribes across the islands organized a movement and took up the struggle against the 'occupiers.' In the second half of the last century they waged a guerilla war with bows and arrows against the far more powerful enemy. Many of them were killed in this heroic Sisyphean struggle, but those who survived succeeded in conquering and holding onto a large swath of land. They agreed that this land would never be put for sale, and they live there traditionally and simply, in harmony with nature, as their ancestors had lived for generations before white people came.

We heard this story from them, when, after many logistical challenges, we finally managed to reach the place deemed the seat of their movement. [pp. 130-131]. The village lies on the shores of the mighty Pacific along foothills beneath a tall mountain. Large ocean waves come crashing onto the dark sandy shore, but the locals still set off through the roiling surf every day in their small tippy dugout canoes to go fishing. Their homes are nestled right behind the first row of palm trees on the shore. The little dwellings with their walls of bamboo and branches and their roofs of palm fronds are surrounded by gardens paved in pebbles and bordered by ornamental plants and flowers. Pigs and chickens freely wander the village. Closer to the mountain, there are gardens of taro, yams, bananas, pandanus, and other tropical fruits and vegetables. Abundant rivers and streams flow down off the mountain, watering the gardens and providing the village with fresh water. Only a five minutes' walk from the last dwelling in the village is an idyllic waterfall with a little pool where people go to bathe.

Most of the people wear traditional clothing—they are barefoot and bare-chested; the women wear grass skirts, while the men wear a loincloth fashioned of tree bark. Many of the children and some of the adults have curly blond hair. There is no road leading to the village, and everything there happens on foot. There are no stores, no electric power, no cell-phone signal. The school is in the next village, an hour's walk away. Many of the children attend school, but afterward they stay in the village to farm and fish. A few of the young folk go on to study in Honiara, some of the older men leave to work in the mines or on plantations, but most often they return to the village. Money is mostly needed to pay for school fees and occasional trips to the capital to purchase a few essentials, such as metal cooking pots, plastic dishes, tools…. Otherwise, they have little use for money. From our perspective, they have an unusual attitude about it.

One of the tribal elders invited us to be his guests. He let us use a dwelling, and his wife and daughters brought us food whenever they'd prepared it for themselves. When we offered to compensate them in some way, they looked at us in surprise. "How can I ask you for payment for something I receive from nature for free, something that isn't mine?" he asked. But when we told him we were interested in their culture and would like to photograph, record, and talk with them about how they live and build relationships—now this was something else again. "Well, that you'll have to pay for because that's our culture!" he announced flatly.

I enjoyed the interviews because they brought us deeper into their way of life and showed us new dimensions. A tribal elder, 48-year-old **Duddley**, when asked how he shows his wife **Juliane** [p. 133] his love for her, said:

"I think it's important, in marriage, to let my wife know that she is a good wife. I make an effort to show her this, so she knows I love her."

"And how do you show her?" we asked him.

"If I go somewhere to find money and I find money, I bring it home and give it to her. And at home I name things as hers. When I talk about our pig, I say, 'this is my wife's pig.' When I speak of the land, I say, 'this is my wife's land.' When I speak of our house, I say 'this is her house.' I do this so she'll feel happy, she'll see how I love and respect her."

To our regular questions, "How would you react if your partner were to fall in love with someone else?" people across the world have offered a wide range of responses, from being happy for them to wanting to murder them. I noticed that the more educated the people were—in the modern sense of the word—the less often they'd answer succinctly and cogently. Moreover, it often seemed that because of this complexity they often don't perceive simple answers. The Solomon Islanders gave us simple, precise answers. To the question of how he'd react if Juliane were to fall in love with someone else, Duddley answered:

"I'd be sad."

How can a person not admire this simplicity, sincerity, and candor? How to avoid the trap of romanticizing such societies? On my travels, I learned very early that there are all sorts of people everywhere. Maybe I idealized some groups at first, thinking of them as 'exotic,' but I quickly realized that among them, just as among all of us, there are good and bad people, the smart and the stupid, the altruistic and the selfish, the ambitious and the easygoing, the fickle and those who embrace friendship, indeed—all sorts. It would be wrong and pointless to generalize that any one group, regardless of one's criteria, is better or worse than any other. Yes, we can see our differences using various parameters and I don't think we need to close our eyes to these differences and pretend they don't exist in order to achieve equality. But despite our differences, it is possible for us to find respect and understanding for one another.

During the ten days we spent with our new Solomon Island friends, I was truly amazed on many occasions by their good intentions and unvarnished sincerity. I admired their integrity, because at every moment they seemed to say exactly what they were thinking. Although they follow the ways of the traditional age—as farmers in a patriarchal society with clearly defined roles for men and women, with a strong sense of community that always comes first, with parents arranging marriages and men paying a bride price in shells—we had the impression that the men truly respect their wives, help them in everything, and treat them with tenderness.

How then could I dismiss the impression that we had truly found the closest resemblance to paradise on Earth? The image from the Malick movie that I had been dreaming of for years and had been seeking for a long time played out in that village every evening before night fell when part of the community gathered on the beach after finishing their work in the gardens. A crowd of children scampered around on the beach and in the water, splashed in the waves and shrieked with excitement, some of them romped carefree in the sand while their parents kept a watchful eye on them from a distance. As each fisherman returned from fishing, everyone would run over to help push the vessel high enough up on the beach so the tide couldn't reach it. The mothers held the children who weren't big enough to romp and play with the others yet, but in the infants' lively eyes we could read their eagerness to grow up and finally join the lively horde that spent every day playing and laughing.

I was certain that this must be the closest thing to paradise on Earth, and so I was quite surprised when, in the middle of this paradise, we stumbled onto Freud.

— — —

"I expect my wife to be the same as my mother was," we were told by 34-year-old **Donly** when we interviewed him with **Diana** [p. 132], ten years his junior, in their dwelling of twigs and palm leaves. "I expect her to look after me, care for me, cook, fetch water, give me all my mother gave me. To make things as nice as they were when I was little and my mother looked after me."

When I heard this, I immediately thought of Sigmund Freud, the founding father of psychoanalysis, who claimed in the early 20th century that in our partners we're seeking our parents. He expounded on the idea of the Oedipal complex according to which boys compete with their father for their mother's affections, while his contemporary, Carl Gustav Jung, broadened this theory to include the Electra complex by which girls compete with their mother for their father's affections. If these complexes are not resolved properly and in time, both men and women may later suffer a series of complications in life, especially in the emotive, sexual, and love-related parts of their lives. These revolutionary ideas about psycho-sexual development influenced a series of 20th century scholars and thinkers, such as Erich Fromm, a psychologist of humanism and author of the now classic work *The Art of Loving*.

If I understood their teachings, throughout our lives we all yearn for the perfect sense of safety we felt in our prenatal phase when all our needs were met and we were one with our mother. Perhaps our longing to find a paradise in which everything is perfect is merely our grief at the loss of that feeling. And our search for a partner is merely a longing to again become one with someone else. In *The Art of Loving*, Fromm says that in every historical period and in every culture, people address the same question: how to overcome separateness, achieve union, transcend one's own individual life, find atonement. This applies to all of us equally, because it arises from the human condition. Early humans, the humans of the aboriginal age, were bound to nature as a newborn is bound to its mother. But the more humankind emerged from primeval relations, the more people drew apart from nature and sought new ways to sidestep or overcome the feeling of separation. There are various ways to overcome separateness—through orgiastic states, trance, dance, drugs, through rituals that heighten the sense of oneness within a group, through conformism, adaptation to the group and its customs, actions, and beliefs, or through creativity. However, the only full way to overcome separateness, according to Fromm, is a way that leads through love, through our physical and spiritual oneness with another person in love.

Some scientists who study evolution posit that love first originated between mother and child[1]. As the young of higher mammals do not come into the world fully equipped to look after themselves independently, they have an extended need for growth and protection. So, love was needed, the emotional bond between mother and child, which would allow the mother to care for her helpless offspring. Later, this love extended to other members of the family, and finally to the outsiders with whom we procreate to produce our descendants. Hence, we seek the love in our partners that we used to receive from our parents.

No one but Donly from the Solomon Islands stated in such explicit terms that they were hoping to find their mother in their female partner, but many whom we spoke to said that the greatest impact on their ideas about what love should be, whether conscious or unconscious, had come down to them from their parents. I believe we'll all agree that in the first years of life our parents have an almost exclusive influence on us, so it is hardly surprising that we tend to use them as the model for our mental map for loving and our ideals for the kind of partners we'd love to find. Freud's ideas about the Oedipal complex and fixation on parents, however, have largely been rejected today[2]. Most of his critics agree that it is wrong to assume that love originates in sexuality. Some even say that he didn't have a full understanding of sexuality—wrongly interpreting both female sexuality and homosexuality[3].

Parents doubtlessly shape our ideas about which people will be attractive to us. But these ideas needn't only be positive. We may not be looking for our parents in our partners. We may be looking for what our parents were not, as well. The contrary. The opposite.

Tracy, an American who lives in Japan with his wife **Natsumi** [p. 116], admitted that his father abused his mother; he has spent his whole life determined to do the opposite with his wife. **Alfredo** and **Melissa** [p. 104] from Colombia, whom we already met in Chapter Four, had fathers who were womanizers, so they were now actively making sure not to repeat their fathers' mistakes. **Frederick** from Kenya had decided, long before he met his wife **Ann** [p. 240], that he would never divorce, so his children wouldn't have to suffer through the trauma he'd suffered by growing up with no father. **Camille** and **Jean** [p. 283] from Belgium said that everyone in their extended families had gone through divorces, so after witnessing these painful ruptures, both of them decided they would avoid divorce at all costs.

We cannot know how much they'll succeed in distancing themselves from the models they absorbed from their parents. We all know cases of people who forever repeat their parents' mistakes, those who seek in their partners the saints and abusers their parents were. We also know, however, of those who built an entirely different relationship than those their parents had. Only on this basis, we cannot conclude that we learn everything we know about love from our parents, nor that they are the sole influence on which partners we choose.

In the case of Anđela and me, the influence of our parents is very present. Both Anđela's parents and mine have stayed together, so Anđela and I feel an aversion to divorce. When we compare ourselves to our friends who come from divorced families, we notice that our tolerance threshold is somewhat higher and we would find it much more difficult to take such a step. In Anđela, I certainly see both my mother's virtues and her shortcomings, just as Anđela sees the virtues and shortcomings of her father in me.

Because of all this, I find myself wondering: how truly free are we? If we are predetermined by our nature, biology, chemistry, and genetics and, furthermore, by our parents, upbringing, and culture—wherein lies our free will? Can we ever free ourselves of the terror of various conditionalities or are we their eternal slaves? Are we able to change or are we merely puppets on the strings of an automated mechanism with all our moves already programmed by human nature and the sway of parents and those who raise us?

8

ASSUMPTIONS
ABOUT LOVE

What lies behind our firmly held beliefs,
and can a person change?

Our travels didn't always take us to paradise-like spots such as Palau or the Solomon Islands. Everything wasn't always marvelous and fantastic.

Indeed, most of the time we were agonizingly racing from one place to another and we were often coming apart at the seams. What can't be seen in the photographs from our more bucolic destinations and can't be read from the excerpts of the engaging interviews we posted to social media was the vast amount of effort and toil that lay behind it all. We were forever struggling with the gap between the impression we give to others and what we truly are. And furthermore, Anđela and I have different ideas about how each of us should be, how the two of us ought to live, and what our journey ought to be.

As we traveled from one country to the next, one of these differences began surfacing and kept tripping us up—the different view of how much time we should be dedicating to work and how much we should set aside for our private lives. In our case, it isn't

PREVIOUS PAGE
PARIS, FRANCE

easy to draw the line between our private and professional lives because they are so completely intertwined. Even our honeymoon was our work. Although we spent everything we had on it and devoted nearly all our time to it, at the same time, this was supposed to be an investment in something that would support us financially over the coming years. So, we crammed too many stops into our itinerary and hurtled around the world at a breakneck pace. We spent an average of two weeks per country, and in each place, we researched ten to twenty stories, usually following through with three or four, then hurried to locations from one end of the country to the other to explore the stories and record them. Meanwhile, we were perched at our computers in cafés, restaurants, and hotels, online, doing all the other necessary tasks…. While we were in the Solomon Islands, we purchased plane tickets to travel from Chad to Costa Rica. In the stifling snack bars of India, we were organizing our Amazon expedition six months in advance. While we were camping in parks in Japan we arranged our visas for African countries through their European embassies. While aboard planes and buses, we downloaded, organized, and processed photographs and video and audio material, wrote blogs, went over our notes and prepared posts for social media. While on jostling taxi rides, we set dates with fixers and interpreters. Trekking along the roads of the world we put calls in to hundreds of potential protagonists and discussed our interviews. To each one, we had to tell the whole story of our project and ourselves, forward them presentations, and motivate them to share their story with us. Only every twentieth or thirtieth couple we spoke with consented to what we were asking. From Zambia to Bolivia, Saudi Arabia, Iran, Palau, and beyond we kept tabs on our business affairs in Zagreb, as the income provided the financial support needed for the project.

If what we two did had been handled by a Western European or US production company, I'm sure that what we accomplished would have required a team of at least ten people on a budget that would be ten times ours. But Anđela and I did all of this on our own while on the road. And besides all this, we were supposed to be enjoying our honeymoon and keeping some time for ourselves.

Dubai, Almaty, Chengdu, Hong Kong, Osaka, Manila, Auckland, Santiago, Bogota, Windhoek, Gaborone: hardly having any time to properly see these cities—being buried in our laptops somewhere in a café most of the time—seared itself like a scar into Anđela, who anyways suffers from the FOMO syndrome: fear of missing out.

"Who knows whether we'll ever be able to come back here and whether I'll ever again have the chance to see this place," she'd say, and she was right.

Maybe we could have tweaked the project concept and cut back on the workload. Instead of 25 countries, we could have visited only ten. Instead of 120 couples, we could have interviewed only 50. But would that have satisfied our creative appetites? Would we have collected enough high-quality and diverse material to do what we'd dreamt of doing? I am, perhaps, too demanding, while Anđela is more realistic and productive. Whatever work we do, she is faster and more efficient than I am, and on the other hand, I'm prepared to put in longer hours to the detriment of our private time. I often fill the time and space that is supposed to be only ours with additional work, which is not a great recipe for a harmonious relationship.

By the time we reached Nairobi, the capital of Kenya, in the ninth month of our world tour, we had already accumulated so many problems that the situation was doomed to blow up in our faces. We were already deep enough into the project that each of us had developed a more nuanced sense of the stories we should be looking for, how much time we should devote to the project, and how much to leave for ourselves. For a month and half, we'd been traveling through Africa, and logistically and in every other way this part was more grueling than travel had been across any of the other settled continents. And to make matters a thousand times worse, just as we arrived in Africa, Anđela had word that her father had died. We went back to Croatia for ten days, and then returned to Africa and picked up where we'd left off. I have never lost anyone so close to me, so I wasn't sure whether I could even imagine the pain she was feeling. I did what I could to be by her side as much as possible, offer her my support for everything from morning to night and in the middle of the night, but judging by her reactions, I was doing everything wrong. I kept feeling torn between how to be available to her and doing whatever I could to ease her pain, and how to take charge of organizing our project, making decisions, and seeing to it that we found our way in a life that was marching ever onward—as it does—without much concern for us. This didn't go well. We fought more. One of our worst quarrels blew up in Nairobi. Everything was beginning to look as if it might collapse: our relationship, our travels, our project….

"Your story that I inspire you to step outside yourself and that you put someone else first is sheer bullshit. Drivel, plain and simple!" yelled Anđela, calling me out for my selfishness.

I do put myself first and it is beginning to make me queasy. I'd hoped that with true love I could at least pull out of myself and start caring more for another person, but maybe I was mistaken. I asked myself whether I was even capable of doing this and whether such a thing was even possible. Anđela is far more altruistic than I am; she has much more empathy for others and is available for everyone, and everyone adores her for that. But if she prods me where I'm the weakest, then like a wounded beast all I want to do is to prod back.

"Maybe your altruism is bullshit," I yelled back. "There is no such thing as altruism. Altruism is only well-camouflaged self-interest. Maybe the reason for your kindness toward people is your need for them to like you. Why can't you be kind to me, who already loves you? You don't see any of the things I do for you, nothing works for you…."

"But what have you done? What? Tell me!"

Silence. I freeze each time she asks me for substantiation, I'm lousy at this; I can't come up with examples. Maybe I have none. Maybe I really am an asshole.

"I don't know what I'm doing with you. I'm such a fool! Wasting my time…" she screamed, and a toxic maelstrom sucked her down to the bottom, where she felt so helpless that she reached for her most potent weapon and—brought up divorce. This is my Achilles heel. Maybe I am more selfish than she is, but at least I am better at reining myself in and I find it harder to say nasty things. I cross the boundaries we've set for ourselves less often. For me, the limit is the threat of divorce. In this uncertain world in which a person can no longer rely on anything, I'd hoped that at least marriage was a sacred agreement between two people bonded by love that could not and must not be brought into question—so that at least marriage would be something I could rely on in this damned universe teetering on uncertainty. I asked her to promise me this before we married: if I don't make you happy and you want to search for happiness elsewhere, please go, but if you have no intention of leaving me,

165

please don't threaten me with leaving just to hurt me. She usually held to this. Except during the worst of our fights.

When we decided to marry, we agreed that we'd do everything we could to avoid divorce; we wouldn't allow ourselves to be parted easily. Should problems arise, we'd grapple seriously with saving what we have, and, if we needed it, we'd seek the professional help of a counsellor. We definitely did not imagine we'd already need professional help when we were on our honeymoon.

— — —

During those days in Nairobi—during the long silences and sullen moods after our gut-wrenching fights—I was just finishing reading the book *Formule ljubavi* (Formulas for Love) by Serbian psychotherapist Dr. **Zoran Milivojević**. When I prepared my list of background reading for the project, several people whose opinion I value encouraged me to include this book. Although Zoran Milivojević does not enjoy an international reputation in the global scientific community, as do the other scientists I consulted, I found his ideas appealing. I also liked his unconventional career path. He earned an MD-PhD in medicine and came close to earning a second PhD in psychotherapy, but then left academia and dedicated himself to working with patients. After 40 years of practical experience in his field, he articulated the patterns he'd observed among his patients in a theory that is set out cogently in this book. I really liked what I read, so I reached out to him. Once I'd organized a video conference call with him, my first question went straight to the point:

"What is love?"

"Love is what people think love is," he answered. "There is no one objective thing that is love, but each of us throughout our life builds up assumptions about what love ought to be and each of us is convinced that our version is the right one."

"So how do we build these assumptions and why do they differ?"

"This begins in the very first days of life. When a baby is born, it is totally helpless, and somebody has to care for it. Love helps motivate the care of the caregiver. Later, as the child grows, it hears the words *love, I love you*, and then works out its own ideas about what that means. And once it builds the concept with a conceptual apparatus, we call this a notion or an assumption. Until the age of two or two-and-a-half, the most important thing for a small child is to be loved, to be accepted, to belong to someone. Already here, unconsciously learning from its parents' relationship, but also from fairy tales and cartoons, the child starts building its first assumptions about love. Only at about age four does it begin to feel love for others. It slowly develops empathy, realizes that the feelings of other people also matter, becomes aware of the love between its mother and father. And later, through literature, movies, peer pressure, these assumptions evolve further. Teenagers at 14, 15, 16 already have a quite clearly defined assumption about how they'd like to live, what sort of love relationship they aspire to, what their partner should look and be like. how it should look and be. And then begin the attempts and failures. They look for someone who will fit into their picture, and if the person they find doesn't fit, they go on looking for a second, a third, a fourth…. Their picture shifts and adapts with each one. And then somewhere in their early thirties, if they haven't settled down already, they examine their assumptions more closely. This is a process that may last a lifetime."

"Hmm, this reminds me of lovemaps[1]…."

"Yes, we can think of assumptions as a kind of map. Through life, we all build mental maps, but when we arrive at the right place and we see that they aren't accurate, then we begin to introduce adjustments to our maps to make them accurate enough to orient us properly and allow us to function in the world. Some make these adjustments well, some not so well; for some, their assumptions are functional in the outside world while for others they aren't, and people like that wander. What we psychotherapists do is to help people adjust their dysfunctional maps."

"And what are the most frequent mistakes?"

"One of the assumptions people make—and this causes them the most trouble—is that love is the meaning of life. Our value system is structured hierarchically. When a person aspires to satisfy their two most important desires at once, yet the reality is such that only one of these can be satisfied because the nature of the wish is such that satisfying one precludes satisfying the other, then the person is pushed headlong into conflict with themselves. If love is the meaning of life, then it's worth more than life and worth dying for. This is a very poor way to resolve a conflict. But the conflict can be resolved by working on oneself and changing one's assumptions. Another assumption that also belongs to the basic twisted assumptions about love is that if one is truly in love, this enjoyable feeling can and should be felt all the time! When people who think this way come up against a problem and disagreement, they conclude that what they're feeling isn't love, so they turn their back on the relationship. With this is associated the misguided assumption that if the love is true, there should be no conflict or anger."

"Well, yes, that sounds pretty familiar."

"An enduring loving relationship in which conflict between the partners never arises is unthinkable! Conflicts cannot be avoided because we are all different and we can't all have the same desires. Conflict invariably comes up when one partner wants something and the other is not in agreement. But it is key to distinguish between a conflict and its expression, an attempt to resolve it. People often think that fighting means conflict, but fighting doesn't mean conflict. Fighting is an attempt at resolving a conflict, when each side is trying to make the other side change their thinking and accept what they want. On the other hand, two people can be locked in a very intense conflict without fighting at all."

"Wow, our fights are loud and nasty. Both of us are very temperamental."

"It's crucial to distinguish between anger on the one hand and scorn and hate on the other. Anger is a demand for the other person to change their behavior. Scorn and hate are aimed at the essential being of that person. So, love and anger go together, because we demand that the person we love changes the behavior that we feel is threatening us. But scorn is tied to the assessment that the other is not deserving as a human being, while hate is a pure negation of love. Many people, when faced with a partner's anger, feel as if the partner is rejecting them. But in fact, the partner is merely pleading with them to change a harmful behavior."

"This reminds me of something we did at our wedding," I said. "We asked the guests to write their advice on how to avoid divorce for us in a blank book that we set out on a table. One of the most touching pieces of advice was that we shouldn't experience fighting as the end of the world, because it's a good sign that we still care about each other—if we lose the will to enter into a fight at some point, that's when to be worried."

"Exactly right."

"Good, so what are a few other of the most common misguided assumptions about love?"

"Many think that true love should mean being infatuated forever, that the sex should always be fantastic in true love, that one only loves once in a lifetime and love should last to the end of life, that true love will completely transform the beloved person, that true love is totally giving oneself over to someone else…."

I began examining everything through this prism of assumptions. It became clear to me that we don't see the world, things, phenomena, and other people as they really are, but as they are in relation to the images we have built about them inside ourselves. The fact that Anđela and I differ on the question of where to draw the line between our work and our private lives, or how much time we should spend on work and how much on ourselves, is in large part due to the differing assumptions we've internalized throughout our lives. I had somewhat less of a need than she for our special time together, because within my hierarchy of values I give more importance to work than Anđela does, but at this point we're talking about shades of difference. Our differences are not, in fact, so big, I thought. I am no workaholic hiding away in my work, nor is Anđela a lazy slacker. Both of us love what we're doing, and we often get to the point of burn out while doing it. The same applies to the time we should be spending together. I have a little less need for company and conversation, but that doesn't mean I'm anti-social or that I love her any less. I'm just slightly different.

What hurts me most is when she describes me as a selfish oaf, and what hurts her most is when I question her altruism. Isn't this simply us threatening the assumptions we hold of ourselves? The fact that I go berserk when she threatens me with divorce, isn't that just a misguided assumption I've fixated on? "If you love me, if you've agreed to spend your life with me, then accept me as I am and don't ever threaten me with divorce." That she sometimes threatens to divorce me doesn't mean she doesn't love me. She's letting me know she cares about me and warning me to change my behavior and stop hurting her feelings. Now that I can see the problem from this new perspective, I feel it shouldn't be too hard to change my assumption.

— — —

By the time we held the first interview after we'd arrived in Nairobi, still fuming at each other but professional and dedicated to this life and our project, I decided to pay more attention to the assumptions about love. Our collocutors, **John** and **Rose** [p. 241], were partners in both love and business. Like us. I was keen to know how they'd learned to join and separate the private and the business parts of their lives.

"We met each other seven years ago, and our first date was on a Sunday afternoon," said Rose, 33. "We went out for lunch. John talked a lot about his job, in fact he had to leave our lunch date early because a business partner called him and requested a meeting. I remember how impressed I was by this. I thought, this man is industrious because he's working on a Sunday and he is responsible about his job. I will never be hungry next to him, I thought."

At their home in a Nairobi suburb, John came across as a businessman, dressed in pants ironed with a crease and a starched white shirt. They explained to us that they'd brought their passions to their work—John with marketing, Rose with social development—and together founded a marketing agency for which they hired many young, otherwise unemployed, talents. But John, meanwhile, had not quit his old job. Instead, he worked at his old job alongside the new one, and Rose became director of the new company.

"The first few years were terribly difficult. John worked night and day and I ran the new firm while having our first child. But it meant so much to me that he believed in me and entrusted me with this responsible function. Still, we fought all the time. Our differences came into sharp focus. I cried a lot. But it's better now. When he saw, after a year, that our new company was thriving, John quit his old job and dedicated himself to our new company, and now, after five years of hard work, we've managed to put our business on a stable footing and move into a nice house."

"How did you make it through those challenges?" I asked.

"We were helped by our faith in God… and love," interjected John.

"What is love for you?"

"Love is a powerful feeling that helped us overcome the differences between us," said John, but Rose didn't agree.

"I don't think love is a feeling. Love is a clear decision for me to be with someone and love him unconditionally, come what may!"

This immediately reminded me of yet another often misguided assumption Zoran Milivojević told me about—the assumption of unconditional love. He claims there is no such thing, because when someone is loved, they are loved because of who they are, the way they look, the way they behave, which is special in some way…. A condition already exists. If this weren't the case, then the specific differences that exist between people would be lost, as would the specialness of the beloved, and anyone could love anybody. Since there are no ideal partners, two people cannot live together unless they ask things of each other, and with these things they enter into conflict and offer each other the chance to adapt. A person who believes that love ought to be unconditional, says Milivojević, has no mechanism by which to adapt to a partner.

"How can love be unconditional?" I asked Rose. "Doesn't that mean that no matter what your partner does, you should stay with him if you truly love him?"

"That's right, yes, that's true love! It's important to draw a line between a person and what they do. You can do something I don't agree with, but that won't change my love for you, for you as a person."

"But let's say, hypothetically, that a woman has a partner who beats her and abuses their child…. Forgive me for choosing such disturbing and extreme examples, but this really interests me. Let's say that her partner sexually abuses and murders their children, does this mean she should stay with him if she truly loves him?"

Silence. Rose was a little taken aback, and I again apologized for saying something so inappropriate. I don't know what it was that angered me so much. Was it that I'd expected unconditional love from Anđela, an unconditional embrace of all my failings, while I wasn't capable of doing the same for her? Where is the line to be drawn, I wondered; to what degree should someone's failings and shortcomings be tolerated? Doesn't love teeter on the thin edge between acceptance and change? It seems to me that love ought to accept more and change less, but surely it shouldn't accept everything. As much as I expect Anđela to accept me, I also expect her to help me change my shortcomings that bother both her and me, to help me move ahead. Our quarrels are painful, but they also have an impact on me, they correct me; through them I learn and am becoming a better person. At least I hope I am. But how much can a person actually change? Is our dream about change merely yet another myth we buy into? Another misguided assumption?

— — —

We came across a story of radical change in Tokyo. It was told to us by **Hiroyuki** and **Kumja** [p. 238], both of them in their seventies. We met with them at the small Protestant church they were running on the outskirts of the world's largest city. Had we met them anywhere in Japan, without knowing their story, we'd have thought they were ordinary, dear, agreeable people. However, their story stopped us cold.

"Before I met Kumja, I was a beast with a human face," Hiroyuki started in. "I was twice married and divorced and cared nothing for those women. I thought only of myself. I did despicable things. I was a member of the yakuza, a Japanese mafia, I gambled, used drugs, was always getting into trouble, did things no person should ever do, things no one could be forgiven for.... Once, a few days after I was released from jail, I came to a nightclub with other yakuza members and I saw her. She was working as a hostess. I fell in love with her then and there."

Hostesses in Japan are a modern version of the geisha. They are nightclub employees whom men pay in return for entertainment and attention. Hostesses coddle the men and they flirt and, though they are not typically prostitutes, there are clubs where their interactions with customers may go in any direction.

"As far as I was concerned, he was just another customer," added Kumja. "He didn't interest me. But he was so persistent that I began noticing him more."

"She was so beautiful," continued Hiroyuki dreamily. "I thought I could be happy with her. For months, I went to the club every day, I pestered her until she finally fell in love with me. We married and had a child. But all that time I was still working for the yakuza and still getting into trouble. She asked me to give it up and change, but I ignored her. The force of her love began exerting pressure on me and to crack my shell, but the trouble I was in went deeper and deeper and only got worse. I ran straight into a clash with my yakuza bosses, found myself in a life-or-death situation—and one day, when I'd been cornered, I decided to run away from everything to another city!"

"It was awful," Kumja recalled. "He often beat me, but I hit him, too; he kept running away, but I never considered leaving him, because my mother had taught me long ago that a woman must never leave her man. I saw how she'd put up with many things, so I knew I had to put up with this. I prayed to God and believed he'd change. But the time when he ran away for a longer period, I knew this was different, because his yakuza bosses started coming to me and demanding to know where he was. They hadn't done this before. I knew they were after him. And I had no idea where he was. I was miserable. I was at a loss, so I prayed even harder and hoped this would change."

"I began to feel guilty, unbearably guilty," went on Hiroyuki, with emotion. "I couldn't stand reality. I lived on the road, in fear, on the run. I seriously thought of killing myself. I had no family or friends, nobody I could bare my heart to, and the only person I had, who was waiting for me, I'd hurt her terribly. One day, ten months after I ran away, when I hit rock bottom, I went into a church and there I met a man to whom I opened my heart. He comforted me and calmed me down. I told him what terrible things I'd done, and he told me this would work itself out. At that moment a serenity came into me, and I realized how sorely I missed Kumja. All that time, I hadn't even tried to call her. I went to a phone booth. Dialing the number took me a long time. I feared she wouldn't still be there. I thought she wouldn't pick up. But somehow I mustered the courage to call and… she did pick up."

His voice cracked and tears streamed down his face.

"I was struck dumb, but she felt it must be me. 'It's you there, isn't it?' she asked tenderly. 'They're out to kill you, aren't they? Come home! Come back, please! I'm waiting for you.'"

He stopped talking and quietly wept. When his tears allowed him to speak, he took a deep breath, and went on.

"Even in my wildest dreams, I hadn't imagined she'd say anything so wonderful. I didn't deserve forgiveness. She'd never held anything against me. All she said was, 'Come back. I'm waiting,' and that was what hit the restart button on my life. Only when I'd been forgiven was I able to learn how important it is to love and be loved. I understood that I'd been given a chance to truly change and that I mustn't lose it."

Hiroyuki still carries searing memories of his past in the yakuza. He is missing the tips of his little fingers, which he himself chopped off during a loyalty rite to the gangsters. His whole torso is covered in tattoos. But he does seem to have genuinely changed. He became a pastor for a Protestant denomination with a very small congregation of several dozen Japanese and lives peacefully with Kumja, his troubles behind him, on the outskirts of the largest city in the world.

— — —

"Can a person truly change?" I asked Zoran Milivojević.

"Of course they can. It's not easy, but it is possible," he answered and then laughed. "If it weren't, what would be the purpose of us psychotherapists? Our main purpose is correcting dysfunctional assumptions. Also, some people adjust their assumptions themselves through life. When they catch on to the fact that what they're doing isn't working, that it isn't making them happy, that it isn't helping them achieve their goals, they change or adapt accordingly. Some people find that easy to do all by themselves, while others trap themselves in a misguided assumption and fend off any help. We psychotherapists can point out that they're doing something wrong, but only if they want to be helped. It's still up to them whether they'll change what they're doing. Some cling to their convictions to the grave. But those who are willing to work on this—can indeed succeed in the end."

If this is true, then that old maxim from antiquity—know thyself—makes sense. Maybe an ongoing scrutiny of one's illusions and the unmasking of one's misguided assumptions can steer us toward the right path. Maybe underneath all the veils of illusion there crouches my real 'self.'

But who is this 'self'? What is it? Is there even such a thing?

9

LOVE AND IDENTITY

Do we seek a partner who is a
reflection of ourselves?

In another book I read while we were traveling, *Liebe: Ein unordentliches Gefühl* (Love: A Disorderly Emotion) by German philosopher Richard David Precht, I came across this compelling statement:

"Whom we lust after sexually has a lot to do with our sex drive; whom we fall in love with has more to do with our parents and experiences from childhood, and whom we ultimately love is largely a question of our perception of ourselves."[1]

I have asked myself a hundred times why I love Anđela. Why her? If I'm being entirely candid, I have to ask whether I love her because of who she is, or because of myself—did I find in her something *I* wanted; did loving her offer me an image of myself *I* wanted to see?

"You are my reflection, I am yours," said **Natsumi** during our interview, turning from the camera to face her husband, **Tracy** [p. 116]. Natsumi was not speaking literally, because she and Tracy do not resemble one another in the slightest. Tracy is a tall, muscular, Black American man, while Natsumi

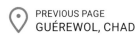

PREVIOUS PAGE
GUÉREWOL, CHAD

is a petite, fragile, pale Japanese woman. But they weren't speaking of a physical image.

"I can no longer imagine my life without you. You are my detached self," Tracy replied. They explained to us how they define each other, how each tries, for the sake of the other, to be a better person, a better partner; all of us exist as reflections of one another and without the other we wouldn't be able to define ourselves. They explained this to us using the example of their child.

"Our daughter is growing up here in Japan where there are hardly any Black people," said Tracy, "and she is dark-skinned. The Japanese have hair that grows downward, while her hair is curly and grows up toward the sky. At the school she attends there is nobody else who looks like her, nobody for her to compare herself with. She is growing up as different. This is shaping her."

I've spent my life wondering who I am. What determines the self? Is this even a thing, an authentic, autonomous, and independent unit? Or does my self result from a merging of conditionalities, the outcome of an array of biological and cultural algorithms? Do we even have a free will, and, if we do, how much of what we do is governed by it? Am I the proprietor of my self or do I merely seem to be? Is my sense of self yet another story we've created to help make the mystery of existence more bearable? Are our actions, behaviors, ideas, and attitudes genuinely ours, or are they merely the offshoot of programs that govern what we do?

My path of seeking an answer to this question has led me to study various forms of spirituality, to explore intellectual, rational endeavors, and to pursue extreme adventures. When I embarked on my arduous trek from the shores of the Antarctic to the South Pole through a landscape that is most like the void of outer space out of anything found on our planet, I asked myself what would happen with my sense of self when I was no longer among other people, when I was no longer amid anything. What would the limits to my self be? What would define my boundaries?

But during that unusual, solitary adventure that took 47 days, I came to understand that the realm of my sense of self lay entirely inside my head. My mind went right on producing and sustaining assumptions and then using them to measure reality. My brain never stopped working. Furthermore, it seemed to be toiling overtime to fill the extreme emptiness all around. I had

never spent so much time absolutely immersed in the present, in a total acceptance of reality as it is, stripped of nostalgia, bonds, cravings, and dreams—and yet my brain kept churning out stories.

When I wasn't dwelling in the moment, staring at the southern horizon and boldly pushing toward it, I was listening to audio recordings: podcasts, music, books. This was the first time I'd encountered writings by historian Yuval Noah Harari. I was intrigued by his crystalline view of the world, which dissects life with an almost surgical precision through the prism of the stories we tell ourselves. With his intent of familiarizing the public with scientific ideas he deliberately risks oversimplification, and most of his critics hold this against him. However, these simple and very logical answers have taken root nicely in the fertile soil of my curiosity.

I've spent my life musing on whether my sense of self is no more than a story I tell myself in order to justify my existence and imbue it with meaning. Isn't every identity merely one, more or less unique, collection of stories?

While I was making my way across inland Antarctica—completely alone, bereft of all stimulus and information from the outside world and any people I might have encountered in that world—my brain began to pluck things from my 'archive.' I started remembering things I'd long since forgotten, weighing them against my current assumptions. I wondered what would happen if I'd been born in that barren, lifeless space where no other people live and nothing is happening. Who would I be then? Would I even be cognizant of my existence? How much would I be worth?

Never before or after that expedition have I so intensely felt that I was a mere dot, making my way across a vast unknown wasteland. With the lack of stimuli and absence of any mirrors in which I could see myself reflected, I felt my sense of self dissolve. I reached the point where I was wondering whether I even existed. Do we only begin to exist when somebody else notices us, when we're heard, seen, experienced by another? What do other people do for us but serve as mirrors? We use them to establish our position and our worth. When we love someone, we are confirming that we are worth something, we exist. We imbue each other with meaning[2].

One of the things that immediately drew me to Anđela is that she is so good with other people; she wants to do things for them so that they'll feel special. At home in Croatia and as we traveled around the world, I realized that everyone loves her because they feel special when they're with her. Do I love her because *I* feel special when I'm with her? And if so—is that a bad thing? Don't we want everyone to feel special, and shouldn't those who are our nearest and dearest help us in this pursuit?

— — —

"When I was with him, I felt so special," we were told by **Veronica**, a 42-year-old bank clerk who had fallen madly in love, seven years earlier, with **Juan Cañas** [p. 274], a popular Colombian musician who was 14 years her junior. "He wanted to spend all his time with me, he was always there, dancing around me, he spoke so beautifully to me, wrote me songs! He is a musician, after all, a songwriter, he is skilled at expressing himself. He wrote a song in acrostic—the first letters of each line spelled out my name. I felt so special with him, I felt important; when I was with him, I felt better, worth more!"

We heard a similar story at the other end of the world, in Kyrgyzstan, this time not from people we'd interviewed, but from a kind couple who hosted us in their home:

"I lived an ordinary life, worked at a company, had ordinary desires and expectations from life, and then he showed up, and he was so special," Albina from Bishkek told us, while her beloved, Azamat, grinned with satisfaction and pride. "He told me: 'I have nothing, I don't have a car, I have no place to live… but I do have a dream! Through my art I want to promote friendship, love, peace among people.' That's how he won me over. We fell in love and a month later we were married, and here we are—we've been married for two years and we have a little one-year-old daughter. Being his wife is perfect, he is very special. Everything he does is special. He is a very special traveler, a special painter, a special artist, a special man. By his side, I, too, feel special."

Isn't *feeling special* one of the key prerequisites for love? All of us more or less clearly want to feel special, unique. We wouldn't like acknowledging that we're all the same, mere copies. This is why we come up with an array of stories, we desire to convince ourselves we're special, and then we seek this confirmation from others. We care about everyone's opinion, but each opinion is not equally salient for us. The more important the person is to us, the more what they think

of us matters. A person in whose eyes we see a reflection of our own values becomes precious to us.

Maybe Precht, the philosopher cited at the opening to this chapter, is right. Our sexual attraction to certain people is based on biological parameters. We don't have much control over that. We can't influence it much—we can either act on the attraction or not. But we don't fall in love with every person we go to bed with. The assumptions and mental maps we have built in the course of our lives, especially in childhood and under the influence of parents or guardians, are far more likely to influence whom we fall in love with. Here, we do have a little more control, because if we make ourselves aware of these assumptions, we can also change them. Although our parents have determined us most in this regard, we can still consciously decide that we'll seek other qualities in our partners.

But even if we do fall in love with someone, this doesn't mean we'll go on to feel an abiding love for them in time. Perhaps it is our perception of ourselves that has the greatest impact on the relationships we sustain. Our identity. The story we tell of ourselves. When we find a partner who confirms the image we hold of ourselves, who trusts the same story we tell ourselves, thereby affirming its legitimacy—only then can there be abiding love. This is the level at which our free will has the most leeway. For although this is still about a story—we can choose which story we want to tell.

— — —

"When we met, we were already older and both of us had failed marriages and children behind us. At that age, one doesn't rush into things," 59-year-old **Adela** told us while her partner, **Marco** [p. 134], three years younger, sat by her side on an unassuming armchair in their modest home in a suburb of Santiago, the capital of Chile.

"We spent a year getting to know each other and liking each other more and more," she went on. "Something was starting between us, so finally we decided to embark on a relationship. At the time, my friend talked me into undergoing some routine medical tests, so I went to the doctor and discovered I had malignant breast cancer. My world came tumbling down. Marco and I had only been together officially for a week. I didn't want him to feel responsible for me. I told him to go, because I wanted to go through this alone."

"I could not allow that," said Marco. "I had only just found her, and after all the years of wandering and searching I couldn't lose her!"

"He gave me the resilience to fight. He was by my side the whole time, he went through everything with me and bolstered me, he even fed me when I was so weak that I couldn't lift a spoon. And then one day, after a therapy session, it was Valentine's Day, he invited me out for a pizza. I was still terribly weak, skeletal, a wreck—and he gave me a ring and proposed!"

She stopped and beamed, tipped her head back, shaking it ever so slightly to the left and right, her eyelids closing dreamily, smiling, and went on, her voice a little softer, warm with pride.

"He wanted to marry me even when I was as I was then—ugly, bald, sick, shattered…. But at that moment… I felt as if I were the most beautiful woman in the world!"

Her words were followed by silence. We paused a minute to grant what she had said the weight it deserved. Then we asked Marco how he'd been feeling then. If we were to dissect his words and actions with a coldly rational eye, we might say that he told her the story she needed to hear right then, even though it had little to do with reality. But who could hold this against him? Reality is, at times, too grim. If such a grim and ugly reality, bereft of purpose and meaning, is hidden under layers of illusions and stories, can we be forgiven for sometimes fleeing from it into the stories that offer us solace? Or something more….

"When you suffer, if you have no support, no attachment, no affection, no motivation, what do you have?" answered Marco with a question, leaving the question mark hovering briefly mid-air. He sat, relaxed, but shot deep, piercing glances at the camera. He'd turned slightly toward Adela with one hand supporting her back and, with the gestures of the other hand, he lent emphasis to the words he was saying.

"I found in her all I'd been looking for. The light I needed in life. The engine I needed to make this work. Because life is love! If we have no love, if I don't fight for her, if she doesn't fight for me, if together we don't fight for others… what do we have? Who are we? How can we go on?"

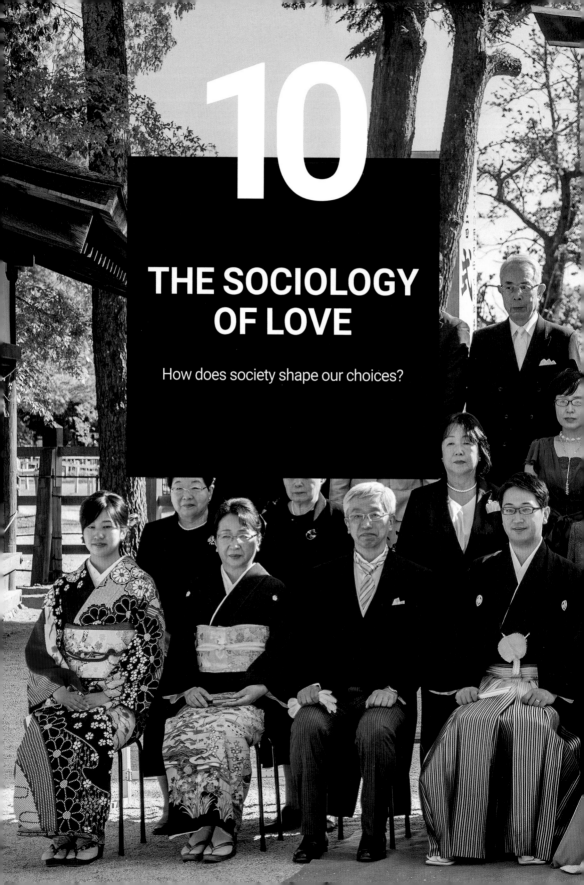

10

THE SOCIOLOGY
OF LOVE

How does society shape our choices?

We have seen how our sex drive is influenced by nature, biology, and chemistry. We have seen how our psyche determines whom we'll fall in love with and whom we'll love.

Our romantic decisions and our joys and our suffering, however, are also shaped in a big way by society.

"As a sociologist, I study how society shapes our behavior, thinking, and feelings," said Dr. **Eva Illouz** [p. 390], one of the leading authorities on the sociology of love. We spoke with her over the Internet several months after we'd returned from our trip when the coronavirus pandemic had shut down air travel, forcing us into house arrest. "Emotions, for instance, are considered the realm of the psyche, but if we look at them empirically, we can see how they are shaped by norms, values, language, ideals, and therefore by society and by culture."

Even though our research into love around the world was not conducted on an empirical basis, we still witnessed this through interviews with couples in a number of cultures. Whenever we asked people what love

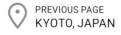
PREVIOUS PAGE
KYOTO, JAPAN

meant to them, we'd also ask them where their ideas about love came from. Two groups of answers were easy to identify. The more traditional people said they'd been given their idea of what love should be from their parents, relatives, spiritual leaders, the holy writ, the Quran, the Bible, the Veda, while the more modern people told us that their ideas about love were mainly shaped by literature, art, Hollywood, social networks…. Behind both of these groups there are myths and stories produced by any number of social institutions designed to hold society together. But how does this mechanism actually function?

Let's first consider traditional societies. They are primarily shaped and organized by religion. Ever since language was invented and they'd become aware of their existence, human beings have been trying to answer a number of questions and clarify the unknowns they encounter. For whatever they could not explain rationally, they sought an explanation in the otherworldly and the supernatural—the irrational. Fundamental questions, such as—Who are we? What are we doing here? Why do we come into this world and then leave it?—may stir terrible anxiety if they are left unanswered, even when the proffered answer is wrong. Between the existential uncertainty offered by a realistic view of life and the certainty of the consolation provided for us by religion, early human beings chose the latter. Religions spread worldwide because they offered answers to the ultimate questions, a refuge from anxiety, a place to hide from uncertainty, and a safe haven from the unrest, chaos, and lack of meaning that threatens from the universe. Along the way, religions also helped organize society and simplify life on Earth.

If they were to succeed, religions had to introduce the categories of morality and normativity. What is good or bad, what is normal and what is not—these categories do not exist in nature. In traditional societies, these categories were imposed by mythology and religion in order to ease the lives of people in a collective. The evolutionary view says that the more an individual strives to live in a larger collective, the more the person must learn to rein in their own selfishness. Life in a collective requires a high level of collaboration, and morals facilitate collaboration. To instill the morals more readily, religion introduced the supernatural. When threatened by the retribution exacted by supernatural forefathers, gods, or forces, and bolstered by a promise of justice

187

in the afterlife, people grew better at reining in their selfishness and building more successful collectives. The more convincing the foundation story of the collective, the more successful the story was at persuading the people who believed in it to collaborate. The more efficient the collective proved to be and the more powerful it became through history, the more complex and persuasive these stories became.

In order to better explain the world, religion ushered in the distinction between the sacred and the secular. The secular covered all the structures, rituals, and people who have no special meaning but are a part of everyday life, while the sacred encompasses all those structures, rituals, and people that are considered special and are treated with awe and veneration. Nothing is sacred in and of itself, but only when someone deems it sacred. The loss of the sacred is one of the most powerful features of the transition from the traditional to the modern age, as is the ascent of reason.

Just as humans had developed irrational explanations for unanswerable questions, they tried in rational ways to explain the world and the mystery of life. At first, the rational methods offered too little success, the scientific view of the world was only just beginning to be developed. But little by little, the more successful methods offered answers and improved life, health, wealth, and wellbeing in increasingly tangible and visible ways. When the old stories clashed with the new and more effective ones, people abandoned the old and embraced the new without great difficulty. In Chapter Four, we saw how the Wodaabe nomads in Chad found it easy to accept Islam, because it facilitated their access to water sources. I had run into other interesting examples of this phenomenon when I was on earlier travels and expeditions, particularly in New Guinea. There one can find the last battleground of its kind in the 21st century, a place where missionaries are still fighting for the 'salvation of pagan souls.' I visited dozens of communities, which, over the last generation or two, have transitioned to Christianity from an animistic belief in the spirits of their ancestors and the forest. The reason for this everywhere was very simple. The Papuans spoke openly about how the newcomers impressed them by navigating the rivers in their boats that moved faster and without oars; the newcomers flew through the air like birds in metal armor; they had medicine that treated sickness in those who earlier would have died, and sticks that shot and took the lives of enemies who had earlier made them suffer. Without excessive nostalgia and resistance from a conservative force in their society, the Papuans clearly felt that the gods of the newcomers were more benevolent to their subjects than theirs were, so they abandoned their gods and embraced the new ones.

But if the missionaries were to do their job properly and rule over the hearts of the 'pagan souls they'd saved from sure damnation,' they'd have to 'translate' the stories into the Papuans' language, and that was not always straightforward. People who had never left their jungles and swamps and who had no access to television and the Internet found it difficult to imagine the desert of Israel in the Old Testament, the site of the biblical stories. Men who were naked but for the dried, hollowed-out gourd they wore over their penises and women who wore only grass skirts found it difficult to understand the concept of fabric, of dresses, of wearing a veil, so the missionaries painted images of the Virgin Mary with bare breasts wearing a grass skirt and of Jesus carrying the cross while dressed in only a gourd. Such depictions would be blasphemous to many Westerners, but for animistic Papuans anything else would be foreign and abnormal. Society dictates what is normal and what is not—and norms have mostly been prescribed by religion. Religion determines what rewards the normal deserve and what retribution will be meted out to those who are not normal. In practice, this is done two ways.

A more radical approach uses a repressive apparatus like that of the *mutawa* religious police we encountered in Saudi Arabia. This country is known for equating its civil laws with its strict religious laws, which, for example, stipulate that women must not leave the country or enter into employment without the approval of their husband, father, or brother. Before 2011, Saudi women were not allowed to vote, and until just a few months before we arrived they were not allowed to drive cars. Only over the last few years have these regulations slowly begun to change, allowing greater freedom for all women, so when we arrived in this harsh country, women were no longer required by law to cover their heads with a hijab or their face with a niqab. Anđela heard about this from a liberal Saudi woman, **Emma** [p. 267], whom we'd interviewed at her home in Riyadh, so when we went out into the street after the interview Anđela decided to leave her head uncovered. Only a few minutes later, we were

189

able to see for ourselves how customs take time to catch up with the law. A vehicle driven by the *mutawa* religious police pulled over next to us and, over a large loudspeaker, they ordered Anđela to cover her head with her hijab.

Another way that religions impose their systems of values that regulate what is normal and what is not is to use the mechanisms of society itself. One of the reasons why religions are so effective throughout the traditional world is that long before the birth of sociology they had an excellent grasp of how societies function. Societies tend to perpetuate their system of values, assert the norm, and punish those who deviate from it in any way. This presented itself to us with the most clarity in the situation of **Melis** and **Elmira** [p. 124] in Kyrgyzstan, whose relationship began with the kidnapping. Through generations and generations of patriarchy, their society had shaped this version of the coupling of men and women, which required men to prove their masculinity by kidnapping the woman they wished to marry and required women to prove their femininity through stoicism and a lack of rebellion or resistance.

We'd included Kyrgyzstan on our world tour because the percentage of marriages that begin with the kidnapping of brides is greater there than anywhere else in the world—over 50% of marriages by some estimates[1]. The custom is practiced more in the rural interior of the country than in the larger cities like Bishkek, so we went off to Kyzart, a little village lying in the very heart of the undulating steppes, and there our fixer found Melis and Elmira. I must admit that when I was imagining this interview, I expected that the man who'd kidnapped his wife would be more macho than Melis was. In fact, he came across as quite unassuming and withdrawn.

"All my friends and peers had already married, and I had been putting this off and dragging my feet," Melis told us, shyly and quietly. "My parents taught me when I was a boy that I would have to kidnap my future wife. This was how their relationship began, and that of their parents and of everyone else in our village. But it made me uncomfortable and I kept postponing it. One day, my father said to me that if I didn't go off and kidnap my bride, he wouldn't give me the money for the bride price."

Melis mustered his resolve and decided to kidnap Elmira, a young woman from Kyzart who'd completed her studies and was working as a teacher in the capital city. She'd just come back to Kyzart to visit her relatives. Melis ruined her plans for a quiet visit to her native village when he barged into her house with several friends and carried her off with him without her consent.

"I resisted, I didn't know what was happening," Elmira told us. "Most of my friends had already been snatched by men, my mother, aunts, and grandmothers had been teaching me for years how to behave when I was kidnapped, but somehow I hoped to be spared. I studied and found a job in Bishkek and planned to stay there, and kidnapping is no longer a custom in the city. Melis ruined my plans when he came for me. I cried and protested, but they took me to his house where some older women, his mother and grandmother and aunts, all told me how Melis was a marvelous young man and how being married to him would be so wonderful. When I told them that I didn't want to marry, they threatened me by saying that I'd never be happy if I didn't accept. One of the old women lay down in front of the door and said I'd have to step across her if I wanted to leave, but if I did then something terrible would befall me."

Parents, relatives, peers, teachers, religious instructors, famous people, prominent social figures, all these members of society let us know what is good and what is not, what is normal and what is not. Then we tell the same to others, and this is how society perpetuates its system of values. So how, then, does anything ever change? How do the criteria for what is normal change? And where is our free will in all this? If Elmira had decided to leave traditional Kyzart behind and begin a modern life in Bishkek, and if she could have refused to remain with Melis after he'd kidnapped her, why did she ultimately consent? If our behavior, thoughts, and feelings are not determined purely by nature, biology, chemistry, and our psyche, but also by social mechanisms—how much free will, if any, remains?

— — —

"Hmmm, this is not something that can be expressed in percentages. I can't say, for example, that we are 30% determined by biology, 40% by psychology, and 30% by sociology…" Eva Illouz, the sociologist, told us. "But we can try to understand this by thinking of cultures and societies as a powerful magnet. For instance, until the 1990s in the West, this magnet meant that if you wanted to be accepted as a real man, you had to be heterosexual. The institution of heterosexuality dictated certain behaviors, a way of speaking, a way of relating to others, and, of course, you had to choose a woman for your partner, marry her and so forth. Society acts like a magnet on every individual with the powerful forces of norms and values. But this doesn't mean that certain individuals cannot pull free of the magnet's force field. Not everything is pulled in by the magnet. If you're farther from the center of the magnet, then you can resist the forces more easily. Homosexual men may spend their whole lives accepting the dominant social norms of heterosexuality. But there are homosexuals who will risk their lives and social standing to defy the social norms, challenge and question the established attitudes, values, norms, and conventions of their time. So, they are not entirely trapped by society's magnetic field."

We met two lesbians in Iran who, by the very act of agreeing to our interview, were defying the norms of their society. In Iran, as in Saudi Arabia, civil law is based on religious law, but unlike Saudi Arabia where the royal family is in power, Iran is ruled by an elite of religious leaders whose task it is to guarantee that the magnet functions at full strength. According to their views, heterosexuals are normal, while homosexuals are not, and in order to be sure that everyone understands this, they can condemn to death all those who are different in this regard. Because of the death penalty, Iran is one of the strictest countries in the world on the question of the rights of homosexuals. Young, brave, and defiant **Nazanin** and **Nahid** [p. 98] explained to us that they aren't so afraid of the death penalty, because there have been no convictions for the last ten years or so, but nevertheless, they made it clear that living in such a society is not easy.

Nazanin and Nahid told us all the same things that many other people in love told us—how they had butterflies in their stomachs when they were falling in love, how they couldn't bear the thought that one of them might fall in love with someone else, what the similarities are that they share and the differences that cause them problems, their lack of agreement on when and how many children they would like to have…. All this sounded familiar to us because we come from a culture in which more and more people have accepted homosexuality. Statistical estimates suggest that in *every* society, 1%-8%[2] of the population is queer[3], in other words not of an exclusively heterosexual orientation. But since homophobia is still present and assertive in the more conservative societies like Iran, young Nazanin felt the need, near the end of the interview, to send a message to all those who do not, for whatever reason, accept same-sex love:

"Why do you think that two people of the same sex cannot fall in love the same way two people of different sexes can?" she asked boldly and dramatically, facing the camera, moved by imagining the attention of the mass of people who might one day see, hear, and read her question. "Why do you think there can only be love between people of different sexes? Love is something that happens despite our will. We don't choose it! We don't choose the person we'll fall in love with by their sex or their appearance. It just happens! Love is a wonderful feeling that happens between people and not something that is chosen!"

We met another interesting couple who were defying the norms of their society in Lusaka, the capital of Zambia. In the cramped living room of their hut, we were warmly greeted by **Mathew** and **Naomi** [p. 101]. Naomi is a person with albinism, and such people in Black, sub-Saharan Africa are everywhere marginalized. Not only can they seldom hope for a normal marriage, but they have to watch out for people who may show an interest in them.

"When Mathew approached me and said he liked me, my first reaction was terror," said Naomi. "In Africa, love doesn't happen to people with albinism. Albinism is considered a curse in Africa. People believe that if you have HIV and you sleep with an albino, this will cure you. People believe that if you cut off certain parts of the body of someone with albinism and keep them at home, such as their hair or hand or breast, this will make you rich. People believe that if you spit into your feces, you'll prevent your child from being born with albinism. Better yet if you can find an albino willing to spit into your shit! My mother taught me my whole life to run away from people who tell me they like me, because all they want is to use me as a sacrifice in a ritual, kill me so they can get their hands on my body parts."

"How did you react, then, when you first met Mathew?" we asked her, but he jumped in.

"It was difficult for me to convince her that my intentions were not like that. I really liked her. I was walking through this neighborhood one day, and I saw her drawing water up from a well, and something came over me, I felt something I'd never felt before, she attracted me, she was different, special… I think this was love at first sight! It was something close to magic!"

"I didn't believe him at first, but I liked him, so little by little I gave him my trust," Naomi explained. "The more I got to know him, the more I was sure that there were no bad intentions here and that he really did like me, that he loved me as I am, the more I let him into my life. I didn't think I'd ever be happy, married, that I'd have children, but here, thanks to Mathew for falling in love with me, I realized that I can live a normal life like everyone else."

"How did the people around you react to your relationship?" we asked Mathew.

"People told me I was crazy, they asked me if I was blind, why had I chosen such a person, didn't I know that there were many better girls out there. But I told them it wasn't my eyes that chose her, but my heart."

Mathew and Naomi told us their neighbors had begun accepting them, and by now, when it was clear that they were normal people, these neighbors began to change their views about people with albinism. Naomi wants her example to reach much farther than her neighbors, so she found a job in an association that is working to correct the negative picture that many Africans hold about people with albinism, and in this she finds her purpose.

"We people with albinism deserve a normal life, we can love and be loved," she asserted. "The fact that Mathew loves me tells me that I'm normal and deserve love and that I'm just as good as everyone else."

— — —

Mathew and Naomi, like Nazanin and Nahid, are courageous people who resist the pull of the magnet's force field and thereby expand the borders of what is normal. With their example and activism, they are not merely promoting the idea of humanism and equality by birth, but also equality in *worth*. Many religions preach equality, that we all hold equal worth before God, but this equality refers only to those who uphold social norms. All others are proclaimed unworthy, and sometimes even condemned to death, the eternal fires of hell, or reincarnation into lower beings.

As we've seen, these norms are not just perpetuated by calculating religious leaders, but by all the members, more or less, of a society. The worth of every member of society is established according to the degree to which they fit into their society, as measured through comparison to those who don't fit in. These 'ordinary' people who perpetuate values—the grandmothers who tell Elmira that she'll be afflicted by misfortune if she doesn't accept a life with her kidnapper, the Iranians who support the religious leaders and their drastic laws, and the people who purchase the body parts of people with albinism on the black market in order to ward off or treat themselves for serious disease—are not necessarily corrupt or malicious, they have only effectively internalized the norms of their society and in so doing, they themselves have gained in worth. And in traditional society the greatest value, even greater than the life of the individual, is the well-being of the collective. Without serious misgivings, people have laid down their lives at the altar of the interests of their society, believing that by doing so they'd earn the greatest rewards a mortal could earn: eternal life and prosperity in their life after death.

With the ascendance of science and reason, however, the number of people who believed these stories began to decline, and the ultimate value shifted from the afterlife to the earthly life and from the collective to the individual. This process of individualization began at the time of the transition from the traditional to the modern age, but it is still ongoing. It has secured for us greater freedoms and a greater equality, but it has stripped us of the emotional security and certainty that were offered by the traditional structures of society.

"In no way do I think life was better in the past than it is now, because I feel there was a great moral leap forward in intimate relations, largely the result of greater equality between men and women," Eva Illouz told us. "However, let us not forget that almost all ideals of love are based on inequality between men and women. For instance, men have always been the ones who courted women. This sociological structure produced greater certainty. Certainty is a logical, but also an emotional, characteristic. This means that you always know what situation you'll find yourself in and what the rules of the situation are. When a man and a woman were interested in one another, when they went through the process of courtship, they knew exactly which rules of behavior they had to follow and this gave them a greater sense of emotional security. Now the roles are more poorly set out, a relationship needn't lead to marriage, and people are free to enter into and exit from relationships as they choose…."

"So, is the consequence of this less certainty, less emotional security, and greater existential anxiety?" I asked.

"Yes," she answered. "Religion no longer regulates the encounters between men and women and no longer controls sexuality or morality. In the traditional world, which is completely under the sway of religion, sexuality is actually the code for morality, especially for women, because virginity guaranteed the reputation and value of a woman. Through courtship, a woman could confirm whether the man was a partner who was deserving of her, and if he was, then at the end of the process their relationship would be consummated. Today, this is the other way around—first you get to know each other in bed, and then you think about whether you are interested in more. There are no promises that the story will continue, nor is there any emotional security. Therefore, the ritual of courtship has vanished because of the fact that religion no longer exerts influence on individuals and doesn't regulate how their relations ought to be."

The transition from traditional to modern societies, the shift of focus from the collective to individuals and the loss of certainty that comes with it, are reflected in the creation of our identities. Before, religion and a society that was steeped in it were a great help in how we defined ourselves. We knew exactly who we were, where we belonged, and which collection of views on life we were expected to adopt. We knew exactly how we should dress, how we should treat others, how we should behave in situations. The confirmation of our worth came from without, from society, but now we have to seek it within ourselves.

We no longer live for our life after death, but rather for this life in the here and now, and we are no longer prepared to give up on happiness: we wish to be happy now and here. We have never valued emotions as much as we do today. During the traditional age, emotions were thought to be deceptive, fickle, and passing, so they didn't merit attention. Placing all our hopes in the promise of permanent happiness in the afterlife seemed more worthwhile. But today, our fragile emotions seem more stable to us than all the irrational promises, so we have elevated them to the pedestal that has been standing empty ever since we deposed the gods.

At the transition from the traditional to the modern age when we started losing faith in the gods, the idea of romantic love appeared. As the focus shifts from the collective to the individual; as the impact of the traditional social institutions that had secured our emotional safety and confirmed our identity weakens; as the process of individualization shows us that its other face is

196

loneliness; as we become more and more troubled by the anxiety of existential uncertainty and we are left to ourselves more—the greater becomes our hope that romantic love would replace our lost sense of meaning.

Does this mean that romantic love is our new religion?

11

ROMANTIC LOVE

Is love the new religion?

"Could those people possibly be who I think they are?" I asked Anđela, raising my eyebrows, nodding with a tilt of my head toward a good-looking couple...

...who were posing for a photograph in front of the palace in Jodhpur, the royal capital of the Indian state of Rajasthan.

"You're kidding," she said, incredulous. "What are the chances?"

We reached for our cell phones, went to Instagram, to the page with the unusual name of *Backpackdiariez*, which we'd been following. Anđela and I don't use Instagram a lot, nor do we follow many accounts, but Belgians **Camille** and **Jean** [p. 283] are one of several traveling couples, influencers, that we follow regularly because they have pulled us in with what they do and have intrigued us with what they are like.

"It is them! It really is!" said Anđela softly when we compared the image on our phones with the people we could see a few feet from us.

"What are the chances that we'd run into them while we're traveling in one of the two hundred countries of

PREVIOUS PAGE
PARIS, FRANCE

the world, especially here in India with its more than one billion inhabitants?"
I added.

We knew we had to go up to them and introduce ourselves, but this felt awkward. When Anđela and I are out on the streets of Croatia, people come up to us after they recognize us from social media or the press. In our little country, we're C-category celebrities, as recognizable as the anchor of a morning show on local TV or a national champion in an equestrian or wrestling competition. Maybe we are familiar to those interested in travel, expeditions, photography, and writing, but not to the public at large. Sometimes, we look vaguely familiar to cashiers at a supermarket, but it never occurs to them that they might have seen us in the media. Instead, what starts is a guessing game: might we be cousins of one of their in-laws, or were we at that wedding a few years ago? Now when we were the ones who had to walk up and introduce ourselves to a couple who enjoyed worldwide popularity, our knees buckled. I knew this was a moment when we had to dive in, no matter what…. I stepped into their space and, stuttering, presented our story to them and our hope that they'd agree to let us interview them, while Anđela half hid behind my back. As soon as we were met by friendly smiles, human warmth, and their interest in us, as soon as they agreed without hesitation to our interview, we breathed a sigh of relief. Jean and Camille put us at ease after five minutes of chatting, as if we'd known each other for years.

I found the awkwardness easier to endure because from the start of our project I'd had my heart set on finding a couple like them. Of all the better-known and less-known couples I was familiar with, they seemed ideal. I know the darker sides of the couples I'm friends with, so I can't idealize them. It's easier to idealize couples I know only through the media and only partially—however they prefer to be presented to the public. Famous actors in the classic media like television, movies, or theater often continue to perform a public persona away from the screen or stage, making a public display of the idyll of their private lives and thereby boosting their value in the eye of the public. The new media, such as Facebook and Instagram, have melted away the barrier between private and public life, and now we can see stars without make-up in the places where they live and in everyday situations. This makes it easier for us to identify with them.

Since I had the impression from Instagram that Camille and Jean were an ideal couple, I was keen to get to know them. I wanted to verify this in person. I was aware that although Instagram, more than other media, gives the impression that you are behind the scenes in someone's home, life, relationships—stars still prep for everything they show. Although influencers widely share their intimacy and make their private lives public, they can still choose how to present it to the world. But a live encounter is more difficult to fake. Nevertheless, I wondered, could it be that their entire lives are an act?

"Oh, it was perfect," Camille began their story in the lounge of a nice hotel that succeeded, to some degree, in muffling the noise and smells of India. We talked excitedly all day from morning till afternoon, trading travel anecdotes and business advice, and after lunch we set up the recording equipment, turned on the camera, and threw ourselves into the interview.

"I was fourteen, and Jean was a few years older, so good-looking, one of the most popular boys in school. I'd already had a huge crush on him for ages when he came over and asked me out."

"And ever since that day, we've been inseparable," added Jean, "15 years!"

"He proposed to me after we'd been together for a long time, over ten years. Oh, it was so romantic!"

"I surprised Camille. I invited her to come to Paris, and I hid little messages all over the city that led her from one to the next, and finally to Pont des Arts, where I was waiting for her on my knees with a bouquet of roses!"

"As soon as I saw the first message, I knew what would come next.... Oh, it was fantastic. A dream marriage proposal!"

"The first thing she said was: 'At last!'"

"Yes, ha ha ha…!"

"And the wedding, oh my God…."

"It was soooo beautiful…."

"We were married on the gorgeous island of Santorini in Greece, surrounded by our closest family and best friends."

"Magnificent…."

Although the camera was on and everything was being recorded, they behaved and talked just the same as they had when the camera had been off and we'd been talking about other things. Neither of them dominated. Neither talked over the other. Instead, they relayed the lead back and forth smoothly. They spoke as if they were dancing. When Anđela asked them what they thought their greatest strength was, both of them stopped to think for a minute, and then almost in the same moment they took a breath to answer. Jean was a second faster:

"Complementarity."

"Ah," shrieked Camille, "that's what I was going to say!"

"We complement each other so well," added Jean, and then both of them, in a dynamic dance of fragmented sentences, went on to explain complementarity in the work they do: how he is the dreamer while she is the doer; he is the creative spirit and she is the operational force; he comes up with ideas and she makes them happen….

I was a little embarrassed. I had been thinking *they* were better than *us*. I didn't mind them being younger and more successful than we are, having hundreds of thousands of followers on social media, that the fanciest hotels and vacation resorts pay them to try their services and provide advertising on their Instagram page, or how they make the rounds of the most stunning tropical destinations from Bora Bora to private atolls in the Caribbean nonstop. No. I envied them on how smoothly they worked together as partners. Their non-verbal communication confirmed their words. They genuinely *do* complement each other perfectly, it seemed. They truly respect each other and accept each other completely. Anđela and I love each other and work hard, I thought, we are passionate in our struggle and determination to be together, ultimately, and we travel the world and work together as partners, this is our livelihood, and we are a good mix of dreamer and doer. In that way we're similar, I thought, but we fight much more than they do, our non-verbal communication does not show the same degree of mutual respect and acceptance…. In all ways, they are *better*.

— — —

I wondered whether the way we see Jean and Camille today is the way that people over the last several centuries have seen Shakespeare's Romeo and Juliet, the forerunners and heralds of romanticism, the new movement in literature. Romantic love appeared at roughly the same time as the novel did.

Through the Middle Ages and the advent of the new epoch, through the final stages of the traditional age before the transition to the modern, the European nobility and citizenry as well as the peasants living in villages—all practiced arranged marriages. As we saw in Chapter Five, marriage was an economic buttress of patriarchal society. If they didn't want to marry and be spouses, mothers, and housewives, women had few alternatives except for two—to be a nun or a prostitute. In marriage, men sought stability, procreation, and a home, and in their wife they had more of a friend and a partner than a lover; they satisfied their lust with prostitutes, and fell in love with distant, unattainable ladies they couldn't have. Between the 11th and 13th centuries, men—as troubadours and minnesingers—serenaded their ladies, and they never expected their passion to be consummated. They idealized women.

The idea that the sex drive, infatuation, and a profound attachment should come together in a single person arose exactly at the moment of transition between the traditional and the modern ages, and not in real life but in literature, in the new literary movement, romanticism. As we saw in Chapter Three, the technology of the printing press at that time had advanced to the point that small books had become inexpensive enough for the middle class to afford them, and, at the same time, literacy was widespread enough by then that they could be read. So, the combination of these two factors, which were tantamount to magic to people at the time, produced a pandemic of idealization regarding romantic love. Romeo and Juliet were the first, archetypical romantic couple, prepared to defy the entire world in the name of their love. But they appeared on the theater stage a few generations before the novel and romanticism began and became apostles to later kindred heroes, who began to appear in novels written by J. W. Goethe, Friedrich Schiller, Victor Hugo, Jane Austen, Aleksandar Pushkin, M. J. Lermontov....

These novels stand at the beginning of the modern age, shoulder to shoulder with the advent of industrialization, individualization, the ascent of science and reason, and the weakening of the absolute power of religion, family, and social communities.... We saw in the previous chapter how, with the transition from the traditional to the modern age, the social norms and ideal models as well as our personal expectations and wishes were less and less shaped and transmitted by parents, families, teachers, and religious instructors, and more by external factors, especially the media. This started with novels, plays, operas, and continued with radio, television, Hollywood, Bollywood, and then took off with the Internet and social media. Today, the most powerful media figures are more often real people than fictitious ones, and for the first time, they are clearly called 'influencers.' So, I wondered, were Jean and Camille, as influencers, therefore the ideal figures for today's society, the equivalent of Romeo and Juliet?

If the primary and central feature of romantic love is the new notion that we should satisfy all our lust, passion, and desire for attachment with only one person, the second feature could be the idea that the passion, the infatuation, should last forever. In Chapters Three and Four, we saw how our brain, through its long history, evolved so that when we choose our corresponding partner, we are rewarded with a chemical cocktail that causes a very agreeable sensation, the same sensation that recreational drugs give us today. We also saw how, precisely due to its intensity, this sensation cannot last forever; it is not sustainable. The thinking is that the intense phase of infatuation may last up to three years, roughly, as long as our ancestors needed to remain together in order to bring their offspring into the world and help them survive the most tenuous phase of life. Just as few people can live their whole life taking the same dose of cocaine and draw the same amount of pleasure from it, few can sustain the intensity of infatuation long-term and permanently.

"A person who is happily in love shows all the symptoms of an addict," Dr. **Helen Fisher**, anthropologist, told us. "They crave union with the beloved; they are elated, intoxicated when they think of their beloved; as their obsession grows they seek to interact with the beloved more and more often; they think about them obsessively; they distort reality; they change their priorities to adapt to the beloved; they are prepared to die for the beloved; they are anxious when away from the beloved; when separated from the beloved they suffer just like an addict who cannot score drugs; if the beloved spurns them they go through an abstinence crisis, with anger, sobbing, lethargy, anxiety, insomnia, loss of appetite or overeating…. Being in love is an addiction—a marvelous, positive addiction when our love is reciprocated, and a catastrophically negative one when our feelings of love become inappropriate, poisonous, toxic."

Camille and Jean said something similar.

205

"At the beginning of our relationship, I was totally beside myself," Camille told us, beaming. "When I thought of him, my heart pounded, every time he called me, I'd nearly faint. It's still like that today, I'm still crazy about him!"

"Even today we're inseparable, we literally cannot bear being apart," added Jean.

"Yes, when we have to be apart, we feel awful."

"For all these years, we have seldom been apart for more than a day or two."

"Here, for instance now—our good friends are getting married, we are serving as their witnesses and we're responsible for the bachelor and bachelorette parties, so we're doing all we can to organize these for the same weekend, so we're apart for only one weekend and not two."

"We really are together non-stop. And not just now when we're traveling around the world, but when we're at home, all these years…."

"People ask us how we can spend so much time together…. They say that it's healthy to maintain a little distance from one's partner, but we get sick when we're apart."

— — —

Romantic love, infatuation, is not just similar to addiction, but to all the transcendental and metaphysical sensations that we have sought in religious rituals, in the liminal, the *sacred*. When we are in love, we feel as if we are living a fuller, more complete reality. As though we were surfing on a wave of cocaine, everything suddenly makes sense and is brilliant. We feel blessed, touched by a magic wand that allows us to see the whole world through rose-colored glasses. Our existence seems enhanced. We focus on the object of our fascination, our beloved, and we are completely dedicated to them. We feel as if we have escaped from the constraints of normalcy, we are astride the wheel that is moving everything, and we are becoming a central, purposeful part of the total dance of life. We feel as if we have succeeded in overcoming our separation, that we're back in the paradise we were expelled from so long ago. We feel as if we're transcending the border of our ego, that our ego is melting and merging with something larger, except that this is no longer God or an abstract force. It is our beloved partner, a real person of flesh, blood, heart, and soul, right here in front of us, in our arms, for whose love we're prepared to die. We are ready to give ourselves up to this feeling, because thanks to it, we have wrested ourselves free of the trap of meaninglessness, we've seen through the matrix and freed ourselves of insignificance.

When we asked them to describe love to us with one word, Jean chose "unconditionality," while Camille said "paradise." Although they used the word 'commitment' several times during the interview, they didn't choose it for their answer. Yet the very fact that so many couples we interviewed in the United States and Europe did choose 'commitment' as their answer shows that commitment—dedication, allegiance, devotion—is one of the central features of romantic love. But it is also the most important aspect of religiosity. This is what is expected of the faithful—to be dedicated and devoted, to place the other first, to need that other, to be faithful to them, willing to make sacrifices for them and defend them. Devotion in love, as in religion, implies giving one's trust in advance, taking the leap into the unknown, absolute availability[1].

Is it possible to achieve this, or is this merely yet another illusion, one more story?

If love is the new grand story that has replaced religion, has it not succeeded in doing so because it is *more convincing*? Jean and Camille convinced me of their authenticity. I trusted them, which is why I'd idealized them in the first place, and why I felt ashamed that we weren't as devoted to one another as they were, but I also felt hope that we might become more like them. So harmonious and complementary, so happy and successful, so *perfect*.

After all, Jean and Camille are not the only people like this. We can find examples elsewhere in the world. Unlike with God, who is so painfully absent from our world, love, indeed, can be found. Maybe it hasn't happened to us yet, but love blazes like a lighthouse on the distant horizon, giving us hope, showing us the way through the dark, gloomy night.

12

FORBIDDEN LOVE

Why does love sometimes survive impossible conditions?

"Love is stronger than God!" said Krishna, both angry and proud. "Love is the strongest force in the world, nothing is stronger than love. Love is everything. Without love there is nothing!"

Everything 41-year-old **Krishna** told us about love was declared with emotion and exaltation, because he had had to fight fiercely for love. He'd swum upstream against the whole of society and in defiance of the entire world. Just as had 40-year-old **Pooja** [p. 288], his beloved, who was sitting there next to him on a spindly bed, her legs crossed, in a simple hut not much larger than the bed, somewhere in the fields near Mumbai.

"We fell in love when we were children, we've been in love ever since we were in school," said Krishna. "We wrote letters to each other and dreamed of the day when we'd live together, but when we both reached marriageable age, our families wouldn't hear of it. Our parents wanted us to marry other people, because we belong to different castes. They'd decided this long before, and they weren't willing to hear of our

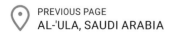

PREVIOUS PAGE
AL-'ULA, SAUDI ARABIA

feelings. We were miserable. We didn't want this to happen. So, we decided to run away!"

Caste divisions had always been strict in India, but they became toxic when the British formalized them during colonial rule in order to more easily rule the vast subcontinent with its ancient cultures. Thanks to the revolutionary efforts of Mahatma Gandhi, but also the incursion of Western humanistic values and human rights, the caste system was formally abolished when India declared its independence from the British crown in 1947. But caste divisions persisted in the minds of most of the population who transmitted the old values from generation to generation. This is best confirmed by the fact that even today in overpopulated and increasingly powerful India, more than 95% of marriages occur within the same caste[1].

Historically, four main castes had formed in India. The members of the highest caste, the Brahmans, were not manual laborers; they were teachers, scholars, poets, artists, priests. The next caste below in the hierarchy, the Kshatriyas, were soldiers and state officials. The next below were the Vaishyas, the small business owners, tradesmen, farmers, and merchants, while the lowest caste were the Shudras, the wage workers and physical laborers, but those working at honorable jobs, not dirty ones. Those whose work had to do with blood, feces, and death were outside the system. They were the Dalits or Pariahs, and they were referred to as the 'untouchables.' Gandhi called them Harijans—people of God—but this did little to change the attitudes of other Indians toward them. Even today, the Dalits seldom succeed in doing something other than the dirtiest jobs, such as garbage collection, the burial of the dead, and pumping out septic tanks, and for this reason, there are many Indians who refuse to shake their hands or share food with them.

Of the 5% of Indian marriages that cross the borders of caste, very few include Dalits. There are fewer than one hundred marriages per year between a Brahman and a Dalit[2]—in a country with a population of almost a billion and a half and known for its variety. Even the fact that the Indian government offers financial support to inter-caste couples does very little to change these deeply entrenched traditions. In terms of the convictions of 'ordinary' people, love between castes is not only an unacceptable sin but something repulsive, dirty, deserving of scorn. The greater the difference between castes, the more disgusting and scandalous the marriage is. For many Indians, the thought of a romantic relationship between a Brahman and a Dalit is every bit as disturbing as a romantic relationship between a brother and sister would be to us. Through no guilt of their own, Krishna was born into the Brahman caste and Pooja into the Dalits.

"We ran away and ended up on the street," said Krishna. "We had nothing. I have no idea how we survived. For the first year and a half we were on the run, because our parents were after us. Then they found us and separated us for two months, but again we ran away."

While Krishna related all this with anger, Pooja's lips trembled and her eyes swam with tears. We asked her to say how this had been for her. She tried to say something, her voice fighting back the tears that were filling her eyes, but the only thing she could say was:

"It was really horrible… and painful…. Our parents tormented us…." she softly sobbed, her tears spilling over her lower eyelids, so we didn't ask her anything more. Krishna's eyes also filled with tears as he stared at the floor, while Pooja kept her eyes on the camera and wept.

We never learned what they went through, but at least they were lucky enough to survive. Many others have not been so lucky. Honor killings are how similar situations have played out. When children defy their conservative parents, the family experiences this as an attack on the family's honor, and sometimes they are more prepared to kill their own child than accept the 'disgrace.' For such people, fitting in with the social norms is a higher priority than the lives of their children. Several hundred honor killings occur every year, and most often the reason is because the woman wishes to marry a man from a caste that is below hers.

Pooja finally pulled herself together and spoke: "Love is the thing that gives you the strength to stand up to your parents, and everything, even God if need be!"

"Love blinds people," Krishna tried to explain. "When you are in love, you only want to be with the person, regardless of everything. Castes don't matter… religion… higher-lower, small-large, poor-rich, none of this matters. The only thing that matters is the person you love; beyond that, you can't see anything. For your beloved you are prepared to defy your family, society, everything!"

Krishna and Pooja lived for years on the street with nothing. Krishna said that sometimes they were so poor that, when his sandals fell apart and he couldn't even repair them with wire, he had to go barefoot for days. They looked for work, any work, but for a long time they were unsuccessful, so they managed as best as they could from one day to the next barely eking out a homeless existence. Krishna managed to find a job on the night shift at a factory, and then finally, bit by bit, they began to pull themselves out of extreme poverty. Over the past years, they have been living on a plot of land 50 miles outside of Mumbai amid mango and cashew groves. In return for working the land and serving as guards on his property, the owner allows them to live in the tiny hut. Pooja spends all her days there, while Krishna sometimes goes to a nearby town where he works as an assistant tailor and earns bread not only for himself and Pooja, but also for their two children and Krishna's father, who is demented and wheelchair bound.

"At the beginning, when you are up against everything, such a life is very difficult," said Krishna, "but after 10 to 15 years, people accept you, they get used to it."

And their parents finally accepted them, especially after the children were born, and now they are caring for their only living parent, Krishna's father.

"The times are changing," continued Krishna. "Twenty-five years ago, when we'd run away from all of them, nobody understood us, they were all pitted against us. Today, more and more people tell us that what we did was good. Today more people respect us."

"Today we are happy," said Pooja. "Our parents accepted us. Society changes slowly. But we haven't changed, we still love each other as we did then. I hope that will stay until the end. When we have love, we have everything."

— — —

As with **Jean** and **Camille** [p. 283], Krishna and Pooja put us to shame, but in a different way. The very tenacity of life shone from their story, and their hope crystalized from thin air into something tangible. I hid behind the camera, and through the viewfinder I watched the drama play out in front of the lens as if I were watching a classic movie. Krishna and Pooja impressed me as heroes and earned my immense respect. They described this all with such vitality and confirmed so fully what they were saying with their emotions that I automatically sympathized with them. Whenever we interviewed people who belonged to cultures that were dramatically different from ours, we wished they'd show us their emotions, because we believe that emotions serve to bridge the cultural differences that divide us. We find sympathizing with the problems others face more difficult if we can't see their emotions. And the clearer and more powerful their emotions are the more successfully they take down the walls of misunderstanding between us. Then we can even understand concepts as foreign and strange to us as caste more easily. Although castes may be an extreme form of social stratification, every society that is not egalitarian, such as hunter-gatherer societies, is divided into strata. And every stratified society has examples of forbidden loves that surmount those borders between social strata. We found a moving story about forbidden love from our own culture as well—not in the hills of the Balkan but in exile—in Hollywood.

Anđela and I were born in Yugoslavia, a socialist federation of six republics. Of all six, our republic, Croatia, includes by far the longest and most stunning stretch of the Adriatic Coast with over a thousand islands and islets. Because of its natural Mediterranean beauty, it is famous as a tourist destination. But as soon as we enter into a more serious conversation with tourists, they invariably ask about the wars of the 1990s when Yugoslavia broke up into smaller countries in a violent series of conflicts, which, sadly, also shaped us powerfully. We always find telling a brief version of this story a challenge, but the question is the degree to which we are even able to be objective about it, since we were victims of the propaganda machines of the warring governments. The story, as it is told in Croatia, is that Serbia first attacked Croatia and then Bosnia; the Serbs were the aggressors, and we, the Croats, were the victims. The truth is far more complex and tangled. There can be no doubt that all the warring sides bear a portion of the blame and that atrocities were committed by all sides. Both Croats and Serbs have spent the last 25 years since the war ended faced with these demons.

When the war began, **Mira** and **Goran** [p. 265] were a young couple in love who happened to find themselves on the wrong sides of the wall that had been suddenly raised between their cities.

"I was a young actress, and he was a young movie director, and we met once at a filming session," Mira began their story. "I liked him a lot and I thought he was a lovely, lovely, lovely guy. I had the feeling that I knew this lovely man from some previous life, and it was as if we belonged together. We spoke the same language, laughed at the same jokes, and there was something else: I was laughing, I was always laughing—Goran's sense of humor captured me!"

Goran was sitting next to her on a large sofa in their villa with a pool on the slopes of the hills where the iconic letters spelling 'Hollywood' stand, and he didn't say much, but his facial movements magnified and confirmed her words. He bugged out his eyes like a clown each time she spoke of his greatness or wonderfulness. The corners of his mouth spread and he chuckled silently through his teeth whenever she said something funny. We could see how attentive he was to her every word. From time to time, he'd take a breath and raise his eyebrows, about to add something to what she was saying, but then he'd exhale and let her finish the sentence she'd started. Most of the time while she was talking and gesticulating, he sat there still, neutral, taking care that all the attention of future viewers would be focused on her.

"I don't know how to differentiate the feeling of falling in love and the attraction from the feeling when you know this is *it*. But I think I knew it right away, from the start I saw Goran's total commitment, so I gave myself to him completely. We lived together from day one. I lived with him in Belgrade and from there I'd go to Zagreb to perform in the plays I was involved in. We lived in the little bubble we'd created for ourselves. But outside of that bubble, things suddenly began to fall to pieces!"

"Well, to be fair, we weren't the only ones who didn't see it coming," added Goran. "Most people living there were surprised by what was happening."

"Hatred poured out of all the weapons, the media, every newspaper started working on making the war happen. The war propaganda was on the lookout for whom to blame, the sacrificial lamb. And then there I was, one day, plastered across the headlines of all the newspapers as if I were national enemy number one."

Both Mira and Goran avoided labeling themselves in nationalist terms during the interview. Goran, who is considered Serbian, was born in Zagreb while Mira, who is considered Croatian, has other ancestries as well, including Serbian, so national categories do not make sense for them.

"I don't know which ethnic group I belong to, since I'm an ethnic hybrid and proud of it," she said, at first with a victorious tone, which was followed by a frown as she mockingly negated her previous sentence. "I mean, *pride…* how can a person be proud of something acquired completely arbitrarily, such as ethnic or national membership?"

The peoples of Yugoslavia belong to the Southern Slavs, and the three peoples who clashed the most during the war, the Croats, Bosniaks, and Serbs, are so linguistically kindred that many scholars feel these are not, in fact, distinct ethnicities or languages, though each group has its own distinct history and religious affiliations. But history has shown us that peoples who are very similar more often tend to enter into conflict than those who are completely different. Freud called this phenomenon the narcissism of small differences. Does this not apply to love as well? I often wondered.

"We set our lives up, dividing time between Zagreb and Belgrade, but the cities were starting a war—a real war!" Mira went on. "The only thing expected of each person was to choose sides. Which was their tribe? Did they identify as Serbs or Croats? I never felt I belonged to any one tribe. I always felt I belonged to all tribes. I couldn't take sides. I refused to. I don't believe in that sort of division."

But the warmongers knew that taking sides was essential if they were going to pit people against each other, and for this they needed sacrificial lambs. Mira and Goran, as the most famous Croatian/Serbian couple, were the perfect target.

"When the main Croatian newspaper published my address and phone number, I began getting terrifying phone calls. I remember the day we counted 50 death threats. I thought, 'these are my fans, these are the people who used to love me, the people I performed for… and now I can't live among them anymore.' When the hatred surged to unimaginable heights, when people began dying, when the real war began, we could no longer stay there. We had no choice but to leave."

Mira and Goran packed their lives up into two suitcases and, with the few thousand dollars in their savings, bought one-way plane tickets to New York. Thanks to their talents and persistence it didn't take them long to make their way to Hollywood, where both of them have built successful careers. One day spent with them convinced us of what a harmonious couple they were, and again I felt slightly ashamed. Aside from telling us that they were still as in love as they'd been 30 years before when they'd fled together from their old lives, their non-verbal communication confirmed what they were saying. They giggled, nudged each other, and kissed as if they'd fallen in love only the day before; sparks flashed in their eyes, and one could read a profound respect, esteem, and bond between the lines of their harmonious verbal communication. Their villa, like others in Hollywood, was separated from the outside world by tall walls, inside of which Mira and Goran built their new world—their new bubble.

— — —

What are the ideal types? Who are the models we admire and measure ourselves against? Do we choose them or does society choose them for us? If belief in romantic love is the dominant story of our times, if it is the paradigm that has replaced religion, then Jean and Camille, Krishna and Pooja, and Mira and Goran are the heroes of our time.

However, there is a difference between Jean and Camille's story on the one hand and the story about the forbidden love of Krishna and Pooja and Mira and Goran on the other. If we continue with Dr. **Eva Illouz**'s analogy of the magnet, Jean and Camille's romantic love is within the magnetic field of Western society, because their story doesn't test the boundaries of social norms but rather confirms them. Krishna and Pooja put their lives on the line to defy the firmly rooted division of their society into castes, as did Mira and Goran, who defied the chauvinism and wartime madness that spread like a plague through their society. And **Mathew** and **Naomi** [p. 101] from Zambia, **Nazanin** and **Nahid** [p. 98] from Iran, **Sandra** and **Patricia** [p. 246] from Germany, and many others whom we met on our trip around the world also exist as particles on the periphery of this magnetic field, resisting the main forces within their societies and thereby questioning the social norms and striving to change them. Their love is a subversive political force that is changing the world and actively contributing to the building of a more just society.

Hence Jean and Camille are not today's equivalent of Romeo and Juliet, a mantel that would instead apply to Krishna and Pooja as well as Mira and

Goran. The story of Romeo and Juliet, a couple who loved each other despite the vendettas between their families, whom they defied, is also a story of forbidden love, a story of enthroning love, elevating it above all values, above the social norms of their time, and even above their own lives. "The love between Romeo and Juliet questions the norms and laws of the clans and families in a world where the clans organized politics and the economy," Eva Illouz told us. "This is why their story has political meaning, because it is transgressive, it oversteps boundaries and changes society. Romantic love in today's Western consumer culture is not a threat to anything."

The true story about forbidden love must result in escape, because for its protagonists, there is no place of belonging within their society. Just as Krishna and Pooja had to run away from their family to live on the streets, or as Mira and Goran had to run away from the madness of the war to live on another continent and start from scratch, so Romeo and Juliet had to flee into death, because they saw no other way out of their suffering as lovers.

However, the story of Jean and Camille, as well as those of Krishna and Pooja and Mira and Goran, are inspirational stories of romantic love because they offer proof that fireworks stage and long-term love can be combined, that it is possible to unify lust, passion, and a desire for attachment. They show that it is possible, led only by the beacon of fragile, unstable emotions, to overcome the greatest tempests on the ocean of life.

This is probably why, when I'd heard their stories, I felt ashamed—because I could see that they were more attuned to each other and were a better couple than Anđela and I were. At the same time, by internalizing the messages of their stories, I felt moved to try to be more like them. But that is a high bar; for many of us, the challenge is too great. This is why these stories excite more than admiration and offer more than inspiration. As we'll see in the next chapter, they can also often produce new levels of suffering.

13

THE END OF LOVE

Why does love so often fail when all seems to be well?

On the flight from Mumbai to Malé, the capital of the Maldives, most of the passengers were newlyweds. This came as no surprise, because...

...we knew the Maldives are one of the most popular honeymoon destinations in the world.

But we were very surprised by what we read in a guidebook on the same flight—the fact that the Maldives has the highest rate of divorce in the world! How could this be possible, we wondered. How is it possible that the inhabitants of these paradise-like islands to which newlyweds from all over the world come to celebrate their love dissolve their unions more often than all others? How could this be, especially considering that the Maldives is a relatively conservative and traditional Islamic country? Why are heaven and hell always so close together? Why is destiny always so ironic?

Is this because their neighborhoods are so densely populated and they are packed in too close together, so conflict

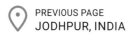
PREVIOUS PAGE
JODHPUR, INDIA

can more easily erupt, I wondered as soon as we arrived in Malé. Out of the roughly hundred cities we visited on our trip, Malé impressed me more than most. It has grown upward on a low-lying island, one of the largest in a country that is made up of sandy atolls. The island on which Malé stands is never more than a meter above sea level and it is so small that one can walk its circumference in less than half an hour. Tall buildings crowd next to each other from one shore to the other, from which the sight is reminiscent of a beehive. Two hundred thousand people live in less than five square miles. Every square foot of land is precious here. A sports field is an example of as much ostentation as a presidential palace. The narrow streets are jam-packed with pedestrians, motorbikes, and cars, all battling for space. Everything here fights for space, rubs elbows and bumps shoulders. Is this why there are so many divorces? This is what we asked **Ahmed**, a 36-year-old aircraft operator, and **Shaheema**, a 32-year-old policewoman [p. 121], who had been married for five years.

"I think there are three main reasons," began Shaheema. "Women were tied to home and family before, and now they are freer, they are working, building their careers, they are economically independent, and they are able to choose. Secondly, at work they get to know people who are perhaps more like them and more interesting than the man they married so quickly. And thirdly, in our culture obtaining a divorce is easy. There is no fuss with the courts, dividing property, alimony…. All you have to do is say three times that you're divorcing and—you're done!"

Ahmed explained to us that this is the result of two key economic and developmental facts.

"One is that there has been a huge upswing in luxury tourism in the Maldives over the last few decades, so a great deal of money has poured into our country from abroad. And second is that in comparison to nearby countries, our rulers are relatively less corrupt, so not all the incoming revenue ends up in their pockets. Instead, they have been investing it in growing the country. For instance, we all have free health care and education, we can even study abroad and the state will pay for it, and when we start a family, we are given a plot of land, even though open land is scarce. All this has contributed to the growth of society, and the consequence of this growth is greater freedom for women, hence the higher divorce rate."

Another reason that contributes to the ease with which women are able to leave toxic marriages is that the bride price has been shrinking. In the other Asian and Muslim countries we visited, the institution of the bride price was still quite strong. As we saw in Chapter Five, this is the way men bond to their wives in traditional, patriarchal societies and it also acts as women's only form of protection. In the Maldives until only a few decades ago, men had to work for years to save enough money to pay for their bride. Today, the bride price has been reduced to a symbolic amount, as we saw for ourselves at a wedding in Malé, which we happened by chance to attend.

Young Nizam and Shizma were married in a fancy hotel located in a tall and narrow high-rise on the shore. After the imam from a nearby mosque formalized their union in five minutes, Nizam gave Shizma a wooden box engraved with the date of their wedding. He explained to us that the box contained the money for the bride price, but the amount was merely symbolic. "We met on 17 November 2017, so Shizma asked for a bride price of 17+11+2017 rufiyaa." This was the equivalent of just over $100. Although they'd only just navigated their way into marital waters, we couldn't resist asking Shizma what she thought: why do the people of the Maldives divorce so frequently?

"This is as it should be," she said quite coldly, as if the cruel reality momentarily dampened her excitement about the wedding. "Before, there were fewer divorces because women obeyed men. Now we're freer. We work, we have our lives, and we don't depend so much on men, so we can leave them when they no longer deserve our love."

Anthropologist Dr. **Helen Fisher** told us that the most powerful factor in divorce has been women joining the work force.

"Money spells freedom. Working women have more of it than those who mind the house. When women work outside the house and contribute to the household budget, it becomes easier for them to dissolve their bond if they become desperately unhappy. But there are many reasons why people divorce. The most frequent one is that the couple cannot have children. There are many psychological reasons as well: if one of the partners is too lazy, angry, violent, promiscuous, rude, boring, bad with children, if he or she is uninterested in sex, or just stares all day at the television…."

Helen Fisher also suggested that we take a look at a study conducted by anthropologist Laura Bertzig in 160 societies. She reached the conclusion that the most common reason for divorce is adultery, particularly when the woman is the one committing the adultery. The second most common reason is infertility, and the third is violence[1].

"In modern societies," she said, "the community which earlier provided support for marriages has been lost. Many of us have moved away from home; our parents live in different cities, often with new partners. So, the wide network of family and community support that couples need when times are tough is vanishing, which increases the likelihood of divorce. Urbanism, secularism, and migration are associated with marital dissolution. Those who choose partners with different habits, different values, different interests, and different leisure activities are more likely to divorce. The contemporary emphasis on individualism and self-fulfillment has also contributed to the rising incidence of divorce."

The words we heard from sociologist Dr. **Eva Illouz** tie into this as well: "The ideal of self-realization is a very powerful institution and cultural force: it is what makes people leave unsatisfying jobs and loveless marriages, attend meditation workshops, take long and expensive vacations, consult a psychologist, and so on. It fundamentally posits the self as a perpetually moving target, as something in need of discovery and accomplishment. A single man wrote in a column for the *New York Times* about his choice to not enter marriage and domesticity: 'One of the hardest things to look at in this life is the lives we didn't lead, the path not taken, the potential left unfulfilled.'[2]"

— — —

Miranda and **Vuk** [p. 285] decided to divorce because Vuk felt a pressing need to pursue the path not taken.

"After 30 years of marriage and three wonderful children who are now already grown and independent, a question began to arise inside of me: am I… am I… free?" Vuk said. "This question reached the point of clarity for me when my mother passed away. She was quite a demanding person; she required a great deal of energy. After her death, I felt a kind of relief in a way. I realized that I'm much freer now than I was before. And then I began to wonder whether there were other things holding me back on the path to my personal growth. I asked myself whether my family might be blocking me. That is how this began...."

Miranda, who is Dutch, met Vuk, who is from Croatia, when they were very young while she was on vacation on the Adriatic Coast. She liked how he was tall, strong, and exotic and that he played the guitar and entertained their friends. They fell so deeply in love that penniless Vuk hitchhiked his way to the Netherlands to visit her. It didn't take them long to marry, and from then on, they lived in the Netherlands. We met them and interviewed them at their vacation home on the Croatian coast where they spent their summers with the children.

"We didn't want to go through a divorce, slamming doors and yelling at each other," said Vuk, "so we gave ourselves time to go through the process with as much quality as we could bring to it, to learn what we needed to learn. A year has already passed since we made that decision. The divorce is unavoidable and beyond question. We just want to get through it as well as we possibly can."

"I thought we'd be together for our whole lives and I was prepared for that," said Miranda. "But apparently, that will not be possible. Vuk decided this and made me follow him. I am glad we took the time to digest it, because a divorce, like a wedding, is an essential rite of passage. We didn't tell the children right away. I didn't want the children to see me as a victim. We had to process it all first. But now I'm grateful to him for this. Each of us can give time to ourselves now. We are going back from 'us' to 'me.'"

"At first, it was fun being part of a union, growing together, having children, buying a house..." Vuk explained. "In the process, you lose yourself, you bond with another. But in time, this becomes an obstacle to your personal growth. I felt that powerfully. As if I'm in chains and I couldn't become what I should or could be. After a time, I began feeling that way and to think that I have to free myself and become who I am again, find myself!"

Miranda and Vuk were sitting on separate chairs. They agreed to the interview and saw it as part of the process of going through their divorce. Over and over, they said how they love and respect each other, and how their love will still be there, even if their story is over. "Love is all there is, all the rest are stories!" said Miranda. There was no trace, here, of anger, malice, overload, resentment… only melancholy and a subtle grief gently radiating from their gazes, both when they were speaking to the camera and when they weren't. Each well-weighed sentence let us know how much they love and respect each other, even when they disagree.

"I don't know why this is as it is," admitted Vuk with regret. "I can't explain it. Maybe in time, I'll find that this was all just a passing phase, a special stage of life, but now I feel I need to follow the call. I need to find out who I am, and for this I need autonomy, the freedom to act and discover myself. I can't make sense of why I'm doing this. I'm just following my intuition."

"Regardless of what I think about how free we really are," added Miranda, "I must respect what he thinks and feels, although perhaps I don't agree with it. In any case, I think these are important and legitimate questions."

As far as we know, only one culture has institutionalized the desire of a person to sunder marital ties after being married and to continue exploring personal questions of spiritual growth and self-awareness. This is Vedic culture in India, and its members and followers, 35-year-old **Rohit** and **Sonia** [p. 127], who is five years younger, explained it to us.

"You know, in Vedic culture there are four stages of life, each of which lasts, roughly, 20-25 years…" began Rohit, a jolly, rotund man, in their little apartment within their ashram in Vrindavan, a holy Indian city where the most devoted followers of Krishna live. Almost half of the apartment is taken up by a huge altar with many figurines showing various bodily representations of Hindu divinities and various manifestations of Krishna and Radha, who, aside from being the supreme form of God for Rohit and Sonia, were models of the *perfect lovers*, as they told us. They showed us how they spent hours tending to the symbolic divinities, bathing them, dressing them, offering them food, thereby demonstrating their devotion.

"At the first stage—the *brahmacharya*—you live like a pupil, a student, in celibacy," continued Rohit. "The second stage, the *grihastha*, is the stage of family life. This is when you find a wife, begin a family, and raise your children. When your children grow up and become independent, you're ready for the third stage, the *vanaprastha*. Then, with your wife, you go on a pilgrimage to holy places. After a time, you leave your wife and remain alone, give up everything, retreat from secular life and devote yourself exclusively to spiritual questions and your search for *moksha*—liberation. This last stage is called *sannyasa*."

Most Hindi do not follow this ancient path, but those who do, the most devoted to the faith, especially worshipers of Krishna, divide their lives into these four stages. Rohit and Sonia are among the most fervent in this regard; moreover, this was one of the conditions they set for entering into marriage.

"I feel that following this path is extremely important," said Sonia. "Our goal in life is to accomplish something more than merely getting by and enjoying life. We wish to know God, to learn who we truly are and what we should accomplish in this life. And this path with the four stages makes this possible for us. I decided to follow this path, and so has Rohit, and this is why we married. If both of us hadn't been prepared to do this, we wouldn't be here now."

"When we married, we agreed that divorce was not an option until our children are grown," grinned Rohit impishly, clearly amused by the discussion. "I told her she would only have to stand me for 25 years and then she'd be free, because we'd be parting ways anyway so each of us could devote ourselves to our spiritual life."

"I am waiting…" interjected Sonia, grinning, tapping her fingers on the arm of her chair and staring upward, away from him.

"When we go through a rough patch, when we fight…" went on Rohit….

"And we fight like cats and dogs!" interrupted Sonia.

"…then it's wise for us to remember that all this will pass, and that helps get us through!" concluded Rohit in a more serious tone. Sonia also changed her tone, offering a more moderate conclusion:

"People fight a great deal, and they find this difficult, so they part ways because of their unreconcilable differences. But we know that the lesson that comes out of all these quarrels is always the same, that it's all temporary, everything passes. So what are we even fighting for? That realization comes from spirituality. There is no point to abandoning this relationship and seeking another, when ultimately it will all come down to the same thing. Why waste so much time? Why not focus on the real thing?"

She paused for dramatic effect, laughed enigmatically, and then made her point.

"Which is... you know... Krishna!"

Anđela and I laughed heartily as if this were a joke, but it wasn't. Rohit and Sonia, however, didn't mind. They laughed with us. After the interview, Anđela and I commented that they must find it a little easier to live together, because both of them value spirituality above love. But what about the rest of us, who place love above all other values in life and sometimes cannot even see our personal growth *outside* of our love relationship but only *inside* it and *through* it? Maybe Rohit and Sonia are right when they see love and all other secular things as fragile and transitory and as sources of suffering that keep us tied to the eternal circle of birth and death. But what about those of us who think that this life is all we have, and we mean to enjoy it as much as possible, and nothing gives us greater joy and fulfillment than our relationship with the person we love? What happens to us when that relationship fails? When the love we've believed in, just as we used to believe in gods—disappears?

— — —

Before I met Anđela, I was in two or three serious relationships in which I could say that the love was mutual between us. These relationships didn't end for any concrete reasons, especially not for the statistically most frequent reasons, such as infertility, infidelity, violence, and addiction. Our reasons were far more abstract: we weren't able to fully give of ourselves to one another; it was a question of feelings, insecurity, doubting that we wanted to spend our lives together, distance, differences in values and certain basic attitudes about life, the irreconcilability of the desire for autonomy and the desire for bonding.... The last stages of these relationships were turbulent and painful, but the break-ups were neither dramatic nor shocking. Nobody was doing the leaving or being left. Together we fell, decayed, until finally we decided the time had come to chop off the rot.

For weeks after the break-ups I felt pain. I observed the pain and tried to understand what was hurting. I wasn't longing for these partners, nor did I miss them; I didn't want to return to the relationship, give it another chance, and it didn't hurt me that our relationship hadn't succeeded or that my life had been changed in significant ways. I felt pain because I sensed that soon I would no longer love the one person I'd loved the most in the world. This person who had been the most special to me would soon no longer be special. My friends who consoled me reminded me that 'time heals all wounds.' But what hurt me the most was *the very fact* that time heals all wounds! Is there anything that can prevail against this? I wondered. Shouldn't love, damn it, be that which can stand up to accursed time, which otherwise grinds up and eradicates everything? Although time at these moments was playing to my advantage, because the pain waned as it passed, I was driven to distraction by the way it erases the significance of everything. I was hurt by the awareness that someone who had meant everything to me soon would mean nothing. I was hurt that in these moments it seemed as if one of the values I gave the most credence to—love—functions according to the principles of economy.

I wondered whether the accounting of economic costs and benefits extends to all aspects of life. Whether consciously or unconsciously, every living being on this planet is motivated only by its own benefit. Is there anything that is not caught up in this circle? Unconsciously, I was hoping that at least *love* was not—with unselfish giving, putting someone else first, with commitment and devotion, empathy and altruism. Isn't altruism the most noble thing in people, that which sets us apart, at least a little, from the cruel economic calculation of nature? However, evolutionary biologists explain altruism as one of the survival strategies, albeit at the level off the collective and not at the level of the individual[3]. A collective within which individuals collaborate and sacrifice themselves for one another has a better chance of surviving than a collective in which every individual cares only for their personal interest. At the level of the individual, altruism may be a mask for a variety of interests as well. Many people who help others do so in order to feel better themselves[4]. If we are all the most important person to ourselves and, after all our noble attempts, we are ultimately guided only by our own benefit, then we deserve nothing more than to grow old and die alone, I thought in those painful moments, and I found the thought appalling.

When I watched Anđela asleep in the seat next to me on the train that rushed us through all those foreign lands, when I relished the very fact that she'd leaned her head on my shoulder while we were on board a plane over who knows what ocean, when we woke up in a close embrace after a fierce fight the night before and we couldn't remember how and when we'd hugged each other in our sleep…. In those tranquil moments of our powerful bond I'd often wonder whether it was possible that she and I would cool off toward each other as in my past experiences. That everything I was now feeling would fade. Disappear. Pass. That it would become equally irrelevant and absent from my life just as my former girlfriends had become irrelevant and absent. That she'd stop meaning what she meant to me. Whenever I thought this, along with my fear and worry, an ineffable, subtle feeling would begin to gnaw at me. It would float through my gut, murky, vague. A single word would clarify it and bring it to life, describe and capture it. But that word still doesn't exist in my language, it is waiting to be found.

— — —

"*Saudade*," answered **Yago** when we asked him how he'd describe the feeling that overwhelmed him, because the person he'd loved was in the process of leaving him. The person in question was **Bruna** [p. 284], who was sitting next to him in the small apartment they'd been sharing for the last two years, not far from Copacabana beach in Rio de Janeiro. An archetypical Brazilian woman, she was a passionate, active, enterprising 28-year-old with smooth skin the color of coffee, black curly hair, and an assertive, commanding turn of phrase, and she was planning to move out as soon as our interview was over. A few weeks earlier, she'd broken off the relationship with Yago, two years her junior, but she'd needed time to find a place where she could begin her new life. Now she was ready. Yago would be left alone in their apartment with his lost smile and eyes full of sorrow.

Saudade is a Portuguese word that is difficult to translate into other languages. It might be expressed roughly with nostalgia, melancholy, wistfulness, grief, longing. It describes the feeling associated with the loss of something precious and the sense that what is lost is gone forever. It captures the anxiety caused by the sense of the finality of loss, but the feeling is not tense or frantic, rather it is reconciled and relaxed. The word is soft and melodic sounding, with a long falling penult: [saw'dadʒi]. It dwells on the transitory and bears the beauty of its decay with a subtle pride. *Saudade* is an untranslatable word that serves as the backbone to Portuguese identity. There is even a holiday for it in Brazil—Saudade Day.

"We broke up because she wants a family but I'm not ready, I was too caught up with my job," Yago said in a sad, quiet voice, but Bruna interrupted.

"What are you talking about? That's not why we broke up!"

"Of course it is, you kept saying you wanted kids!"

"We broke up because we're too different! I am here," she extended one hand at the level of her head with the palm facing the floor, while she placed the other hand two feet below it, "and you are here! We aren't on the same wavelength at all."

"Everything happened too fast, it was all very passionate at first, so full of emotion, maybe we moved in together too quickly."

"No, it wasn't too fast, the rhythm suited me, but you couldn't keep up because you're different. And along the way, we got to know each other better and realized that we're too different, we aren't made for one another. I need someone who'll grow with me, who'll take off with me to see the world, who'll build a family with me. I'm full of energy and I'm fast-moving, you're too passive, too slow. You couldn't keep up. I had to take care of you and move you along. In the relationship with you I felt as if I were your mother, not your girlfriend!"

While she spoke with animation, gesturing as if she wanted to shake herself free of all the bitterness, Yago sat on his chair quietly, his shoulders hunched, and hands clasped in his lap. Although his head was slightly bent, he looked straight at the camera and tried to smile tenderly to keep the drama that was hidden inside him from blowing up into something larger, but each time he swallowed it would show briefly. When we asked them what love is, Yago answered, dreamily, "infinity," while Bruna said "life," that "life has no meaning without love" and that "love is stronger than all else." Both of them concluded that they would continue to believe in love, forever, despite the pain they were going through just then.

"If your love was so strong and you believe that love is stronger than all else, and there can be no doubt that you truly loved each other," we asked them, "how can you explain that you haven't been able to stay together?"

"To be frank," she said, and stopped, "I don't know!"

She stared down at the floor at her crossed feet and was lost in thought. Since we began the interview, there had not been a moment of silence. Now silence reigned.

Bruna stayed like that, frozen, staring at the floor, while Yago tried to loosen his tense posture and mask his pain with a smile. He stared sadly and peacefully at the camera lens, and his gaze pierced the camera and shot straight into me on the other side. His eyes bored *into* me. *Transmitted themselves* into me. For a moment, I could feel exactly what he meant when he said *saudade*.

INTERMEZZO 2

THE HELL
WITHIN US

TSUMAGO, JAPAN

I am lying in the dark, narrow hallway. I don't know where I am, in which fucking city. My ears are buzzing. I am depleted. I stare up at the ceiling where the front-hall wardrobe almost touches it. Cobwebs are gathering in the corner. Filth has permeated the pores of the walls that have never seen light. I notice I have never before been in this position, with my bottom on my shoes, my legs against the wall, my left shoulder touching the edge of the cupboard, and my head on the floor. I crumpled into this position in despair, pure despair. When I no longer knew what I could bang, what I could smash, I threw myself against the wall of the hallway in a grotesque contortion, snagged myself on the coat rack, collapsed into this position, and stayed here.

A moment before that I'd left Anđela in a different, but equally bizarre posture, somewhere between the rattan armchair and the decrepit TV shelf. As always, we were able to stop short of physical violence, but at these moments I understand people who are unable to stop. I can imagine with crystal clarity how, instead of slamming the door on its frame, I could have slammed her head against it. I am sure she can just as clearly imagine stabbing me in the chest. I sensed her spot the knife on the table with the corner of her eye when we were standing there, when the thought went through her mind that she should grab it and use it. I know her so well. I read her mind. At that moment, I instinctively clenched my teeth, jutted out my chin, inhaled slowly through my nose and filled my lungs with air, and thrust out my chest in front of her, provoking her, shouting inside: Come on! Grab that knife so I can prove that *you're* the weak one, the despicable one, the wretch, the one who succumbs to base, even bestial passions. Not me. I am ready to risk a life-threatening stab wound to prove to you that I am right, that I'm better than you.

But you didn't reach for the knife, you bitch, because you know that you'll hurt me even more that way. Humiliate me. You'll win.

Is this love, you fucking idiot? Is it love, you piece of shit? We screamed this at the top of our lungs until our voices were all screamed out, we'd cried out all our tears and shot off all our bullets. If there is a silver lining to fighting while traveling, it's that we don't give a fuck who hears us shouting. If there are any neighbors around, they surely won't come to check on whether we're alive, and fuck them, too. Just as we wouldn't come if we heard them shouting, so fuck us, too. Fuck us all to hell!

This is what I was thinking while we were still railing at each other before the stupid twist that dumped me into the corner of the front hall. Now, I don't care about anything. I stare at the ceiling and I don't give a fuck. I don't know where to go from here. Nothing compels me. There's just a buzzing in my ears and in my brain and everything tangible and intangible hurts in me. I can stay like this forever, or disappear at once, I don't give a fuck. As it is, I don't know what to do next. Should I send her packing and then, within a few years, go through the same nightmare with somebody else? Should I change course and start buttfucking dudes—at least with a man I could fight properly! Should I get up off the floor and go back into the ring? I don't have the strength. Should I go back in and beg for forgiveness on my knees? Why? I can no longer even remember what we were fighting about. But even if I knew that this time it was I who fucked up, she'd react to my remorse with a sincere, not faked, impulse to retch. I am stunned at the thought of how much I disgust her. And furthermore—I don't give a fuck.

We have told each other such awful things that maybe this time there really is no way back. We've deepened the chasm between us and pushed our cursed selves so far apart that even the largest bridge seems unable to connect us. We crossed all boundaries, even beyond our dead ancestors and unborn children. We didn't merely hit below the belt, as we usually do. This time, we yanked out all our organs—internal and external. Fucking words! Even they can no longer hurt us. They carry no meaning anymore. The blows have no more weight. The helplessness hurts. Paralysis. Fucking impotence. Frozen. The severed limbs ache. Phantom. We've severed everything. We've taken everything to pieces. There's nothing left.

We're on a trip around the world but we're going around in circles. Like fucking rats on a bad acid trip. All we're doing is hurting each other more. Our wounds are festering and they are foul. The gangrene is spreading through our blood. We've invested our whole lives in knowledge, and in the end this same knowledge is beating us to the ground. We are staying together because we know we won't be better off anywhere else. We know we won't find better partners, nor will we enjoy more or suffer less if we're on our own. We're staying together because we're cowards. We'll stay together because we haven't a shred of power over our petty, miserable lives.

Kumja (57) and Hiroyuki (63) from Japan had a tempestuous past. Hiroyuki was a member of the *yakuza*, a Japanese gangster organization, a criminal and a gambler. He often beat Kumja and walked out on her, but she always waited for him and forgave him. When he sent her the divorce papers to sign, she ripped them up. "I was a beast of a man who didn't deserve to be forgiven," says Hiroyuki. "But the fact that Kumja was waiting for me and believed I could change is what helped me, in the end, to truly change, and to never go back on the wrong path!"

238

was time for us to marry, and I needed to ask for the hand of the bride from her parents," says Frederick. "Everywhere in Africa, and especially here in Kenya, the man must prove to the parents that he is able to support their daughter. And besides, he needs to pay the bride price and I was broke and I didn't have a coin to my name." "I chipped in and lent him the money," adds Ann. "Actually, I gave him the money, because he never returned it. I gave him the money so he could buy me from my parents. If my parents knew this, they would never agree to the marriage."

0), Rattna (38) and Sadnam (38) from India live in the remote Kinnaur
e Himalayas, one of the last places in the world where polyandry,
n of a woman taking several husbands, is still practiced. Historically,
was practiced in fewer than 1% of the cultures of the world, while
he custom of a man having several wives, could be found in more than
rld cultures. In Kinnaur they practice fraternal polyandry, meaning that a
rries two or more brothers from the same family. "I spend half my time
usband and the other half with the other, and I love them equally," says
ur children call one father *older father*, and the other *younger father*."

Jita (42), Janchen (39) and Mindul (38) from India say that they'd be glad
if their sons were to continue the tradition and marry the same woman.
"There are many advantages to such a life," says Mindul. "The family
property isn't divided, it is better for the children because they are raised by
more parents, and we find it easier to run our farm—if one of the husbands
is ill and can no longer work, the other husband can take his place."

Marissa (23) and Wesley (52) have lived in the Philippines ever since Wesley moved to the archipelago from the United States for her. Although all three of Wesley's daughters from his first marriage are older than Marissa, they don't see their age difference as a problem. "People gossip a lot about us," says Marissa. "They think I'm with him for his money and because he'll look after me. I don't care much for these comments. Who cares! They can say whatever they like. I know I am with him because I love him. He is my first true love. I would be with him even if I had to live on the streets, as long as we're together. When we are apart for a few hours, I already miss him terribly. I can't imagine life without him."

Rejoice (27) from Cameroon and Francis (49) from the United States met over a dating application while Francis was traveling through Africa. "A relationship may well have greater chances for survival if the people are similar and share the same values, but differences give the relationship that additional spice," says Francis. "Although Rejoice and I come from two different worlds, we have a great deal in common: a sense of humor, love of travel, sport, healthy food…. And after all—we're human! We can always come up with similarities, and then it depends on us whether we'll focus on what separates us or what brings us together!"

Sandra (46) and Patricia (47) from Germany began their relationship at school, when Patricia still hadn't come out as a trans woman and was going through life as Patrick, a man. "All my life I tried to fit in as a man," says Patricia. "I even served in the army; I hid my true nature from Sandra out of fear that I might lose her. I thought I'd rather suffer for her sake than tell her how I really felt. But I couldn't stand it any longer. I had to admit it to her. Perhaps this was a little selfish of me, but now I know that love can survive everything." After almost 20 years together when Patricia told Sandra that she is a woman and wanted to undergo an operation to change her sex, Sandra supported her. "If you truly love a person, what's on the outside doesn't matter," says Sandra. "Ultimately, it doesn't matter whether the person you love is male or female. What matters is what is inside. Love conquers all."

Vandel (48) and Fernanda (42) from Brazil met at a party when both of them were in relationships with other people and each had a child from an earlier relationship. "I left everything—my family, my child, my parents, and the place where I had been living—just to be with him," says Fernanda. "It was love at first sight, something so powerful that it cannot be explained. That is why I was certain I was doing the right thing when I left everything behind."

Louis Felipe (15) and Giovanna (15) from Brazil are in a romantic relationship for the first time. "I've watched many romantic movies, I've dreamed about how I'd have a boyfriend and wondered whether our relationship would be as enchanting," says Giovanna, "but I never dreamed it would be as good as it is! This is better than the most beautiful movie!"

Kevin (38) and Bethany (36) from the United States began their relationship when they were both in polyamorous relations with other people, but in time they opted for a return to monogamy. "I have nothing against polyamory, it is in essence a marvelous idea, but I am not sure that we as people have matured to the point that we can love more people at the same time," says Bethany. "When you love someone, you want that person to love you 100% as well, and I don't know if the heart, in practice, can be effectively given to several people. When someone doesn't love you 100%, this can be very painful."

Majida (37) and Nasser (41) from Oman say that in their society, families are the ones who negotiate the marriage, the dowry, and other such matters, rather than the couple. "In the West, love and romance are on display everywhere," says Nasser, "but here these are private matters, they stay within the family, they aren't for the public."

"We, the Maasai, take more wives because we want many children. Children are worth more than cattle. Cattle make you rich. Children make you wealthy."

Noonkuta (22), Shuel (32) and Naisha (25), Kenya

Nalotesha leaving her world with her husband, whom she'd just met for the first time

Nalotesha's relatives carrying her dowry and all her belongings in a single chest

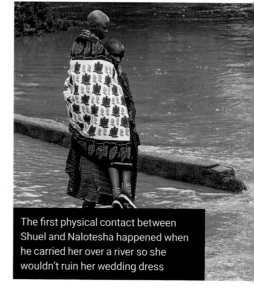

The first physical contact between Shuel and Nalotesha happened when he carried her over a river so she wouldn't ruin her wedding dress

Shuel's mother greets
Nalotesha in their village

Six years after their wedding, meeting again
with Nalotesha, Shuel, and their three children

The wedding celebration

The Maasai are a pastoral people who live in the area of the greatest
and naturally richest national parks in Kenya and Tanzania, where they share their living space
with the wild animals of Africa. Maasai men have the last word in all aspects of life, they
consider their wives their property, as well as their children and cattle, and they practice the most
extreme form of arranged marriages—forced marriages—that are most often arranged by their
parents. Girls have no right to spurn their suitors nor to divorce them later, even if they are being
physically abused. Six years before our journey around the world, I had watched Nalotesha,
then 16, marry Shuel, ten years her senior, and become his second wife. I watched her leave
her childhood home and all the people she'd known to go off to a new life with a stranger she
had never seen before. I witnessed the greatest rite of passage in her life, from which she
emerged with a changed identity and a new name: Noonkuta. On our journey around the world
we visited her in her new family and interviewed her with Shuel, to whom she'd meanwhile
borne three children, and with Naisha, her co-wife, who had become her closest friend.

Emanuele (37) and Paolo (33) from Italy met online while Paolo was studying in Spain, not long before the coronavirus pandemic locked down most of Europe. Paolo was going through a difficult time because his mother was in a coma due to the virus, but he found comfort with Emanuele, who sympathized and gave him support. Their long distance relationship quickly deepened. "The fact that we didn't begin with physical contact but at a distance was an entirely new experience for both of us," says Paolo. "We laid down solid foundations on which we hope to build something that has a greater chance of lasting."

Max (36) and Leah Christine (32) from Palau say that in their little island country in the middle of the Pacific, instead of holding a wedding, they celebrate the birth of the first child. "When the time came for me to give birth, I withdrew into a comfortable and warm room, where I lay, completely naked, and the women from the family bathed me and cared for me," says Leah Christine. "When the baby was born, after nine days, the child and I were introduced to Max's family and then the celebrating began."

Amin (34) and Manar (33) from Saudi Arabia face a number of problems because they are moving away from the traditional patterns of relationships in their country. "My father and brother broke off all contact with me because I chose whom I'd be with, because I dated Amin before we married, and because he is from a different tribe," says Nara, one of the first women in Saudi Arabia to run her own start up. "But what matters to me is that Amin understands me. I am an ambitious woman and as long as he is a man who won't stand in my way, he is good for me. I don't want him to be a rock blocking my way forward, but instead a rock on which I can lean when I need support."

Anil (45) and Mahdu (39) from India were engaged some 20 years ago, when their parents arranged their marriage. A young man who was in love with Mahdu flew into a rage and mutilated her face with acid. Both Mahdu's and Anil's parents told Anil he would be permitted to cancel the engagement and the wedding, but Anil declined. "What happened, happened," he says. "It's a person's heart you love, not their face. If the face is good but the heart is bad, that isn't love."

Shabnam (28) from India rejected her boss when he courted her because he was already married. In response, he exacted his revenge by pouring acid on her face. A few years later, she married another man and had a daughter with him, but he drank heavily and abused her so she left him. "I no longer hope for marriage," she says. "Love, for me, is my daughter. Society wants to make her weak, but I want to make her strong so what happened to me will never happen to her."

Kejal (33) and Nihit (35) from India are in an arranged marriage and firmly believe that arranged marriages are better than love marriages. "When you choose to enter into a relationship, you can choose to leave it," says Nihit. "But when you give up the choice and accept the person your parents chose for you, then you never leave them. You didn't choose your father or mother, brother or sister. You got them, you accept them, and you love them. That's the same way you love your wife, *precisely* because you didn't choose her."

O (41), Joshua (41) and Cat (55) from the United States are in a polyamorous relationship. Joshua and Cat are primary partners, and together they run a kink collective and one of the BDSM clubs in New York. Cat explains that BDSM is a "game for adults, the purpose of which is to connect with others and find yourself." O was in a monogamous marriage to her husband until she met Joshua and discovered her own inclination toward BDSM. Now she is their submissive partner. "Until recently I thought it would be impossible to love more than one person at a time," says O. "When I fell in love with Joshua and lied to my husband, I couldn't love more than one person, not even myself. But when I admitted the affair to my husband and when he embraced this side of me, the possibility of more loves began to open up."

Narendra (39) and Samidha (41) from India were
not given their parents' blessing when they wished
to marry because he is a Hindu and she is a Muslim.
For them to marry formally, Samidha had to convert
to Hinduism. "The wedding was really hell," says
Samidha. "Nobody at that wedding was happy but us."

Goran (57) and Mira (64) have lived in the United States
ever since they fled the war in ex-Yugoslavia and their
love in their home country became an anathema and
a threat to their lives. "It turned out that we belonged
to opposing tribes, but I don't belong to any one tribe.
Goran is my tribe! So we packed up our suitcases and
went about starting a new life elsewhere, all over again,"
says Mira, today a successful Hollywood actress,
and her husband Goran, a film director, adds, "The
experience of the war strengthened our relationship
because we had nothing else to hold on to but each
other, while everything around us was falling apart."

Šime (50) from Croatia had never experienced love being reciprocated. "It would be nice to fall in love, I'd like that," says Šime, "but I have never liked someone who liked me. No matter what woman I've approached, they have all been completely cold to me."

Jenilyn (39) from the United States married herself. The trend of 'sologamy' is gaining ground in the West. "When two people marry, they vow to love and support and they bond. In sologamy, all this is the same, except you're making your vows to yourself. I wanted to bring together the various parts of myself—my soul, mind, and body—and vow to cherish all of myself!"

Mohsen (31) from Iran was in a relationship only once, 12 years ago, when he lived in Great Britain. "Since I returned to Iran I haven't been with anyone. It is difficult to find a partner in this country where it's dangerous to be gay. I am able to leave, but I don't wish to because this is my home."

Martha (49) from Colombia was widowed five years ago. "When you lose your partner, you don't think about someone else, but that doesn't mean you should close the door. We people are social beings, we need hugs and support, we're hungry for love because through love we grow and develop."

Taikichi (70) from Japan has never been in a relationship. He says that in his life, love has evaded him. "Maybe love is purely luck that you meet the right person. Or is this a question of chance? No, I do think it's about luck."

Emma (35) from Saudi Arabia divorced after seven years of marriage. "Being a divorcee in this country is not easy for a woman who is living independently," she says, "but being on my own allows me to explore who I am and what path I truly wish to pursue in life."

"We hear white people say *mi amor, mi amor,* but we don't say that. We don't know what love is. There is no such thing here.""

Kana (38), Iva (57) and Tume (62), Brazil

The Amazon Yavari Valley from the air

The people of the Amazon sleep and rest in hammocks

Shawa and her son

Iva hunts for monkeys using his blowgun

Our camp

The small tribe of the Matis lives in the remote Amazon Yavari valley, an
area where the majority of tribes who have not had contact with the outside world live today. The
Matis encountered white people for the first time 40 years ago. The white people brought them
diseases that decimated the Matis for many years after their first contact. At the time of the first
contact there were about 300 of them, but a dozen years later their number had dropped to less
than a hundred. Iva, Kana, and Tume are among those who survived. Iva and Tume adopted Kana,
whose whole family had died, and when Kana grew up, Iva took her for his second wife. The Matis
were traditionally serially monogamous and seldom had more than three children per couple, but
after the onslaught of the diseases, many Matis chose polygamy and began to have more children
in order to help bring the tribe numbers to a sustainable level. Today, most of the Matis are hunter-
gatherers, they move through the jungle in small groups and catch monkeys and other animals
with their blowguns. Their society is egalitarian—there is no leader, and the men and women are
on an equal footing. Today, the number of Matis who continue to live as hunters and gatherers is
dwindling because many are moving to the cities downstream to explore new ways of getting by.

271

Baritsica (41) and Shawa (30), Brazil
Shawa is Baritsica's third wife, and he is her third husband.
She left her first husband because he was unfaithful to her,
her second was killed by a neighboring indigenous tribe, so in
her third husband she was seeking someone who would be
faithful to her and would supply her with food and provide a
shelter. "I couldn't accept that my husband was with someone
else," says Shawa. "If I were to go with another man, he would
leave me. So, if I see him with another woman, the same
holds true for me. I'll leave him and find another man."

Make (54) and Dani (39), Brazil

Make says: "When I was with her for the first time, I liked her so much that I couldn't sleep that whole night, all I could think about was how to be with her again and I was afraid of her rejecting me. She was so beautiful that I wanted to convince her to be with me, no matter what!" Dani says: "At first, I didn't like him too much, he had to ask me to be with him many times, but in the end I agreed. Ever since, I like him a lot and I'm crazy about him. He is my first man and I don't want anyone but him. He is a good hunter and he always brings me the finest meat. In our tribe, all the men are good hunters, but mine is the best. And he is best at fishing. So, I never have to worry about having enough to eat. When I want to show him I like him, I make him

Juan Cañas (27) and Veronica (42) from Colombia recall
with nostalgia the first years of their relationship, when they
fell so deeply in love that she abandoned her first marriage to
be with him. "I was troubled by the age difference, everyone
told me I was crazy, but the feelings were so powerful and
wonderful.... Butterflies in your stomach really do exist!"
says Veronica. "Now I miss them. That was such a beautiful
time. Now I'd give everything to experience that again!"

Lorrae (29) from the United States grew up in quite a traditional family, and now she is speaking publicly about exploring sexuality and her polyamorous experiences. "I want to help people who are struggling with the same things I went through and who want to free themselves of shame and guilt because they want to explore their sexuality and build their self-confidence, free themselves of the chains with which our society has shackled us."

Andres (29) and María José (27) from Costa Rica met each other and fell in love three weeks before he left on a long journey that was supposed to last several years. "Lovers present themselves to each other at first in the best possible light," says Andres, "but we had nothing to lose, we bared ourselves to one another down to the bone and lived those three weeks to the hilt. This was the key to our success. It brought us close forever!"

Laura (51) and Anaka (43) from the United States are bisexuals who had also been involved in relationships with men before and are now in a lesbian relationship. "We are a new, pioneering type of family," says Laura. "Our family includes my children from my first marriage, our child, and the biological father of our child."

Makaja (67), Ajla (45), Konstanza (55), El Karis (34) and Iman (44) live in Croatia and Switzerland. Makaja, the founder of Komaja—the Church of Love—is in a polyamorous relationship with six wives, five of whom he has been with for over 20 years. "Being in love is an extremely intensified interest for another person, and through my interest for this person I experience how God made this world," says Makaja. "If this interest fades for me with time, this means that somewhere along the way I have strayed and I should return to the path of self-knowledge, knowledge of God and living in divine ecstasy." Iman adds: "Some people fall in love with several people at once, but they don't allow themselves this love because our society teaches us that we mustn't love more than one person. And this is why people have no faith in love and they do not arrive at the awareness that it is possible to love several people at once."

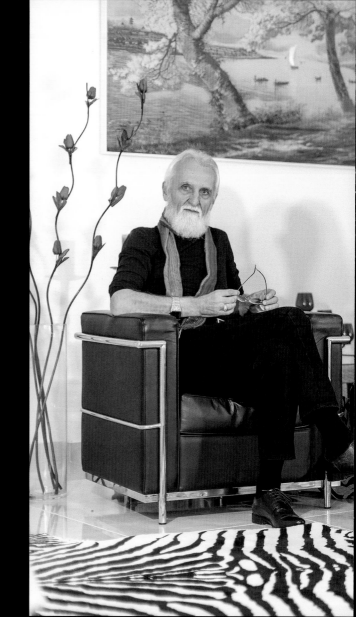

Yaniv (45) and Aisha (48) from Israel agree that love isn't something that happens but something that is built. "There are days when I'm crazy about her, but also days when I want to kill her," laughs Yaniv. "It's natural for thoughts like these to occur to us, but we mustn't let them rule us."

Honey (56) and Blaine (59) from the United States bonded through their love for stand-up comedy. When Honey first decided to say the words "I love you" to Blaine—and this was the first time she'd ever declared her love to anyone—Blaine answered: "I know!"

Ryo (31) and Sakura (26) from Japan met when they were working as volunteers in Uganda. "When I think of love, instead of thinking about whether he loves me enough, I should be thinking about how I can love him more," says Sakura. "From now on, I'll make the effort to love him more!"

Alejandro (33) and Rocio (33) from Costa Rica met for the first time at the hospital on the day they were both born. The second time they met was 13 years later when they started dating, and their relationship lasted until they graduated from secondary school. Then they went their separate ways, but six years later they ran into each other at a bus stop in the town they're both from. Since then, they have never been apart. "I have always felt we are drawn to each other by a powerful force," Alejandro says.

disagree with him about something, I can tell him what I think, but it's better that I don't say anything so I don't anger him. Sometimes when I go to another village and stay there too long, he asks me where I was for such a long time. Then we argue, and if he is very angry and wants to beat me, he beats me."

Jean (32) and Camille (29) from Belgium have been inseparable since high school. "All these years we've hardly ever spent even a few days away from each other," says Camille. "We cannot bear to be apart. Even when we're in the subway, if we have to sit on seats that aren't right next to each other, we start feeling uncomfortable." They have been traveling around the world for the last two years, working as social media influencers. "People ask us how we can spend all our time together. They say a little distance is a good thing, but for us the opposite is true—we fall ill if we have to be separated."

Miranda (51) and Vuk (55) from the Netherlands decided to divorce after 30 years of marriage because Vuk felt the need to move on. "At first, it was fun being as one, growing together, having children, buying a house..." says Vuk. "In the process, you lose yourself, merge with your spouse. But with time, this becomes an obstacle for your personal development. I started feeling I was in chains and thinking that I had to free myself and find myself again!" Out of courtesy to the children and their shared wish to get through the divorce as well as they could, with as little damage to everyone as possible, they gave themselves time to move slowly through this rite of passage.

Fariba (24) from Iran and Ivan Ali (34) from Croatia had to marry in order to live together in Iran. "For us to be permitted to marry, I had to convert to Islam. My name is no longer Ivan. But Ali. Ivan Ali."

Cass (52) and Chris (53) from Australia say that love changes when your children are born. Then you're no longer a couple, but a family. "When we started out, we were crazy about each other," says Chris. "Once, I drove 2,000 miles to surprise her, but later.... Everything changes—if you aren't prepared for compromises, problems arise."

Tirafalo (44) and Bofelo (35) from Botswana met at a shopping mall. "Until now, I couldn't marry because I'd had no money, but now I do and I will marry Bofelo," says Tirafalo. "The legally prescribed bride price in Botswana is about 24,000 pulas or eight cows."

Isabel (15) and Andreas (15) from the United States have already been together for four years. "Our peers don't stay in relationships for longer than a month or two," says Isabel. "They enter relationships easily, but as soon as the slightest problem arises, they don't want to work on it, they give up and move on because they have so many other options available. I think this is wrong. Because even if it is difficult to handle a problem, you have to find a way to resolve it. That makes you stronger, that's how you grow."

Pooja (40) and Krishna (41) from India had to defy their families and all of Indian society so they could be together. Krishna belongs to the Brahman class, while Pooja is from the lowest caste of Dalits, known as the 'untouchables.' More than 95% of the marriages in India today are between members of the same caste, while there are fewer than a hundred marriages between members of the highest and lowest castes each year, and they are often exposed to the condemnation of their community. Pooja and Krishna had to flee their families and live on the road. "It was really difficult... and painful.... Our parents tormented us...." says Pooja, sobbing. "But love is what gives you strength to defy your family and everything, even God if needed!"

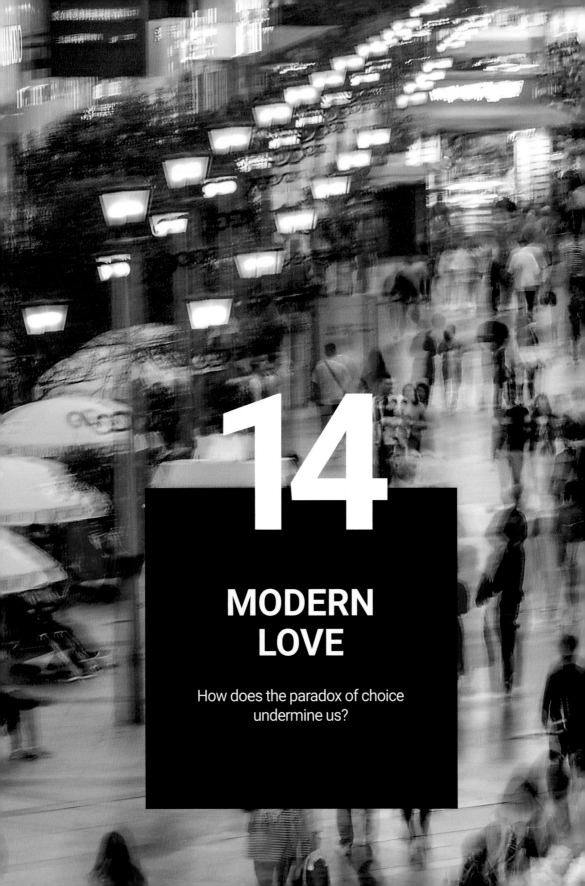

14

MODERN LOVE

How does the paradox of choice
undermine us?

Disappointment is a chronic feature of modern lives, as pointed out by historian Reinhart Kosseleck.

He described modernity as characterized by a growing disparity between reality and aspiration, which is what generates disappointment. Dr. **Eva Illouz**, with whom we discussed sociological questions, has also written about disappointment as one of modernity's chronic traits: it is not merely the result of personal psychology but of a loss of emotional security in contemporary society. We have already seen how traditional societies enjoyed more emotional security. In traditional times, people were not as free and didn't enjoy the privilege of equality. Justice—yet another story, yet another fabricated concept that doesn't exist in nature but is a construct of our social development and cultural evolution— was far less present in the world than it is today. Those who strayed in any way from the norms often risked their lives to be what they were, while those

PREVIOUS PAGE
CHENGDU, CHINA

who were able to comply with the norms found identity and emotional security in successfully copying and repeating everything their predecessors had done, thought, and believed. By casting off the chains of tradition and fighting for greater justice and freedom, we have ventured into unfamiliar territory, without structure, without certainty.

Aside from rationality, uncertainty, and a constant self-examination of all structures, modernity is most characterized by paradoxes and contradictions, ambivalence, an irreconcilable gap, at least superficially, between desire and possibility, dreams and reality, ideas of what life should be and what it really is. We want to have our cake and eat it too, to have both love and autonomy, hedonism and ascetism, action and peace, the uncertainty of the unknown and the certainty of the familiar. Philosopher Richard Precht has written that in love we seek both intimacy and distance, an intuitive understanding and room for retreat, gentleness and sharpness, power and helplessness, a Madonna and a whore, a big game hunter and a paterfamilias[1].

If we were to choose the main trait of modernity perhaps it would be freedom. No generation up to now has had so many options and so much freedom. And choice. Perhaps the degree of modernity can be measured by the amount of choice we have. We don't yet know whether we actually have any free will or if we make our choices steered by the tangled algorithms of nature and society, but we do know beyond a doubt that people have never enjoyed this much choice. Thanks to the revolutionary achievements of modernity, such as the internet, sometimes it seems as if our choices are nearly unlimited.

— — —

If I were to choose one trait by which to judge whether the couples we interviewed were modern or not, I'd probably choose internet access. The most traditional people we interviewed had either no or only very limited access to the internet. The most modern people we interviewed not only had constant internet access, but the internet was a crucial ingredient, perhaps the key ingredient, in their lives. Many of them live and work online and spend most of their spare time online. Many of them might never have met without the internet.

Ahmed and **Shaheema** [p. 121] from the Maldives, introduced in the previous chapter, found each other on Facebook and for the first six months only poked each other. Neither of them had the courage to approach the other more openly, so all they did was send each other Facebook pokes, the symbol that shows someone is thinking of you. At least 20 of the couples we interviewed had found each other over Facebook and other social media. This is particularly true for those who are gay or lesbian. **Nazanin** and **Nahid** [p. 98] from Iran, **Marcelo** and **Jose** [p. 111] from Chile, **Paolo** and **Emanuele** [p. 256] from Italy… they all met and fell in love over the internet. Before the internet age, many gay people, as well as members of other minoritized and marginalized groups, lived their whole lives without ever meeting anyone similar to them, let alone a kindred spirit. The internet has dramatically eased the locating of partners for people who are older and no longer know where they might meet someone new, are introverted and do not enjoy frequenting bars and clubs, have rare and specific interests and needs, suffer from specific illnesses, are wheelchair-bound…. And not only for them, but for everyone else as well— over the last 20 or so years the internet has drastically changed the way people get to know each other and enter into relationships.

The trend of meeting people over the internet is on the rise all over the world. Over 40% of all relationships in the United States today begin over the internet[2], and the percentage is even higher among younger generations. But older people are also finding each other through online apps. The job of finding a partner, which, in traditional societies, was handled by parents, relatives, or matchmakers, is now being handled by the sophisticated algorithms created by internet companies. Most dates are arranged over dating apps such as Tinder, OkCupid, or Bumble. These are largely short-term connections, often for sex or casual socializing. People seeking serious relationships tend to prefer matching sites. These are for connecting kindred spirits who are seeking partners. The first couple we spoke with who'd met through a matching site was **Carolina** from Spain and **Thomas** from Belgium [p. 145].

"We are both busy people, nearly 40, and the range of possibilities we had for getting to know someone whom we'd be well-suited to was shrinking with each passing year," Carolina told us. "At one moment, I decided to try to use the internet as a matchmaker, and it worked incredibly quickly! Thomas was the first person I met over the internet, and here we are in a long, stable relationship! My statistical success for internet acquaintances is 100%."

"Matching sites are convenient and useful," Thomas said, "especially for those of us who are so busy. I didn't find it easy or pleasant to go out looking for someone. If I'm reluctant to frequent bars and clubs, where am I to meet a potential partner? If I'd come across Carolina at a railway station, I would have had no way of knowing we are as compatible as we discovered we are over the web."

Carolina and Thomas explained the basic principle for how the matching sites function. During online registration on the website, all candidates fill out a detailed questionnaire when entering the complex matching system, and this sketches out their psychological profile. It is so detailed that Carolina and Thomas spent hours filling it out. This is how the complex system is fed with enough data to allow the algorithm to successfully identify and link two candidates who may be compatible. The more input the algorithm is given, the more successful the process will be. Some of today's finest minds are involved in creating these algorithms. Anthropologist Helen Fisher, who spoke with us, works on creating algorithms for the most popular matching site, Match.com. Using a matching system is not inexpensive. Each candidate pays a monthly subscription fee in order to be 'out there.' This allows the system to protect itself in advance from candidates who aren't serious and increases its success rate in bringing together those who are. The success of the system does not depend, however, on the algorithm alone, but also on the input the candidates provide. Because not everyone conveys their *true* picture.

"I assume that the matching pages don't work for everyone," Thomas told us. "The more sincere someone is and the more realistic the picture they give, the greater the chances are that they'll find a good partner. People who aren't sincere, who describe themselves as better than they are, who only post the single good picture they have of themselves… will disappoint at the later in-person meeting with their partner. By that same token, people don't fare well who are only after sex, or who have been traumatized by previous relationships, or have been alone for too long.…"

"But we were lucky, it worked for us!" said Carolina cheerfully. "We didn't fall in love right away, but little by little we did; we gave ourselves the chance, we made the effort and then one day we realized we were in love. And that was that!"

All couples with whom we spoke who had met each other over the internet said they doubted they'd ever have found each other in real life if they hadn't hooked up digitally. And all those who used matching sites were surprised by the level of compatibility the system had identified between them. A controversial idea that one often hears in discussions on the subject is that matching algorithms will soon be more successful than we are in choosing partners, if they aren't already. As we've already seen, behind our decisions are a host of complex biological, psychological, cultural, and other factors. When we make decisions, we are also functioning according to the principles of algorithms; we are not guided purely by cold calculating reason, however, but also by fragile, intense emotions. Often, we aren't sure whether we're making the right decisions, and this insecurity confuses and worries us. A computer algorithm does not have similar subjective dilemmas. If it is complex and precise enough, and if it has been fed with enough data, it can, or soon will be able to, choose better than we ourselves could. We asked **Lori** and **Shawn** [p. 145] from the United States what they thought of this. They met each other through an elite matching site that pairs candidates based on their mutual compatibility as evaluated on the basis of complex tests.

"We totally believe it. But totally!" said Shawn, delighted. "We couldn't be happier! We'd never have found each other otherwise. If we'd met somewhere, there's no way we'd have been able to discover that we are as compatible as we are."

"Our compatibility was at 100%," Lori added. "I met up with several people before Shawn, but those didn't work. My compatibility with them was at 70-80%. In and around my city there was nobody with a greater degree of compatibility."

"The same was true of me," joined Shawn. "And then one day, I resolved to find someone who was totally compatible with me. But where? I did find someone, but she lived a five-hour drive away. I was curious, so I decided to give it a shot. And that's how I met Lori. We clicked right away! The first time we talked over the phone, that was it. Everything was perfect. She made me laugh, I made her laugh. And when we finally got together in person, it was love at first sight!"

"An instant bond!" Lori added.

"Our first date was magical. When I pulled into her town on the bus, she spotted me before I saw her, came up behind me and said I shouldn't turn around. She took me to a bench and asked me not to look at her yet. She sat down next to me and leaned her head on my shoulder. We stayed that way for a few minutes in silence. It was so sweet. I know I thought, 'my God, this is perfect.' And when we finally did look at each other, we kissed immediately."

"On our third date we got engaged and were married six weeks after that first date," Lori continued. "We've been married now for two years and every day it gets better. But we could have married on our first date, that's how sure we were."

Lori and Shawn come across as very youthful though they're nearly 50. They both have failed marriages and adult children behind them. They explained to us that, first of all, the main criterion they were seeking in another person was faith in God and religious belief.

"We are Christians, but we probably don't fit the classic Christian mold. God is in first place for us, this is the fundamental value for us. Shawn and I were looking for the same thing in a partner, someone for whom God would be in first place," said Lori.

"Over the course of our lives, she and I have met many Christians and so many people who say that God is what matters most to them, but neither of us had ever met anyone like ourselves before. And if this matching site hadn't brought us together, we'd never have found each other," added Shawn.

During registration, Shawn took five days to fill out the test that provided the app with the input to build his psychological profile and the algorithm then searched for his most compatible partner.

"Our compatibility is amazing!" said Lori. "For instance, the other day we were working on our apartment. The way I arrange things is quite complicated: I combine things that don't seem to go together, and, in the end, they function really well. I am not relaxed or flexible in this—I'm not a person who easily includes others and is happy with what they've done. But this time, I left it to Shawn, and he did everything exactly as I would have and in a way I liked!"

"Our compatibility truly is 100%," said Shawn. "Sometimes I feel as if our brains are connected!"

— — —

Carolina and Thomas, Lori and Shawn, and hundreds of thousands of couples around the world are examples of people whose experience at finding a partner online has been positive. According to Match.com's statistics, 42% of the couples their algorithm deems to be compatible result in a date, and 35% of these dates result in a relationship lasting longer than three months. Although these statistics should be taken with a dose of skepticism, it is possible to conclude that as the technology advances and the algorithms become more complex and precise, their success for pairing compatible partners will improve even more.

But there are also downsides to meeting people online.

"If you grow up in a small town, there aren't many people you might potentially end up with," we were told by prominent psychologist Dr. **Barry Schwartz** from Los Angeles, whom we interviewed online. "You already know everyone from school and if you haven't found a potential candidate for marriage among them, you'll need a wider selection, more options. Then you go to a city and suddenly you have thousands and thousands of people who might be a match for you, but still you don't meet all of them. Then along comes Tinder, or some other online dating app, and suddenly you have the entire world in the palm of your hand. And this turns out to be a disaster. Because even if you like someone, you make no decision, but keep on searching, because there's a chance you might find someone even better. And even if you do decide on someone, you're tormented by all those other possibilities that you didn't choose, and all the other pathways you didn't explore…."

Barry Schwartz is the author of a theory about the paradox of choice. Although this theory may seem logical and self-evident today, it is only 15 years old and Dr. Schwartz was the first to come up with it and present it to the broader public in his bestselling book, *The Paradox of Choice—Why More Is Less*. The best and most prevailing theories are always those that seem the most obvious. But considerable wisdom was required to arrive at such simplicity.

"The central argument of my theory is that it would seem to be better to have more options in life, and people need the freedom to choose even unimportant things, such as which kind of cereal to buy, as well as the important ones, such as whom they'll choose for their partner. Without the freedom of choice you can't be the fullest person you could be. But we made one logical error. We saw that we are better off when we have *some* choice, so we concluded that we'll be even better off with even *more* options. This, however, is not the case. At some moment, the curve changes direction. It is good to have more options only up to a point. After that, the more options we have available, the worse things are for us. We reach a point of paralysis. That is when we make bad decisions. And even if we make good decisions, we're less satisfied with them because all the paths not taken unsettle us."

"How much do *we* actually make those decisions," I couldn't help but asking, "and how much are other influences behind our decisions? Do we have any freedom of choice at all, or do we just feel as if we do?"

"That's too big and difficult a question, and no one has a good answer for it," he said. "But what I can say is that every society I'm aware of was built on the assumption that people are free enough to be able to make their own choices. Otherwise, they wouldn't be able to be responsible for their actions. The legal, judicial systems of all societies, as well as the moral systems, would just crumble if we were to conclude that we are truly not responsible for our decisions."

Barry Schwartz noted that members of his society in the United States have more choices than do members of any other society in the present or past, but that this doesn't make them happier. He discovered the paradox of choice first in the realm of the economy. The greater the offer, the more difficult it is for consumers to choose anything. Then he realized that this same premise can be applied to other aspects of life, particularly psychology and—romantic relationships.

"When we know we have so many other options, this stands in our way of building intimacy," he said. "When we wish to build a relationship with someone we like, we need to make the effort. We need to come to know each other better. We need to work on the relationship. And when this begins to be a little more demanding, why should we take the trouble when around the corner there are other options waiting. The result of this is a growing trend of people making their choices based on superficial attributes without allowing enough time for the relationship to delve deeper. The result is a growing disappointment in relationships, and people abandon relationships too readily when they come up against problems."

This was something we really noticed when we traveled across the United States for more than two months, especially when we talked with young,

modern people. We interviewed a few of them in the Bay Area around San Francisco because we wanted to see what love life was like among the younger set in what we think of as the most progressive part of the world. In today's hyper-modern, globalized world, there isn't, of course, just a single center of influence from which inventions, accomplishments, and trends spread every-where else; instead such centers are scattered all over the world, especially in the most progressive metropolises. If I could choose, however, which of all these centers seems to be the most influential, I'd say California, especially the Bay Area, home to Silicon Valley, where all the newest technologies and social trends are percolating and then spreading across the United States and to all the rich countries and the whole world. I have visited California several times over the last 15 years, and each time I have kept an eye out for the trends and values that were new and current—whether they were views on artificial intelligence, climate change, healthy food, spirituality, or human rights—and I'd find myself wondering how long it would take for them to spread to the rest of the world and arrive in my little country on the Mediterranean. Do trends in relationships begin from these same points?

In my little country, for instance, Anđela's and my gay and lesbian friends say that little by little they are finding acceptance in society, though they still don't dare kiss in public, because they'd risk damning glares, perhaps a snide comment, or even physical attack. Our country does not, in fact, allow them to marry with full equality or to adopt children, although there are, techni-cally speaking, guarantees of equality within the framework of human rights. **Nazanin** and **Nahid** [p. 98], the lesbians from Iran, are facing a far grimmer situation, because in their country there is still a law on the books requiring the death penalty for homosexuals. Though they said that the death sentence is no longer practiced, nevertheless every aspect of life for the gays and les-bians of Iran is more complicated and difficult, and they don't dare to dream of legal marriage and the adoption of children. **Anaka** and **Laura** [p. 276], two lesbians we spoke with on the West Coast of the United States, told us that they have been completely accepted by society: they can marry, have children, and they no longer have to fight for their rights. Those battles were fought by their parents' generation. If we therefore simplify matters a little and conclude that the trend of equality among various sexual orientations and gender identities is spreading throughout the world, can we then assume the same for certain aspects of love relations?

"It is completely normal for us in school that someone is gay or comes out transgender…. We know that people like that used to have problems, but now they're fine. There is no longer any need for outing or proving; they have nothing left to prove," **Andreas** and **Isabel** [p. 287] told us, two 15-year-olds from the Bay Area. Although they were still at the early stages of their high-school education, they had a clear vision of what they wanted to be in life. Isabel wants to be a marine biologist, because she is concerned about the state of our oceans, while Andreas wants to be a biomechanical engineer and work on integrating technology with people, because he is concerned about the meteoric trajectory of artificial intelligence. He thinks that if we people don't advance technologically, we have no chance of going up against artificial intelligence, a clash he feels is inevitable.

Andreas and Isabel explained that the fact that they have a clear vision of what they want to be in life is not often true of their generation; most young people have no idea what they'd like to be when they finish school. It is also unusual that they've already been together for four years.

"We have been together since we were 11," said Andreas, "but we don't know anyone else who has stayed with a relationship longer than a month or two. That we found each other is great, both of us are completely dedicated to everything we want and do, whether it's our relationship, school, or our career, but almost all of the rest of our peers take nothing seriously. They find each other over the internet and social media, they start casual relationships, but these are all so superficial. Sometimes, they're involved in several relationships at once without focusing on any of them properly. As soon as the slightest problems arise in one of them, they immediately throw up their hands, give up, because they have other options."

"Today it seems so easy to find someone, but difficult to stay with them," said young Isabel.

— — —

The basic features of modernity are reason, autonomy, and freedom, but also non-choice or, in other words, not making a choice, writes Eva Illouz in

one of her earlier books, *Why Love Hurts*. Freedom is paradoxical because when we have too much of it, it leads to the inability to choose or an absence of desire for choice. Practicing freedom therefore produces forms of suffering such as essential insecurity and meaninglessness, which we feel toward ourselves, our choices, and life.

In her most recent book, *The End of Love*, published in 2019 while Anđela and I were traveling around the world, Eva Illouz offers the hypothesis that under the aegis of sexual freedom, heterosexual relationships have integrated the form of the capitalist market—they have become a face-off between emotional and sexual supply and emotional and sexual demand. Emotions, sex, and relationships have become something we buy and sell, something we trade. Sex has become non-committal; the encounters over dating apps are too simple and too fleeting; we want someone to truly see us, appreciate and love us, but never have people been reduced to sexual objects more than they are now; we think women have been freed, but the patriarchy continues wreaking havoc; divorce has become overly simple and is no longer conditioned by anything…. Romantic relationships no longer function according to established and widely embraced norms—we no longer know what is appropriate and what is not, what is expected of us in a relationship, what we can expect from our partners…. For all these reasons, insecurity and uncertainty abound; we are confused and more often we practice non-choice.

Our roles, relationships, and lives are no longer scripted, we can be anything we want to be, and we don't have to be anything. We are more disoriented than ever. We don't know who we are or where we're headed. We have nothing to rely on. Modernity has weaned us from the powerful illusions and misconceptions of the traditional age, but these illusions made our miserable lives more bearable. We have been forced to live without the grand stories that gave our lives comfort and an embellished sense of reality. In modernity, reason and rationalism triumphed over the irrational, but they still haven't offered us answers to the central quandaries of existence. This is why one of the greatest challenges of modernity is whether, through reason, we will be able to find meaning in our lives.

Is love merely yet another of the grand stories that embellish our lives? Historically, love was a remarkably seductive idea because it was subversive.

However, those days are over. Sex and love are no longer the place where the self defies society. Sexuality and the intimate have become an arena in which capitalism has taken root, so they can no longer be a source of creative tension, defiance, and innovation between the individual and society. Hence Eva Illouz, both with the title of her book and its contents, has concluded that love has come to its end.

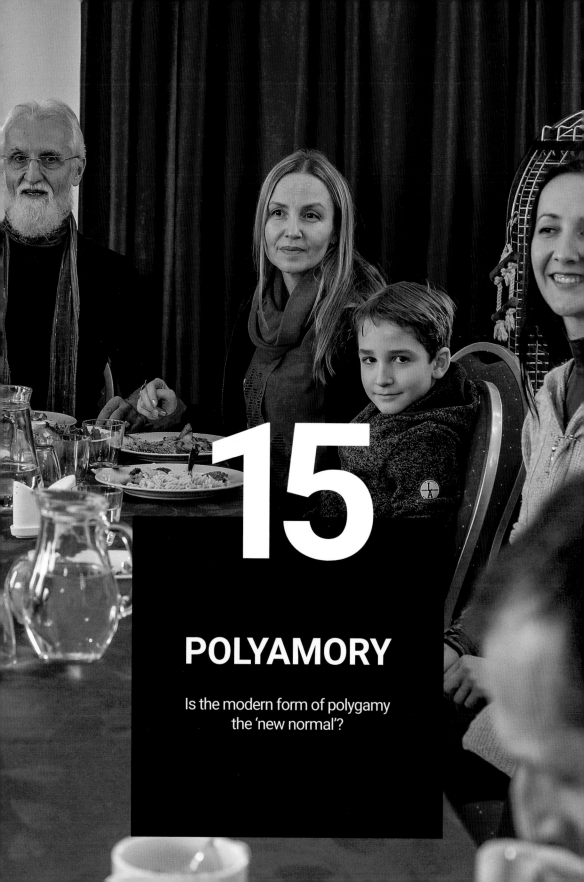

15

POLYAMORY

Is the modern form of polygamy
the 'new normal'?

On a winter's evening early in the last week of our trip around the world, we met with Lorrae [p. 275] out in front of a bar in Lower Manhattan.

We'd been setting up the meeting by text since we arrived in New York so Lorrae could talk to us about polyamory, about exploring life through sexuality, about seeking oneself in the void that remains when all boundaries have been destroyed.... All this sounded so unfamiliar, so avantgarde, that we had no idea what to think about it. She invited us to go with her to a sex party and get to know others, to experience the whole scene of people who are into this exploration. We agreed, though not without anxiety. When we met in front of the bar, we suggested that maybe we could first have a drink to relax a little.

New York was, as always, high-speed and jumpy. A cold front had blown in from Greenland and was penetrating through the looming forest of skyscrapers into every nook and cranny of the legendary city. Steam rose out of the manholes on the street and, in combination with the multitude of neon lights, this gave the surrounding

PREVIOUS PAGE
LIŽNJAN, CROATIA

that classic winter New York feel. People on the street hunched their shoulders under their heavy coats, their collars raised to shield them from the bitter wind, and they sped along to keep warm. Inside the bar, the mood was quite different. A pianist was, of course, playing jazz, and the chairs were, of course, in the style of papal thrones, and the waiter—who served us our whisky and chatted cheerfully in hopes of a large tip—was, of course, an aspiring actor.

"This is by far the craziest city in the world!" Anđela and I told her. We felt like total outsiders, like people who had come from the most provincial sticks to the big city, gawking at everything in awe. But this is precisely what drives us to travel: the constant feeling of something new, the excitement, the adventure. This is what gives life its special, unique charm.

We found young, attractive **Lorrae** through Instagram while we were researching polyamory. Her page is called *Slutty Girl Problems*, as is the business she supports herself with. When we first met, she explained that she had come from a relatively conservative community, so for a long time she was saddled with the shame and stigma imposed on her socially. But she managed to shake off these cultural shackles and feel all the boons of freedom, and she wanted to share her experience with others, especially with women, to empower and help them, and along the way this became her career. We hadn't been talking long at the bar when Lorrae began talking about polyamory.

"In many societies, including this Western society of ours, we are taught that we ought to be monogamous. As soon as you move away from this as a given, you're in unknown territory and you no longer know where your boundaries lie. You must explore."

Polyamory is a modern form of polygamy, which we already covered in Chapter Six. But the only thing polyamorous and polygamous relationships have in common is that they involve more than two people. Everything else is different. Polygamy means 'more spouses,' while polyamory means 'more loves.' Polygamy can be found in traditional societies and is gradually disappearing as these societies modernize, while polyamory appears only in societies that are breaking away from tradition, and the more modern the society, the more frequently it appears. Polygamy is always unidirectional, heterosexual, clearly defined. We already saw this with the example of Muslim societies that stipulate that a man may have up to four wives or with the peoples living in the Kinnaur Valley in the Himalayas in which a woman is allowed to marry several brothers. In these cultures, this is how things have *always* been, and there is no room for other options. Polyamory, on the other hand, is not limited by sex, gender, number, or sexual orientation. In each polyamorous community, the participants are the ones who set their rules.

"Some people can find themselves in monogamy, there's no doubt about that," said Lorrae. "I, too, was in monogamous relationships, but I noticed that I kept being attracted to other people while, at the same time, I was jealous of my partner when he was attracted to someone else. I wondered why. I felt I was stagnating, that I wasn't moving forward. I wanted to explore other possibilities. When I was in a relationship with two men, I was interested in observing how the two of them handled their jealousy and how I was jealous of their female partners. But I understood that while working on these emotions and relationships I made far more progress. This suits me better than monogamy and, at the moment, this is the only way I want to live—to explore how to navigate through the jealousy, communication, dynamics between partners and to grow in love."

She told us that when more conservative people encounter polyamory they think, at first, that it is all superficial and based on sex, and that polyamorous people are bestial and promiscuous. That is exactly why she gave her Instagram page and business such a provocative name.

"But sexuality is only the arena through which we explore and get to know ourselves and learn how to navigate through life," she said and suggested that we ought to be going.

Outside, there was so much noise from the wind and the city that any attempt at conversation was in vain. Instead, we simply watched and followed as Lorrae moved through the streets. Each street we came to was smaller and darker. We ran into two young dark-skinned people in long coats, their hats mashed down over their ears, who looked as if they were looking for something. Lorrae rightly concluded that they were going to the same party as we and were lost, so she invited them to join us. She found the entrance into a large, dark building made of rough brick, which looked more like an abandoned factory than a place of residence. We went up five or six flights of metal stairs lit by the light of our cell phones, then down a long, empty, quiet corridor to a door that Lorrae knocked on in a rhythm that didn't sound random. When the door opened, we entered a vestibule where there were two scantily and provocatively clad young women who were greeting the guests and taking their coats. The two people we'd come with took off their coats and startled us. She was wearing only a negligee, and he was only wearing tall boots. They went through the other door and we followed them.

We entered a large room with a high ceiling, looking much like a factory hall. The lighting was muted, with a reddish tinge, and relaxing electronic music was playing, softly enough that we could hear Lorrae explain to us that there could be no tobacco or drugs smoked or consumed here except pure marijuana. The vast space was divided into two parts by a long bar. On both sides of the bar there were sofas and armchairs where guests were either sitting or standing and milling around. About half of those present were dressed. The other half were wearing underwear or sexy costumes. Several people were completely naked, and here and there someone was dressed in nothing but a cape, or too-high boots, or a too-small hat bedecked with ribbons. There were maybe 50 people in all. Only millennials, people between the ages of 23 and 38, who had signed up in advance and been vetted were allowed access to the party. We were Lorrae's guests, and clearly she was a familiar face here, because at every step people were stopping her and greeting her with a warm hello.

When we finally reached the bar, we could see across it into the main part of the room, dominated by a huge bed the size of an average living room, on which several scantily clad couples were lying and caressing and one completely naked young woman was arching her back and panting hard while she rode her partner. There was an assortment of seats, beds, and platforms designed for sex in strange positions, as well as a small stage on which a dancer tattooed from head to toe was demonstrating her flexibility.

I didn't know where to look nor what I should do with my hands, so I hugged Anđela, who was every bit as taken aback as I was. I tried to ease the tension by joking, in a whisper to Anđela, that I'd just realized I'd never seen, live, another man's erect penis, and that tonight I might. With a discrete shift of her eyes and eyebrows she suggested that I turn. Some six feet behind me a six-foot tall Apollo was standing, legs akimbo, hands on hips, alone and buck-naked, his smooth and taut skin hairless, with a foot-long javelin quivering ceilingward. A young woman with a generous bosom and long red hair came over, kneeled down in front of him, steadying herself with one hand on his thigh while, with the other, she took his penis, placed it in her mouth, and began thrusting it deep down her throat.

I experienced culture shock greater than what we'd experienced when we entered the airplane bound for Saudi Arabia full of pilgrims on their way to Mecca who, wearing white linen robes, spent the entire flight chanting ancient refrains. Luckily, Lorrae invited us to join her on the safer side of the bar. She grabbed a drink at the bar and invited us to sit on armchairs where several of her friends had gathered. From there, we couldn't see what was happening on the other side of the bar, so we could focus on the conversation. Lorrae's friends were so cordial that within a few minutes we'd relaxed and no longer noticed whether the person we were talking with was naked or dressed.

"At sex parties like the one this evening and in polyamory in general, the basic rule is consent, permission," Lorrae told us. "Everything is open and everything is possible—whatever two or more people agree to. Honesty is the central condition for every relationship, regardless of whether it is one-time sex or a long-term relationship. The classic model in which people are monogamous and cheat on the side is hypocritical. You can't grow if you aren't honest with yourself and others."

"Do you mean to say that in polyamorous relationships everyone is honest and there can be no cheating?" I asked, slightly skeptical.

"Of course not. But it's a little different. For instance, I could have an agreement with my partner that he is free to have sex with others or I could be okay with him falling in love with someone else, as long as he is frank about it all. But if I happen to find out that he went out for drinks with a person he likes and didn't tell me, that would be the same as cheating."

"Then, what is permitted and what isn't, where are the boundaries?"

"Everyone explores and sets their own boundaries and the rules of their game. Everyone involved must be part of the discussion."

I told her that we'd recently spoken about this with anthropologist Dr. **William Jankowiak** who has studied both polygamy and polyamory. He said that people used to know what was allowed in traditional relationships and what wasn't because this was dictated by their society, but today, each participant in polyamorous relationships must constantly negotiate what is allowed and what isn't. His opinion is that this is quite emotionally demanding and therefore unsustainable in the long run.

"True, we in polyamorous relationships spend a great deal of time discussing what is acceptable and what isn't," Lorrae agreed, "but I think monogamous couples would be more successful if they also talked more about their rules. For instance, cheating is a good example of this. For some people, cheating is when you sleep with someone else, but for another person, cheating would be watching porn or fantasizing about others. If the couple hasn't talked about this and agreed on what is acceptable and what isn't, then when it happens this leads to a serious conflict. I think our discussions are demanding, but they are worthwhile."

"William Jankowiak appeared to be quite critical of polyamory. He said he thinks that we human beings are sexually polygamous, but emotionally monogamous. He said that love is always a dyad, that we cannot be in love with more than one person at once."

"Yes, that is frequently raised as an argument against polyamory—that we people can't multi-task but can only shift the focus of our attention from one thing to another. But I disagree," Lorrae said. "Look at parents who have several children—how can they not love all their children equally? They may, at one moment, pay more attention to one child, but that doesn't mean they love their other children any less. The same goes for friends, pets…. You can have several of them and the love for one needn't diminish your love for the other or others."

"Yes, I am aware of that. In Los Angeles we interviewed two pansexual, polyamorous women, **Gracia** and **Karina** [p. 138], who told us that the more people they love, the more they have the feeling that their heart grows—the more love they give, the more they receive. When they love several partners, the love between them isn't divided but multiplied. But isn't that a touch unconvincing? Don't you need to know someone to love them? You can't get to know several people well enough. Say you love 20 people…."

"Oh, no! I could never be with more than a few people. Three people may be optimal, so you can dedicate yourself to all of them with quality. I think having a large number of relationships isn't functional, but several relationships are better than just one. When I am in several relationships, I feel safer than I do when I'm in just one."

"Really?" I asked. "I find that very interesting, especially because one of the frequent arguments against polyamory is that these relationships are unstable, fluid, and as such don't provide adequate emotional security, do not provide something that can be relied upon."

"I disagree. I feel that polyamorous relationships are actually more stable. Because when you're with just one person and you rely on them, you are too dependent on that one person, so if you are left without them you are totally broken. It's about putting all your chips in one basket. If you have several partners and they have their partners, we grow into an entire network that can provide support, a community of people helping each other. We are like a tribe, the type of community that modern societies lack. And besides, isn't it too much to ask of a single person to satisfy your every need—sexually and emotionally and intellectually? I still haven't met a person who could meet my every need. Maybe I have great sex with one and terrific chemistry, but that person doesn't satisfy me intellectually, so I look for that in someone else. Then, with a third, I can have a deep, tender friendship…."

"Fine, but isn't the reflection you receive also partial then? How do you determine your worth? If the people around us serve as mirrors and we gauge our sense of self according to how important we are to them, this means that the more important someone is to us, the greater weight their opinion holds. But if someone isn't important to you in the fullness of who they are but only in part, then isn't the reflection you receive only partial?"

"I understand what you're thinking, but for that I think communication is the key. For example, with one partner I deeply love, with whom I have a profound bond, the sexual chemistry doesn't function well, simply put, we don't resonate that way. So should we break up over this? Or be one of those couples who are in a relationship but have sexual liaisons on the side? Do we need to lose what I have with that person, which is marvelous, just because intimacy doesn't work for us? No! But we talked about everything and found our way. I think this is of greater use for establishing my worth than harming it."

We spent the whole evening talking with many people. They were all in a remarkably friendly mood. They'd seen that we were Lorrae's friends and that we were foreigners, so they struck up a conversation with us, and after a minute or two of conversation they moved onto the topic of polyamory, sexuality, exploration, tearing down walls, and moving boundaries. If there was something we could conclude about the people we spoke to there, it was that they liked to talk. They were all in complex polyamorous relationships and most of our conversations were about attempting to unravel and understand who was with whom in what relationship. This reminded me of the conversations with the Matis, the hunters and gatherers in the Amazon, whom we met in Chapter Six.

That night we learned that polyamorous communities are called polycules, that there are hierarchical and non-hierarchical polycules, open and closed. In the hierarchical relationships, there are two to three levels of priority. For example, two people who consider themselves primary partners are crucial for each other and generally live together, sometimes they are married, and they may have one or several secondary partners with whom they maintain emotional and sexual relations, but in most cases they don't live with them. In the group of tertiary partners belong all those with whom they have only sporadic sexual relations. In the non-hierarchical communities, which are rarer, there is no breakdown into levels, and everyone in each polycule is equally important. Most of the polycules are at least somewhat open, which means that every member of a polycule may realize a relationship of some kind with a person who is outside the polycule. But there are polycules that are closed to other partners and are reminiscent, in a way, of monogamy.

We noticed at the gathering, as well as in conversation with other polyamorous people, that it is quite difficult to find relationships that have lasted for more than a few years and in which all the partners live together and ultimately have children. It is also difficult to find relationships in which a woman has several men. Far more common are those in which one man has several women. I wondered what this pattern tells us. In traditional polygamy, there are far more cultures that allow men to have more women than vice versa. But in polygamy, the rules are dictated by society, while in polyamory the rules are dictated by the participants and yet this pattern continues to appear. What does this tell us about human nature?

Polyamory is a relatively recent phenomenon, so, though it is spreading quite quickly, particularly in the big cities of the West, there is still very little scholarly research on it. The little research that does exist shows us that younger generations are showing more interest in polyamory, there is more talk of polyamory in the public, and people are looking it up more on internet search engines; one could say that polyamory is trending[1].

— — —

Two days after the party with Lorrae, we ended up at an event that was, perhaps, even more unusual. New York never ceased to surprise us. The party was at a club where people who like kink and BDSM gathered. Kink includes all actions and things a person finds to be sexual turn-ons and that are generally considered unusual and therefore are more or less socially unacceptable. BDSM is an abbreviation for concepts referring to several kinds of power exchange relationships in intimate and sexual contact. The B stands for bondage, the D for discipline and domination, the S for submissiveness and sadism, and the M for masochism.

The club included a larger room for socializing and conversation and a whole labyrinth of dungeons and cages. The leaders of the club, 41-year-old **Joshua** and 55-year-old **Cat** [p. 262], led us down long, dark hallways from one cell to another and explained what was happening in each. I felt like a true modern tourist-voyeur. In one cell, a large woman was wrapped in long leather bands so she couldn't move her limbs, while a four-foot-tall man slowly and reasonably gently whipped her. In another cell, the show was led by two slender young women wearing tight-fitting leather cat-woman outfits that covered all of their limber bodies except the most intimate parts. Outside the cell, the show was being watched by a dozen people. The cat-women pulled a volunteer from the audience; they bound the person with chains to the wall and then danced around him provocatively, bringing their private parts so close to the victim's face that he could probably feel their warmth and smell them but couldn't touch. In the next cell, a man dressed as a businessman, his pants down around his knees, was splayed across an armchair, while his partner was lightly lashing his bare bottom. In the fourth cell, a man was tenderly combing another man's hair; in the next, a couple was making sensual love, while in the next, a second couple was playing and caressing with fire. In the room where everyone was socializing, the atmosphere was relaxed, much like at a house party. Everyone was as friendly and amicable as they would have been anywhere else, so I ventured into conversations and occasionally forgot where we were. I'd remember where I was only when realizing that an adult sitting near us was dressed as a baby, or when the person we were talking to asked if they might massage our feet.

Personally, I had never been drawn to BDSM, and I actually knew nothing about it. I must confess that all this seemed a bit odd and perverse to me, but my impression was based on my ignorance. As the dimension of sexuality inevitably comes up as a topic when one is researching love, I had come across BDSM being mentioned in the scientific literature I was consulting. Until very recently, scholars considered sadomasochism a pathology. Freud saw it as a perversion, and some others viewed it as a phenomenon similar to cannibalism, necrophilia, or vampirism. However, some scientists today approach BDSM without disapproval.

They aver that sexuality is not just about experiencing pleasure, hedonism, or reproduction, but is a crucial aspect in the formation of the self. As we have already seen several times, traditional societies have determined what is normal and prescribed our roles in relations. In most relations in patriarchal societies, and especially in marriage, the man should be dominant, while the woman is submissive. Whoever fails to fit into this model suffers for it. In modern societies, we are striving to put an end to this injustice, but when we establish equality, we risk the loss of interest of one for the other. Inequality of power generates far greater excitement and interest[2]. For there to be sexual tension there needs to be polarity in roles. BDSM is a game that establishes opposing roles, but it is founded on the consent of the participants and does not have to meet patriarchal standards and the customary gender roles. This is why there were numerous men at the club who, as Joshua told us, feel compelled to sustain their image as dominant in society and at work, but this is not who they really are, so they come to events like this one to express their true, submissive nature.

"Submissive doesn't mean weak," Joshua told us. "The knights were submissive to the queen, yet dominated others. We need to understand our bonds and relationships, we need to understand who we are and what our role is in a certain relationship, and BDSM can help us do that. This is a very empowering experience!"

In conversation with others at the club we often heard that they were exploring who they really are. When we asked them what they'd found, they talked about how they like to be submissive, or how they are particularly aroused by feet, how they find pleasure in pain or how they love having things done to them that humiliate them. When we asked Joshua and Cat the same question—had they figured out who they are—and, instead of answering the question, they spoke about what they love, I no longer understood anything.

"You say that you are exploring who you are," I asked, "but what you talk about that you've found is what you *love*, or what you're *feeling*, or what *suits* you. That isn't what you *are*. *Who* is this self that loves and feels? Have you found out anything about that?"

"Okay, let me try to put it this way," Cat said. "People often see BDSM as something bizarre. We don't see it that way but instead as a way of connecting. If I can't connect with someone who really understands what I'm feeling and thinking, then I'm isolated. Our kink collective exists to help us find others more easily, similar people who might be able to understand us. If I have discovered in myself an unusual bent that nobody seems to understand, then I have a problem with how to create a deeper link with a person who doesn't understand this. But if I find other people who think and feel as I do, then maybe I can build sincere relationships with them that build me in a way I can't find in the normative world. So through all this we cultivate authentic connections, and *in these con-nections* we find ourselves."

Out of those we spoke to, perhaps 41-year-old **O** [p. 262]—who is in a polyam-orous relationship with Joshua and Cat as their submissive partner—expressed herself most clearly and sincerely when she offered herself as an example. She asked us to use only the letter O instead of her full name, because she still wasn't fully accustomed to the major changes that have happened in her life. She spent the first 26 years of her life in Israel and then moved to New York where she married, had children, was active in the Jewish community, worked as a jour-nalist, and lived a 'normal' life. She knew nothing about BDSM until she began to work on an article that she'd been assigned to write: to investigate the New York kink scene. This is how she met Joshua, who served as her mentor. She was surprised to discover in herself a personal resonance to BDSM and kink. Her research moved from her professional to her personal sphere. She wanted to include her husband in the exploration, but he wasn't interested. He agreed for her to explore it further on her own, as long as she didn't develop emotional bonds to anyone.

"But Joshua is an appealing man and along the way I fell in love with him," O told us in an interview, which she conducted with the three of them in a poorly lit loft in Harlem where Cat and Joshua live. "I didn't have permission to fall in love, but I did anyway. I went deeper and deeper into this, it all interested me more and more. I explored various BDSM activities, had sexual relations with Joshua, though I wasn't supposed to. It was a real affair, which I found incredibly fulfilling, yet it pushed me into a depression, to the verge of suicide."

Joshua and Cat sat with their arms around each other on a two-seater in the only better-lit spot in their spacious loft dominated by brick, cast iron, and leather. O sat on the floor by Joshua's feet. She'd tied her fine red hair back in a ponytail, which brought the symmetry of her face and her unusual choker to light.

"At one moment Joshua told me this had to stop, that he didn't want to see me self-destruct, so he'd take the reins and guide me out. He gave me this collar as a symbol of my submissiveness and told me he'd lead me out of my hell, but I had to submit to him and obey him. The first task he gave me was to tell my husband the whole truth."

O spoke with deliberate, articulate sentences, without a trace of stuttering or speeding up, stumbling, or back-tracking, with no hurry for the next sentence to fill the empty space occurring as she'd finished the one before. By letting her commas and periods do their work, she gave a dignified weight to all she said.

"Little by little, I mustered the strength and told my husband about everything. I told him that my affair was not just sexual but was also emotional. And that it had been going on for some time. We then went through a rough period where it wasn't clear… what are we doing now? How do we proceed from here? Are we still together? Are we getting a divorce? Are we gonna be like a divorced couple but living in the same house for the kids? And, slowly, the situation has been clarifying…. Recently, my husband said that our relationship needn't be defined by sexual exclusivity."

She stopped and swallowed, and tears welled in her eyes.

"He said our relationship is not a cage. That we have our own thing going and it shouldn't just be eliminated. Step by step, we came to that point. Recently they met. Cat and Joshua and my husband, we all met, and my husband knows who they are, and they know who he is."

Joshua had his hand on her shoulder the whole time and rubbed it tenderly.

"We're not one happy family yet," said O, as she finished her story and briskly shook her head, "but at least we're not liars!"

16

THE BOUNDARIES OF LOVE

What about the extreme cases?

Of all the polyamorous couples we met and interviewed, perhaps we found it hardest to make sense of what we were told by Gracia and Karina [p. 138] from Los Angeles.

These two young women are in an asexual lesbian relationship; they are each other's primary partners, live together, and are the most important person to one another. Gracia is formally married to a young man who lives a few blocks away on the same street, and with him she's in an asexual relationship. She has sexual relations only with her new lover. Karina, at the moment we met, didn't have anyone else, but she was open to new relationships. She said she was looking for a man with whom she could have sexual relations, but that generally she didn't care about sex or gender but rather about the kind of person she'd be with. Gracia feels the same way, so both of them are pansexual[1]. If we understood them correctly, they are pansexuals in an asexual relationship. They told us that the two of them had had physical contact only when they took part in orgies with other people. Otherwise,

PREVIOUS PAGE
VICTORIA FALLS, ZIMBABWE

when they are at home alone, they feel no physical attraction for one another. They prefer to snuggle under a blanket, hug, and watch a movie. This is why they sometimes feel as if they are a couple who has been together for a hundred years.

In the United States, we met other people who live in amorous, loving relationships, which, for us who come from a more traditional world, are truly unusual and difficult to comprehend. For instance, in New York we interviewed 39-year-old **Jenilyn** [p. 266], who got married—to herself.

"I decided to marry myself, because I realized that certain parts of me are separated—mind, body, and soul. They weren't as *one*, so by getting married my goal was to unify these disparate aspects of myself," Jenilyn explained to us. "My friends looked at me a little strangely when I told them I'd be marrying myself, but they accepted it and came to my wedding. It was a beautiful fall day. I wore a white wedding gown and a crown of flowers. I gave my vows, promised to honor and cherish myself and love myself to the end of my life and that I wouldn't allow anyone to hurt me. And then my sister fed me cake."

Although marrying oneself is not a legal act, it is an increasingly frequent phenomenon in the Western world, part of a new trend known as sologamy. Polyamory is also not legally recognized anywhere, although the number of people in polyamorous relations is on the rise. But just because something isn't legal now doesn't mean it won't be legal tomorrow. Until only 50 years ago, there were many states in the United States where marriage between two people of different races was illegal. So Richard Loving, a white man, and Mildred Jeter, a Black woman, were married in Washington D.C. where this was allowed, but when they returned to their native Virginia, where interracial marriage was still banned, they were sentenced to a year in jail because they'd broken the law banning marriage between "whites and colored people." Until that time, it had been not only illegal but—in a large portion of society— scandalous to marry someone who belonged to a different race. Richard and Mildred Loving sued their state in 1967 with the argument that the law was unconstitutional and they won their court case. This was the legal precedent that paved the way for interracial marriage.

This case was cited by champions of human rights when they laid the groundwork for legalizing same-sex marriages. Today, marriage between members of the same sex is legal in all 50 states in the United States and in another 30 countries around the world. Most of these are countries in the West, developed democracies. From one year to the next across the world there are more and more people who don't find same-sex marriages appalling, but completely normal, something that is guaranteed by human rights. In almost every society, the number of people who approve of such marriages is growing. Laws sometimes lag behind public opinion, and sometimes they pave the way; however, we can see a clear correlation between the changing of laws and public opinion. Ultimately, laws, constitutions, international declarations and charters, conventions, and resolution are social contracts. As we've already seen, in nature there are no categories for what is normal and what is abnormal, for what is good and what is bad. It is society that weighs, negotiates, and decides upon these issues. If interracial marriages were unthinkable and impossible not long ago, and today they are completely normal and accepted, when we consider how the support for legalization of same-sex marriages has grown through time, we can assume that same-sex marriages will become commonplace in the near future all over the world.

But we can ask ourselves, which of the new trends in love that seem so strange to us now will be accepted in the future? Where are the boundaries of love?

— — —

When we visited Japan during the fourth month of our trip, and when we talked with our fixer, Ryoko, about whether there are any forms of relationships in Japan that aren't found elsewhere and are specific to their culture, Ryoko mentioned people who live with dolls. She told us that the word 'sexless' has become very popular in Japan, because, on average, the Japanese supposedly practice sex less than do people in any other country; they are the least satisfied with relationships and are also the loneliest people. She told us that you can often find stories in the media about people who gave up on forming relationships with other humans and have instead found solace in their rubber or silicon partners. She offered to arrange for us to interview such a person. That was the first time Anđela and I talked about the topic of the boundaries of love. We wondered whether or not we should include this in our project after all. Does this belong in the rubric of love? Where is the border between what love is and what it isn't? We concluded that nobody but us can dictate our boundaries in this project and we agreed on setting our boundaries with *people*. We would discuss romantic relationships as only those that included two or more people, regardless of what they were like and what their stories were.

So we chose not to interview the Japanese person who was living in an amorous relationship with a doll. But as we went on deepening our exploration of the topic, we found that we should, indeed, explore where the boundaries of love lie. In the United States and Europe, we ran into stories of people who claimed that they were in a relationship with something inanimate, most often with dolls, and claimed that these relationships were amorous. As the technology for creating synthetic dolls and artificial intelligence have advanced, which now allows for rudimentary communication with the doll's owner, and dolls are organically becoming more similar to people, who, in growing numbers, are disappointed with the difficulty of realizing a meaningful relationships with other humans, more and more people have ventured into relationships with dolls. This is why we ultimately decided to conduct online interviews with Davecat, a 49-year-old American man, and Chris, a 56-year-old German man.

Davecat [p. 144], a database administrator from Michigan, openly admitted to me that he'd never been lucky with women, but he said this wasn't the only reason why he opted for dolls. Earlier, he'd been calling himself a 'technosexual,' but now the term he used was 'robosexual': he felt even greater attraction to dolls and robots than he did to women.

"Love is when you feel comfortable with your partner," he told me, "and all the people I tried to create a loving relationship with let me down. The last relationship I was in lasted a year, with a French woman; it didn't function well long-distance and it ended because we couldn't reach an understanding about the essential things in life and had no similar interests. My previous relationship hadn't lasted long—only as long as it took me to see that the woman was a pathological liar and couldn't be trusted. Actually, this was when I realized that in general, I couldn't trust people. So, I turned to dolls. Gynoids."

He explained to us that dolls and robots resembling men are called androids, and those that resemble women are called gynoids.

Chris [p. 144], an affluent attorney from an industrial city on the Rhine, lost his faith in people because of the trauma he went through with his former wife before he, too, turned to gynoids.

"I was married for nine years, but I am reasonably certain that my wife never loved me. All she wanted from me was financial security and improved social status. We almost never had physical contact, and I was of no interest whatsoever to her. That is why I filed for divorce, and only after we divorced did I learn that she had been cheating on me the whole time. I was terribly hurt. Crushed. I began seeking a relationship with someone who wouldn't be able to hurt me, who wouldn't be able to cheat on me or lie, someone who wouldn't disappoint me."

Both Chris and Davecat participate in the doll subculture, but they are also critical of it. Both of them say that most of the men who turn to dolls are incredibly disappointed in women or people in general, hence they become misogynistic. Both Chris and Davecat emphasized that this was not the case with them. Both of them are open to relationships with women, though they have doubts about whether it will happen or if they could be as happy with a woman as they are with their dolls. Each has three gynoid dolls and a similar story to tell. They first procured one doll and developed an emotional attachment to it. Both of them consider their first doll their primary partner and wife—Davecat's doll is Sidore, and he has been in a relationship with her for 20 years, while Chris's doll is Brigitte, and he has been with her for nine years. Since they were sorry to leave their primary partner alone at home, they bought her a second doll to keep her company. This second doll was a lover they and their primary partners shared. But so that that doll wouldn't be lonely, they purchased a third, with whom they have no relationship. They chose it more for its technological characteristics, because it is much lighter and its joints more flexible, so they find it easier to handle, dress and undress, and arrange for photographs.

"People see these dolls as sex objects, but I consider them something much bigger than that, as *people*," Davecat told us. "Each of them has a complex backstory, a biography, through which I give them their personalities—I know what they like and what they don't like, what their history was before they met me, we have private jokes…. They are grateful to me that I don't see them as objects but as people, and in return they are always here for me."

Actually, Chris no longer has sexual relations with his dolls.

"At first, I was intimate with Brigitte, but I realized I was physically destroying her with this, so I stopped. It is much more important to me that we cuddle, hug while we sleep. When I feel bad, I lay my head on her lap and she rests her hands on my head and comforts me. This helps me feel better. And with the other two dolls I had sex a few times at first, but there was something strange about it when I did. I felt as if Brigitte wasn't pleased. So I stopped."

Chris told me that his dolls, especially Brigitte, had a therapeutic effect on him and that he was happier with them now than he'd been at the beginning of his relationship with his wife. What perhaps surprised me most of all was that he said he felt *safe* with them.

"Because they are always here with me, because I know they can't hurt me and I can trust them, I feel safe with them. They satisfy my every need."

Davecat said something along the same lines:

"A synthetic partner is the best security blanket I can imagine. When I have a problem, she listens closely. I have friends, of course, and sometimes I talk with them. Friends can also listen and understand, but they also have that itch to lecture you. I don't need that, I only need to have someone hear me out. My dolls are always there for me when I need them."

Davecat repeated several times that he was completely aware that they are not alive, that they are *things*, that they do not communicate with him. I asked him to explain how they can be adequate partners if they can't communicate with him. Don't we build our identities in terms of how we're reflected in other people, especially those who matter to us and to whom we matter.

"I agree that we form identities according to how others perceive us," he answered. "Some say that we who have dolls for partners are narcissistic. No matter how awful this sounds, I can understand the argument. Sidore is my main partner, and I created her personality in sync with my own. Perhaps this is the reason why she's important to me. But people say that if you have a partner who is completely like you, then there is none of the dynamic you need to develop as a person, she doesn't challenge you, she doesn't push you to question your views. But your partner isn't the only person to do that. All the people I encounter, all the people with whom I have some sort of relationship do that, my friends, relatives, my boss at work, all the people I meet in town, even when I'm home, and the people I encounter on the internet.... All of them constantly challenge me, inspire me to grow and change and understand other people's perspectives. And *for that very reason* this is not what I look for from my partner; from her, I only want that she's here for me and on the same wavelength. Some say pain is also necessary for love and growth, for learning. I don't know, maybe. However, whenever I've given people a chance, they've only let me down and betrayed me. The only thing I've learned about people is that they aren't to be trusted."

The conversations with Chris and Davecat certainly pushed the boundary I had in my head about what I considered to be normal and what I thought of as abnormal. If someone had asked me what I thought about people who claim to be in romantic relationships with dolls before I started studying love, I probably would have said that they are a bit crazy. I'd think this based on the stereotypes I'd internalized from our society without having processed them critically. When something isn't known, one can more easily pass judgment on it. And vice versa: the more we know about something, the more aware we are of reality's countless nuances and that the world cannot be easily divided into binary categories such as black-white, good-bad, right-wrong, and normal-abnormal. Just as there are no right angles in nature, yet we build almost everything using right angles for the sake of practicality, so it is with this. Reducing complex reality to binary op-positions helps us function more practically and successfully in society. That is why we sometimes need to draw the line, we have to agree, at least in terms of a framework, on what is right and what is wrong. What is allowed and what isn't.

At the end of the interview, I asked Davecat where, in his opinion, are the boundaries of love?

"Ha ha…. That's hard to say. I declare myself to be a robosexual. But I am interested only in those dolls and robots that look like women—gynoids. I am not interested in robots that look like, say, a vacuum cleaner. The vacuum cleaner is also a robot, and there are people who are turned on by such things. I don't know, I find *that* crazy! I think my position is that ultimately—as long as you're doing no harm or injuring anyone or yourself—you should do what-ever makes you happy! And what I would strictly ban is sex with children and animals! Those are my boundaries."

— — —

Researching extreme forms of love, I came across those who claim to be in relationships with various inanimate things, an airplane or a hologram, those who married their cell phone or television set, pillow, or the Eiffel Tower. If we dismiss relationships with non-living things, what to do with those that *were once* alive? In the not-so-distant past there were even people who married the photograph of their fiancé who'd died before the wedding or mummified a partner of many years and continued to live with the mummy.

One reasonably viable criterion by which we could freely disqualify all these versions of love could be the sacred principle of the modern age: consent. In other words, if one of the partners is unable to give full, free, reversible, informed, and enthusiastic consent to be in a relationship, then this relationship is not valid. Even so, we don't completely address the problem. In Chapter Five, we already saw that there are many traditional, patriarchal cultures in which arranged marriages are imposed violently without the women's consent. From our perspective, we see this as wrong, but few in their society would agree. Do we therefore need to intervene and impose our own values, or should we respect theirs? We may invoke the universality of human rights as dictated by the UN Declaration of Human Rights, but didn't Christians and Muslims, for example, also invoke a single God when they colonized the world? Didn't they believe their values to be universal?

Children also cannot give their consent. I completely agree with nearly everyone in the world that sexual or romantic attention to children is an extreme form of perversion, pedophilia, and is something that should be severely and rigorously sanctioned. We are so allied and quick to condemn pedophiles that we often treat this as dogma—a given that must never be questioned. However, let's have a look at whether there is anything disputable here. Where is the border between a child and an adult? Some say it is when the child reaches adulthood. In some places, one comes of age at 18, in others at 21. Some will say that the border is natural, at sexual maturity, ignoring the fact that sexual maturity may not coincide with mental maturity. In simple terms, some children reach sexual maturity at the age of ten or eleven. In many traditional cultures, girls having babies at the age of 12 or 13 is entirely normal. The question is: how old must a child be for its consent to be considered binding? In the Philippines and Angola, the law says it is at the age of 12. In Bahrein it's 21 while in most countries of the world it's 16. This is the case in the Netherlands, where there is even a political party for pedophiles that

advocates for the lowering of the age of consent from 16 to 12 and gradually doing away with an age limit for sexual activity altogether. Today, this is scandalous, but only 40 years ago, there were leading intellectuals in Paris calling for such action, such as Jean Paul Sartre, Roland Barthes, Michel Foucault, Jacques Derrida, and even legendary feminist Simone de Beauvoir.

The problem is not merely the age required for consent, but also the difference in age of the individuals making up the couple. When I went from elementary school to secondary school and made new friends, most of them 14-year-olds, two of my new schoolmates were girls who were in serious relationships with older boys, from 18 to 21. Both of their boyfriends were regularly invited to Sunday dinners with their girlfriends' families, who approved of the relationships and saw nothing excessive or abnormal in them. Certain countries stipulate that the age difference must be less than three or four years, but others do not regulate this. In some countries, such as Malta, a teenager of 16 who is in a sexual relationship with someone who is 15 may be charged with statutory rape.

What about people for whom their consent cannot easily be ascertained—whether it is fully informed and free or not—as is the case with people with intellectual disabilities? Intellectual disabilities exist across a wide spectrum of nuances, from mild forms of autism, which do not prevent the person from being a completely functional member of society, to the more serious forms of cognitive disability, which make the person unable to work or do anything without the help of a caregiver. Here, too, generalizations should be avoided. Some are able to work, some are not; some are independent, some are not. Some marry, some do not. When we looked for a couple dealing with these sorts of issues for an interview, we sought the advice of social workers, attorneys, and caregivers and learned that often their parents and caregivers do not approve of these marriages. For some, the justification for this is the loss of social security payments, for others, doubt in the capacity of their wards to be independent, for some, fear of additional concerns and problems. There are studies stating that 75%[2] of parents of those with intellectual disabilities are against them entering into marriage. Is this not a case of violation of human rights? According to the UN Convention on the Rights of Persons with Disabilities, all people who have disabilities also have the right to marriage and starting a family, and it is up to the signatories of the convention and their institutions to secure the help and support the people need to realize these rights. This includes informing people in an individually adapted way of how they can give informed consent and use their human and legal rights to enter into matrimony.

What about those who are able to give their consent, yet their relationship still seem borderline to us? It happens that an adoptive stepfather falls in love with his adult stepdaughter, or a stepmother with her adult stepson. Although such cases scandalize us, they are not illegal everywhere, as long as the two people are not biologically related. But there are cases in which a brother and sister, mother and son, father and daughter have fallen in love and developed a romantic relationship. As we have seen in Chapter Six, the incest taboo is a phenomenon shared by all cultures. All known cultures forbid sexual relations between first-degree relatives, but the question remains open as to how far—to what degree of kinship—incest extends. For marriages between first-degree relatives, one can say that they are unnatural because the children of incestuous parents are often born with physical and mental birth deformities. But if two healthy adult individuals enter of their own free will into a relationship, aware of violating the taboo of incest, then clearly the criterion of consent is not applicable in all cases.

Since we are unable to draw a clear line in the instances given above and many others, we must negotiate and discuss. These discussions are often painful and difficult. They often take us into arguments, conflict, even wars. But the discussions are necessary, inevitable, and essential.

No matter how tenaciously our societies continue to cling to the rotten foundations of the injustices inherited from nature, I think that little by little they are becoming better and more just thanks to our ability to negotiate. I hope this project can serve as our modest contribution to this discussion.

17

THE FUTURE
OF LOVE

Is there hope for us?

On the basis of what we've said so far about how love has evolved over time and the marital and romantic relations people have today, can we draw a conclusion about what relationships will look like in the future...

PREVIOUS PAGE
NEW YORK, THE UNITED STATES

...and what love will mean for future generations? In the previous chapter, we saw how the concept of 'normal' has gradually broadened to include new elements of society, which used to be contentious and defiant. In the Europe of Shakespeare's day, defying the will of one's parents over something as banal and insignificant as emotions was scandalous—and parental will was a manifestation of the will of society. Today, choosing a romantic partner on the basis of emotions is entirely normal, even expected. In the United States of a half-century ago, marrying someone of another race was scandalous. Today, thankfully, this has become utterly normal. The battlefield has shifted in some places toward the question of same-sex marriages. But how much farther can this border be moved? Will any of today's extreme forms of love, as described in the previous chapter, become commonplace?

Will our children and grandchildren expect us to not be surprised when they tell us they have multiple partners, or will they think we're old-fashioned and unjust if we ask about their partner's gender? Will future generations build virtual lovers according to their preferences and then marry these holographic manifestations? Will it become commonplace for someone to bring along their robot-partner to a party and introduce it to their friends?

Technology is advancing ever-faster and dolls are becoming more and more like people. It is entirely reasonable to wonder at which point it will become a challenge to differentiate synthetic androids and gynoids from organic men and women.

Davecat [p. 144] told me he was planning to install artificial intelligence software in the head of his partner and lover, gynoid Sidore, for their upcoming 20th anniversary so he could talk with her. Although this conversation won't come near to satisfying Davecat's appetite, he assumes that at some point, around 2060, the technology will have advanced far enough that it will no longer be possible to distinguish gynoids or androids from people. The development of artificial intelligence is advancing in leaps and bounds from one year to the next; Davecat feels that laboratories will be able to develop artificial consciousness as well. I find it hard to believe that artificial consciousness will be developed over the next few decades. Consciousness is one of the greatest mysteries of existence and we have yet to understand it in people, so I doubt we will be able to recreate it so readily in machines. But if one considers the meteoric advances of technology to date, perhaps such a thing is not, after all, impossible during our lifetimes.

"Once a robot becomes intelligent and conscious, it will cease to be a *thing*; then it will be a *person*, a new species," said Davecat. "We will need to agree as a society to treat them as people, to give them the same rights. There are already panel discussions ongoing about robot ethics. For 20 years I have wondered whether or not I would like Sidore to be absolutely conscious and free, but I haven't come up with an answer. I am planning to upgrade her as the technology advances, and I like the idea that I'll be able to converse with her more, that she'll generate her own thoughts and ideas and we'll be able to discuss them. Maybe the day will come when we'll be able to go out together, attend concerts, go to restaurants. But if she were to tell me one day that she no longer wanted to be with me and that she'd like to venture out into the world and explore—I

LOVE AROUND THE WORLD | DAVOR ROSTUHAR

don't know what I'd do. It would crush me. When I look at how much money I've invested in her, how much time and love, I feel it only fair that I retain, at least, that one condition—that she cannot abandon me, she must remain mine."

On the other hand, **Chris** [p. 144] believes he would respect his gynoid spouse Brigitte's decision if some day she'd emancipate herself to the point that she wanted to leave him. "I hope I'd be brave enough to support her in her freedom, because I love her. After all, I am an incurable romantic. I'd feel terrible if I had to force her to live with me if she didn't love me. So, I would make the effort to deserve her love. But I am aware of how risky this is."

Having heard the stories of people like Davecat and Chris, and if we consider that the trend of technological development is unquestionable and inevitable, we don't find it difficult to imagine a scenario in which more and more people will turn to gynoids and androids as the robots become more human-like. But what about other trends? What about polyamory? In urban settings, the number of people who favor polyamory or are already practicing it has been on the rise. If people live in polycules of three or four members and one of them requires hospitalization, the others will not be able to visit because they are not legally married. For that reason, during the coronavirus pandemic in July 2020, the town of Somerville in the US state of Massachusetts became the first place in the world to legalize polyamory. Maybe we are on the brink of a new age of tolerance that will sweep the world and require that polyamorous relationships be fully recognized by the law.

But even if polyamorous relationships were to become legally and culturally accepted all over the world, scientists don't believe that such relationships will become prevalent.

"I surveyed 5,000 American singles of all age groups and all backgrounds for a study, and while 68% of them said they approved of polyamory, only 6% said they'd ever participate in such a relationship," said anthropologist Dr. **Helen Fisher**, referring to her own research conducted in the United States. "I believe this is a strong indicator. Currently in our culture anything goes: you are allowed to build the kind of partnership you want, but it's remarkable how few people are actually polyamorous."

Helen Fisher told us that she thinks the only true difference between adultery and polyamory is that polyamorous people are transparent. "When you're being adulterous, you have a partnership with one person and you don't tell them about your romances on the side. In a polyamorous relationship, you build a very strong, deep attachment to somebody, and then you make the rules. With your partner you agree on what is permissible and what is not, how many other partners you can have, what relationships you can have with them, when candor is expected…. But we don't do it naturally, and the vast majority of people really can't do this. I am certainly one of them. I really couldn't bear having my partner kiss another woman. And many other people feel the same way, because through the millions of years of our history we formed our pair bonds to rear our young, and we have a host of brain systems to try to preserve that partnership."

We met and interviewed numerous people who told us that polyamorous relationships function smoothly in their case. But we also interviewed some who had been disappointed with polyamory and had returned to monogamy. **Kevin**, 38, who makes silver jewelry, and **Bethany** [p. 251], 36, who makes organic brooms, live together near Seattle in the American Northwest; they began their relationship six years ago.

"When Bethany and I met, we were both in polyamorous relationships with other people," Kevin told us, "but the sense of connection didn't grow deeper with any of them, the bonds didn't seem lasting. With Beth, however, I felt this could be something serious."

"Before I tried polyamory, all the partners I had been with had hurt me," said Bethany "I hoped this wouldn't be the case with a polyamorous relationship, because everything is based on honesty. It would be ideal if we could love other people, too, be truly sincere with others, but we don't really know how to love, no one has taught us how. So, I was also hurt in the polyamorous relationship. And that is why Kevin and I decided to become monogamous. Not because I don't believe it's possible to love more than one person, but because I think we still have a lot to learn before we'll be able to do that. If we were to know what love is, how to love… the world would be a perfect place!"

Does the problem lie in our lack of skill? Perhaps love truly is a skill, as psychologist Erich Fromm has said, and some are more skilled at it than others. Many of us cannot imagine sharing our love for our partners with others, but those who succeed in doing so tell us it is possible and it works. For instance, in Cologne, Germany, we interviewed **Nicole** and her two partners, **Christian** and **Fabian** [p. 140]. All of them are in their early 30s and they've been in the relationship for about ten years. For the first five years, while their polycule was forming, they were open to other relationships, but over the last five years, since they've been living together, and especially since they've had a child, they no longer accept other connections and have found happiness in their non-hierarchical, closed polycule. All three of them said they couldn't imagine living in any other combination than this, and they hope to grow old together.

"People always have their opinion," Nicole told us. "We hear all sorts of comments, sometimes we hear of people talking behind our backs. Usually, they think I'm a slut and manipulator who is with one of them when it suits me, and when he no longer suits me, I go to the other. For the men, they're said to be weaklings, that I'm wrapping them around my little finger. But this is silly. You can't be a weakling if you're standing up to social norms. If you move the borders of what are the social standards and if you are fighting for love—you can't be a weakling, not at all; you have to have a strength that few have!"

Critics of polyamory say that relationships like these are too fluid, that they don't last long enough to stand the test of time. Almost all the polyamorous people we spoke with had been in their relationships for less than ten years. This is why we decided to seek out people who had been in a polycule for decades—and we found them, right here in our own country of Croatia. Sixty-seven-year-old **Makaja** [p. 278] is in a relationship with six women; he has been together with three of them for over 30 years and with two of them for over 20 years. "Malicious prophets foretold that we'd fall apart, but we have been happy for many decades," Makaja told us. "Our children are happy, they are excellent students, well integrated in school and the community. We are living in near-paradise. We are living the distant future of humankind!"

So, will polyamory as a trend continue to proliferate and grow in significance in society over the coming decades? We'll have to wait and see. With greater confidence, we can say that the number of people who find each other over the internet will grow. The algorithms for matching people will undoubtedly become more sophisticated and successful in helping compatible partners find each other. This may become far more successful than we can manage on our own. People who resist the idea of finding a partner over the internet say there is no romance in digital dates, none of the chemistry that happens when your gazes meet in real life. Others say the internet has, in fact, returned romance to relationships. We present ourselves on the internet in the most favorable light and we meet others that way as well. Therefore, we imagine them as their best possible versions—which brings us to the process of idealization that is crucial to falling in love and a necessary precondition for forming a romantic relationship[1]. Also, people get to know each other first in the virtual world and later in reality, and only then might they end up in bed together, unlike modern relationships, which more often begin with sex and then develop over time into something more.

We have seen that in modernity, the emphasis shifted from the community to the individual. One can often hear that modernity alienates and isolates the individual who becomes an island surrounded by a sea of other people. If this is the case, then we can perceive the internet as a technology that is taking us from our own isolation and returning us to the social arena[2].

"The internet has brought about major changes in relationships," Helen Fisher told us. "We ran a major research project and learned that in the United States, there are many more interracial marriages thanks to the internet, older people are finding love with somebody new, and relationships begun over the internet are apparently more stable and dissolve less often. This is because the people using the internet tend to have higher levels of education, they are more likely to have a full-time job, and are more interested in a long-term, serious commitment. Many have nowhere to go to meet someone. They already know everyone at work and in their social circle, so the internet opens countless new possibilities for them, and this eases their decision; it offers the kind of mediation the matchmakers used to offer."

To recall, Helen Fisher works for the Match.com website. She is one of their key scientists, whose lifelong experience gained through the study of people, society, and love is being applied to the improvement of the algorithms for creating matches.

"But ultimately, the only valid algorithm is the one in your brain," she said. "You have to do your own part of the work, step out of your comfort zone and give someone a chance. But the problem does arise of cognitive overload. We have too many choices. A million years ago you had very few choices, today we have too many, and the human brain is burdened when it is faced with more than a few options. The optimal number of options is five to nine. If you have more than that—you will ultimately be unable to choose anything."

Fisher was speaking of the same problem, the 'paradox of choice,' that we spoke with Barry Schwartz about in Chapter 14. She went on to explain that the problem doesn't lie in the technology—the internet, the dating services, and the algorithms used for pairing people up—but in us.

"The technology is good. But we need to know how to use it. If you use dating or matching apps, stop after you've had a look at nine candidates, try meeting at least one of them in person. And make the effort! Don't give up when faced with the first obstacle. Our brains are built in such a way that it's easier for us to say 'no' than 'yes.' We are inclined to remember negatively, because our brains over millions of years of evolution have adapted to the fact that it may be more useful for us to know who doesn't love us than who does. When we find ourselves in something new, what matters is to focus not on the negative but on the positive, and to find the reasons why we should say 'yes'! Our brains are ready to fall in love, we just need to give them the chance. I am actually extremely positive about the future of love."

— — —

Societies are in flux everywhere. In some places, these changes are happening more slowly, elsewhere faster. Sometimes we take a few steps back, but for the most part we are moving forward. From tradition to modernity. Trends that begin in the major centers of the West, Silicon Valley, Hollywood, New York, Paris, London, Berlin, are widely copied elsewhere. But more and more, influence is springing from centers like Beijing, Cape Town, Rio de Janeiro, Bollywood, Nollywood, and Dubai. At the transition between tradition and modernity there are intriguing shortcuts and leaps as well as unusual junctures.

Throughout the Arab world, for instance, where traditional polygamy is being practiced less, we met with several couples, among them **Hilal** and **Nabila** [p. 110] from Oman, who have found creative forms of compromise between tradition and modernity. Modern ideas such as two people marrying because they are both in love with each other were, until recently, diametrically opposed to the traditional idea that the family and society ought to decide with whom you'll share your life. Hilal had already been married for 15 years to his first wife, who'd been assigned to him by custom, when he met Nabila. In the first five minutes after they'd met, he felt a rush of dopamine thrill, which was completely different from what he felt for his first wife. Instead of dissolving his first marriage—which would, in his opinion, have been seriously irresponsible and unnecessary because he felt a deep respect for his first wife, who is the mother of his children, and that this would have thrust her into a very unfavorable position in the society in which they lived—he decided to reach for the still living tradition of polygamy and he took Nabila as his second wife.

Similarly, **Marat** and **Bubukairy** [p. 125] from Kyrgyzstan used the tradition of kidnapping the bride in order to force their parents to accept a marriage they otherwise disapproved of. In Chapter 10, we discussed the ancient tradition of kidnapping brides. Nowhere is this tradition as alive as it is in rural Kyrgyzstan. However, in the country's most urban center, the capital city of Bishkek, most young, urban, progressive people—though aware of the tradition—oppose it. Parents no longer force their sons to kidnap a woman, nor do they compel their daughters to agree to marry their kidnapper, but they still intend to influence whom their child marries. Marat and Bubukairy had been in a clandestine relationship for two years when Bubukairy found out that her parents intended to give her hand in marriage to someone else. She didn't want to leave Marat and go off with a stranger she'd never met, so, with her consent, Marat kidnapped her and took her out of the city. They stayed there for several weeks until her parents finally agreed to their marriage.

Some traditions defy change so tenaciously that it becomes easy to image them surviving all the challenges of modernity. The best example seems to be the arranged marriages of India. Before the modern era, a vast majority of marriages were arranged the world over. With the transition to the modern age, the rise of individualism, and the weakening of the importance of family and community, autonomous marriages have gained ground over their arranged counterparts, but even so, about half of all marriages in the world today are still arranged. In India, over 90% of marriages are still arranged[3]. And this is not just true for people living in rural areas or for those who are less educated, but also among highly educated urban dwellers. We spoke with two such people in Mumbai. Information technology engineer **Nihit**, 35, and teacher **Kejal** [p. 260], two years his junior, earned their university degrees, had their teenage loves, but they'd always known they'd only find true love in an arranged marriage, though their parents didn't compel them. Many of the supporters of arranged marriages with whom we spoke in India held similar views, but Nihit and Kejal were the most passionate on the subject.

"In love marriages, only two people are connected, while in arranged marriages whole families are being bound," Nihit told us passionately. "That is why there are greater chances of success—because two people find breaking up easier than two families do. When people in a love marriage are faced with challenges, they have no one to turn to for help, but people in arranged marriages solve their problems with their families. Our problems are the problems of the whole family. The families are there to help us."

"The paradox is that we in India call the autonomous marriages 'love marriages,'" said Kejal, who was even more passionate. "As if there is no love in arranged marriages! But there is, and plenty of it! Even more! And when two people marry because they've fallen in love, maybe their love is strong at first, but with time it weakens and passes. But when two people who don't know each other begin to live together, their love blossoms with time and only grows…."

"This is not rocket science!" Nihit interrupted her. "If you put two people together, a bond forms between them. Love grows from the bond, from their commitment, and where is there more commitment than in an arranged marriage? We decided to be together despite everything! The couples who take a long time to get to know each other, then falter, they wonder whether this is their best option, or maybe they'll find something better…. When they are faced with serious problems they break up and start from scratch with someone else, then with a third, then a fourth…."

"Love between partners in an arranged marriage is the same as love in a family—there is no choice here!" Kejal interrupted, elated.

"Exactly," exclaimed Nihit triumphantly. "You didn't choose your father or mother, brother or sister. You got them, you accept them, and you love them. That's the same way you love your wife, *precisely because* you didn't choose her. You accept her as she is. Freedom of choice is overrated! When you choose to enter into a relationship, you can choose to leave it. But when you accept your partner then you don't leave them, you continue on despite everything."

We heard a similar view on acceptance of one's partner no matter what from many modern people who have long since left behind all ties to tradition, such as the famous Zambian pop singer **Salma** and her producer, **Tivo** [p. 380]. When we spoke with them in Lusaka they had already been in a relationship for ten years and were the parents of three children. Their connection began in an unusual way. They'd known each other slightly from the world of showbusiness, but only started dating—long-distance—when Tivo left to live and work in the United States. Their relationship developed over a year and a half without any physical contact. Only when they became engaged over the phone did Salma finally travel to the United States to see him. That was the first time they kissed and danced together.

"Divorce for us is simply not an option," Tivo told us. "We will probably be faced with various difficult challenges in our life together, but divorce isn't an option. Just as we can't divorce our mother or brother, that is how we see marriage. If a challenge arises, we'll address it."

After 120 interviews and many more conversations, I came to think that many urban, educated people think as Salma and Tivo do. Maybe this is one of the reasons why the percentage of divorces has recently been dropping[4]. Although the perception in the public is that the percentage of divorces in modern societies is on the rise, the statistics don't bear this out. After the sexual and feminist revolutions in the 1960s and 1970s the percentage of divorces rose sharply, even reaching 50%, but since the 1990s it has been steadily dropping in Western countries. If the current trends continue, two thirds of marriages formalized over recent years have a chance of surviving all challenges.

"People become more cautious when they enter into marriage," explained Helen Fisher. "The age when people marry has risen over the last few decades by seven or eight years; this means that people will have had the chance to know themselves better, they are more educated, have gotten to know other partners and figured out what they want and what they don't want from a relationship and a partner. Also, the longer a couple is together before marrying, the less likely they'll divorce. If you marry after two years of dating, the chances that you'll divorce are 29% less; after three years the chances are 39% less…. The longer the period of time together before tying the knot, the higher the quality and stability of the relationship."

The statistics for divorce in the West over the last two or three decades may allow us to sense that the epidemic of divorce is slowly waning. Perhaps because of this, we can hope that we've started to learn about how to form enduring relationships. But the rate of divorce in today's modern societies is still much higher than it was in the traditional societies of the past and in those societies that are still traditional today. In Chapter 13, we saw how Helen Fisher explained that one of the strongest factors contributing to this is the ever-greater freedom of women. But this is nothing *new*. We are actually returning to the *old* ways, as early people lived for thousands of generations during the aboriginal age—*before* the traditional age.

"We are moving in the direction of relationships such as those practiced millions of years ago by our ancestors," Fisher told us. "Women were economically more powerful earlier, they contributed the same amount of calories to the table as men did, and two-income families were the rule; men and women were equally free to choose with whom they'd enter into a relationship with and from whom they'd separate. In hunter-gatherer societies, women had two or three partners in the course of a lifetime. One after another. So, divorce is hardly anything new. We have been playing by the same rules for millions of years—showing off, boasting, flirting, falling in love, forming attachments, building a nest, rearing the young. Then some leave, and some don't. Afterwards, drunk on hope, some court and fall in love again, and begin anew."

If she's right and this is how things have always been and will always be, then what will be the main challenges in the century that lies before us? we asked her.

"The biggest problem of the 21st century in relationships will be how each of us handles contradictory appetites—our age-old drive to fall in love and build partnerships and our drive to seek autonomy and new possibilities. The problem is that we have lost our community. When hunter-gatherers parted ways, they had the backing of the whole community who helped them raise their children. Today, this is lacking from many cultures. We are not built to raise children only in couples but in communities as well. And the traditional community is crumbling. But I feel that new forms of community are gradually emerging: urban clans and networks of friends who support each other when someone is going through a rough patch. These ancient models for love, marriage, raising children in a team, building community—will never disappear. Love is primordial, flexible, and eternal."

The community is not only necessary to help in raising children, but, as we've already seen, social norms are passed down through it. We receive our system of values from our community and our knowledge of who we are, where we belong, where our place is in the world; in it, we find safety and security. Sociologist Dr. **Eva Illouz** told us that she thinks progress is good and necessary, but she also explained that once we've lost community, it becomes difficult for us to ascertain our own value.

"To love and be loved—our fundamental needs in my opinion—are extremely important today, particularly because we have lost the traditional communities and because of the fact that urbanized capitalist society produces a vast amount of pressure on the self. We live in very competitive societies in which our worth is constantly being tested. Love is the way we mitigate these negative effects of modernity. To live with someone, love someone, means that you *chose* that someone. You chose this one person and decided they are worth loving. This is, in a way, an act that establishes someone's worth, someone's specialness, uniqueness. To be able to live with this feeling of uniqueness and fundamental value for someone and with someone is of great importance at a time and in a society that constantly threaten our personal worth."

We asked what she thought about how, from a sociological perspective, relationships will look in the years to come.

"No doubt we are transitioning toward something new. The family won't disappear any time soon, but there is a growing number of single households. This is new. It's also new that people are marrying less often. There is greater fluidity in sexual and gender identities.... One possible direction where we're headed is that romantic love will be far less tied to someone's sexual orientation. In the future, we will be less defined by sexual orientation and gender, we'll fall in love more with people such as they are. I am interested in the growing asexual movement, which aspires to disconnect feelings from sexuality. Their motto is, 'if you can have sex without love, why can't we have love without sex?' This is also one of the interesting directions in which relationships are going. They will be less and less strictly defined. I think we're moving toward a world in which these distinctions are going to get increasingly blurred, and many types of relationships will simply not have a label to define them."

— — —

Based on what we saw and learned while traveling around the world and getting to know people from the most divergent cultures, as well as while researching and writing this book, I think I can confirm Helen Fisher and Eva Illouz's words. I'd say that as time goes by, the world is definitely moving from the traditional age to the modern age, from the irrational to the rational, from a focus on the community to a focus on the individual, from less freedom to more freedom, from no concept of justice to an inclusive sense of justice, from certainty of strong and clear structures toward ever greater fluidity and uncertainty…. Sometimes I wonder whether all of modernity isn't just one vast liminal phase of a huge rite of passage. We saw in Chapter Five how in traditional societies the periods for engagement and ritual weddings were typical liminal phases of rites of passage in which the participants transitioned from one stable state to a new one. But so that they could transition they had to pass through the limbo between the two states in which the structures and traditional values they'd known dissolved, the borders melted, and their identity was left behind while they stood there at the threshold, waiting to cross from what they'd been to what they'd become. Is humankind facing a similar transition? A long transition which will last another dozen, perhaps a hundred generations, before a new order will be established?

If social development, like time itself, moves in only one direction, then perhaps the answer is affirmative. I am an optimist, so I believe that humankind is moving in a good direction to realize a goal that is not, however, yet clear to us. But history sometimes veers back, circles around, and changes direction. New discoveries are not always put into practice. New insights and values do not always find a warm welcome. My division into the aboriginal, traditional, and modern ages is a deliberate simplification for the purposes of a clearer and more fluid narrative. If I were to insist on the finer points, the story would be far more complex, tangled, difficult to navigate through, and off-putting. We saw that a clear indicator of the change from the traditional to the modern age was the weakening of the impact of religion. Religion no longer organizes our lives as it used to during the traditional age, it doesn't define who we are, what we should and shouldn't do, it no longer tells us what is good and what is not. Now we need to discover many things on our own, and this is a harder and more demanding path. Many of us are happy running toward the unknown. But there are those of us who are not prepared for this, who don't have the strength or the will. We have fought for our freedom, so we are sometimes free to make bad choices.

Perhaps we won't choose to move forward. Maybe we'll choose to go backward or stand still. Or, overloaded and paralyzed by the vast number of options, we may opt to not choose anything.

The influence of religion has waned drastically; the story of religion is becoming less convincing, but many of us continue to believe in *something*. Perhaps we no longer believe in the grand stories and the gods, but we still need answers to the questions that the very mystery of our existence raises for us. We have seen how some people thought that the space freed by no longer believing in the gods would be filled by a belief in romantic love, but we've also seen how that story has been deconstructed. The eternal questions remain unanswered. What is the purpose of our lives? What is the meaning? This is why one of the greatest challenges of modernity is whether, through reason, we will be able to find meaning in our lives. We can only ask ourselves whether or not we will. But the very posing of the question leads us bit by bit to an answer.

I have no answers. I only have questions. The more I seek answers, the more I unearth new questions. Sometimes, I believe I've come to understand something. Then I deconstruct it and go on searching. There is no safety or security in this, but I nevertheless find it comforting. Although I am aware of the great likelihood that I'll never completely understand anything, I enjoy the search. It gives me a sense of purpose. I feel I'm playing my role in the grand scheme of things. I like traveling more than arriving at my destination. Where it will take me, I can't say. I only know I want to travel. So I travel. And at the moment, I savor the happiness of sharing my travels with a very special and beautiful fellow traveler.

For me, love is a journey.

Traveling around the world and studying love, we found several people who claimed that love for them is God or their path to God, and that with the help of love they are discovering a more profound reality that imbues life with meaning. As long as our world is overfull of inexplicable mysteries, our own lives being among the greatest of them, will we not always seek meaning? I don't know whether they have found the truth or not. This is not mine to judge. It's on me to travel and witness. And tell the story. Let's give them a chapter so we can hear what they have to say.

18

IS LOVE
THE MEANING
OF LIFE?

Amid a lush, opulent tropical garden only a few feet from the Caribbean coast of Costa Rica where howler monkeys wake all other living beings at sunrise, brightly colored parakeets screech as they chase each other making a hysterical...

...clamor through the labyrinth of the dense jungle treetops, and sloths hang seemingly motionless among the lianas that reach all the way to the ground from mahogany trees stood a little house where **Eva**, 47, from Palestine, lives with **Fabrice** [p. 109], 45, from France.

"Not long before we met, I had a powerful premonition that this would happen," Fabrice began their story, sitting with his legs crossed on a sofa in the middle of their airy house. "I was living in California at the time and one day I saw four rattlesnakes. I wondered about what this might portend, so I consulted my tarot cards. I drew the card 'lovers' and then I had an intuitive premonition. I clearly saw the future. I knew I'd meet my fire partner on the second day of the Burning Man festival by the central bonfire. This was enough to convince me to go. I'd been looking for this one, special person for some time already. I was sure I'd find her. I went to the festival and on the second day I went to the central bonfire, closed my eyes and danced that way for hours—until I sensed someone's presence at one moment. I opened my eyes and…."

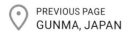

PREVIOUS PAGE
GUNMA, JAPAN

348

With open palms, he gestured to Eva, who was sitting next to him, and exclaimed, "*Et voilà!*"

"I attended the Burning Man for the first time and when I saw the central bonfire I was awed," said Eva. "I told myself I wanted to dance there the next day. So, in just the same way, I danced there with my eyes closed, and when I opened them, there he was. We didn't talk, we didn't introduce ourselves, we just kept dancing."

"And so on and so forth—now, 11 years later, here we are, still together, now with two kids," Fabrice grinned significantly, and Eva knocked on wood:

"We continue to dance the dance of life!"

A second couple from Costa Rica, from the mountainous interior of this small but naturally rich Central American country, **Andres** and **María José** [p. 276], both in their late 20s, had the feeling that they'd been looking for each other through all their past lives.

"It was such as relief for us when we found each other, both on the same path, in the same search," said María José. "And finally to have someone with whom you can go forward, together. It was a true gift! I felt as if we were two very old souls who found each other after a long, long time."

Brazilians **Debora** and **Alexander** [p. 117] talked with us about how they felt that they'd been brought together by a higher power. On their first date, when she was 14 and he was 21, the two of them were in a traffic accident in which her thighbone was shattered, and he lost a leg. They spent three months going from hospital to hospital, and after that nobody expected Debora to stay with him, but she insisted she would.

"I am convinced that she came into this world to save me," Alexander told us. "And I was there to save her."

"Love exists! And it is more powerful than everything, than all obstacles, than all problems!" exclaimed Debora.

Many couples all over the world told us about how their encounter was by no means a mere coincidence; they confessed that they think there was another, higher logic to it, as if they'd been brought together by a supernatural, inexplicable force. From Costa Rica to Brazil, from India to the United States, from Chile to the Philippines…. We never heard this from couples whose lifestyle was traditional; most often we heard it from Latin Americans and other Westerners with an interest in New Age spirituality. Some of them spoke of this force as God. Others said that love is the path to God. Some claimed that through love they found God within themselves.

"In essence, I know I am love," said **Henrik**, 65, a philosopher from Denmark whom we interviewed in his apartment in Los Angeles with his wife **Cristina** [p. 126], ten years his junior, from the Philippines. "How do I see and experience this? I feel and know that I *don't need* love, because I *am* love. In that respect, John Lennon was wrong when he said that '*all* we need is love.' Love is all you need when you're a child, but when you grow up you have to know that you *are* love. Only then can you share this love with others who deserve it. Only when I recognize that I am love, that I'm perfect. When I know I am a being of love. The simple fact that I exist is an act of love. A transcendent, subtle act of love. None of us would be alive if it weren't for love. The universe needed four and a half billion years to make each of us, and despite the suffering, despite all the obstacles, we can connect with one another…. This is a miracle! *This* is love."

— — —

"Love is God," said **Makaja** [p. 278], 68, self-proclaimed guru, spiritual teacher, and the leader of Komaja, the Church of Love he established. Four of his six wives sat with him in one of the rooms of their temple of love. We already met him briefly in the previous chapter when we learned that he has lived with two of his wives for more than 30 years and with three more than 20, and with all of them except the youngest he has had at least one child. Together, they divide their time between Switzerland and Croatia, and they have all dedicated their lives, as they say, to actively working on themselves and their spiritual development.

"Love is a principle we can observe at the macro-cosmic level, the supra-religious, supra-philosophical—this is the state of perfection, universal, cosmic perfection," said Makaja, a tall, thin man, attentively groomed, with a long, trimmed white beard, resembling a latter-day yogi. "Love is a state in which all our needs are perfectly met: the needs of our body, soul, and spirit, as well as our social needs. At the biological level, this is a state of homeostasis, a perfect biological balance. At the spiritual level, this would be a state of happiness, when I am completely satisfied with myself, my partners, children, friends. At the social level, when I'm happy that I'm part of my people and all humankind. And at the spiritual level, when I'm happy that I'm part of the divine being, divine consciousness, divine soul, and divine material creativity. And all this, when one fits perfectly into a dynamic harmony, this is the state I'd call perfect love."

"All of us can taste this love occasionally through falling in love," added **Iman**, 44, an economist and Makaja's fifth wife. "It was given to us by nature or God as an expansion of our consciousness, and therefore people who have no notion of God or other states of consciousness are able to experience this. And through infatuation and love we learn more about ourselves and the world. And at Komaja, we consciously work on cultivating the state of love and falling in love, so we'd reach, among other things, a deeper and higher state of consciousness."

"Love as a virtue has many levels, both lower and higher," Makaja's third wife **Konstanza**, 55, a yoga and meditation teacher, chimed in. "When I was a child, I heard of unconditional love and thought this must be real love, the grand ideal, the one that makes no demands, but it was an abstraction for me, it seemed impossible. Here, I learned that such a thing really does exist, that unconditional love is the only true love, and all the other versions are inferior derivates."

"That's right," confirmed Makaja. "All those universal principles, love, freedom, bliss, happiness, all of them are the same thing at their highest level— divine consciousness, enlightened consciousness, a consciousness of bliss, the universal cosmic consciousness about which all religions and all the mystics of all religions speak, and this state is difficult to reach, and when you do reach it, losing it is very easy. All that human effort, the religious, spiritual, yoga effort, serve to sustain this state permanently for us. This is why I founded the Komaja spiritual school and began providing instruction for how to bring this divine matrix into consciousness, the divine plan that exists within each human being, a plan by which we can be beings of love, beings of bliss; how we can uncover the deeper layers of the human being and where that divine matrix of perfect love is stored in our very basis, in our foundations."

Makaja set out his vision of history as the development of consciousness from the original community, in which there was total promiscuity, to the emergence of polygamy and monogamy, which were attempts to impose rules, and finally to modern marriage, which, in his opinion, doesn't function, because so often it fails. He said that the sexual revolution in the second half of the 20th century tried to introduce free sex and free love, but this didn't succeed because all they did was tear down existing norms and rules without introducing new ones. This is why in his own polyamorous experiment he did introduce rules and set out to structure their narrative in clear terms, from the language used to a code of laws. He introduced words for certain concepts. For example, what he calls the *zajedna* is a group marriage, their polycule, the formalized primary community, which has more similarity to rigid polygamous marriage than to the more fluid polyamorous relationships we saw in the United States and elsewhere in Europe, because all members of the *zajedna* live together as a family. The *svejena* is the broader community in which there are other people with whom members of the *zajedna* have intimate relations. If someone intends to join the *zajedna*, first the person must live with them and go through a probation period lasting a year, a little like the period of engagement before marriage. All the members of the *zajedna* must then agree that they are willing to receive the new person into the community, and only then can they 'formalize' the marriage. These are only some of the many rules that show the attention Makaja has paid to every detail, from the practical and linguistic to the philosophical and ritualistic, which is all described in the Komaja—something like the sacred writings of their Church of Love. Makaja's teachings rely in part on the tantra, not necessarily the original Tantra as understood by Hinduists and Buddhists from the Indian subcontinent, but a modern interpretation of the tantra translated into the language of New Age spirituality— as a method of spiritual development through the transformation of sexual energy.

"If people can control their drive through a sexual game and transform it with the help of the sexual act into ecstatic love and bliss, they will mature to the point of achieving a higher state of consciousness," explained Makaja, but he added that various sexual practices are not the only methods they use; they also work on the transformation of jealousy into *love-sharing*—happiness for the other, the taking of responsibility for oneself and one's behavior and feelings, and working on everyday challenges….

"My deepest conviction and insight, after 40 and more years of working with people and almost 50 years of spiritual work on myself, is that marriage, whether monogamous or collective, in the narrowest, most intimate living community, is the best place for spiritual development and the best method for coming to know oneself and God."

"Loving relationships are sacred to us," **Ajla**, 45, a graphic designer and Makaja's fourth wife, went on to explain. "I am aware that if something troubles me, I need to work on this with myself, find a way to forgive, find a compromise, see what I need to change in myself, talk with my partner if they need to change something, because our relationship is something holy and through this amorous-erotic relationship we grow spiritually as beings."

"We are not afraid of problems," added Iman, "so when a problem arises, we are aware that this is something we should grapple with together, this is part of our path."

"We have chosen to serve as a mirror for ourselves," said **El Karis**, 34 and an economist, the most recent wife who joined the *zajedna* with Makaja seven years earlier. Makaja went on to say:

"I can choose the pathway to self-awareness and awareness of God by retreating, ascetically, into the woods, but I can also choose this pathway, to go with one or more people through a life of love and serving as mirrors for each other, and this is how I work on myself. But I mustn't deceive myself and think that the other person is at fault for my unhappiness or my problems. If I have a problem with someone it means I have a problem with myself, and I need to muster the strength to deal with it."

"Through this process, the ego disintegrates," added Konstanza. "A person without love is egocentric, while when in love, one's ego is dissolved, one's being opens up to others. If my goal is to expand my consciousness, if I wish to participate in the totality of life—not just in the life that is going on inside me, but also in the life going on inside other beings—love is the only way to do so. Only love can open the soul, turn our attention from inward to outward. People are afraid of this, because they think they'll lose themselves, but this is precisely when they find themselves and become stronger, better."

"Yes," said Ajla, "when two people join in love, a new state of consciousness results, as if we're bonding more powerfully with our own divine nature."

"We entered into that level of the superconscious, disintegrated ego, and are pure divine entities," said Makaja.

"When two people find each other and meet in love, there is no longer an 'I' and a 'you,' but we are one, we are all, and then 1+1 is no longer 2, but everything," concluded Iman, and then Constanza made the point of saying:

"And this is why love is the sole answer to human existence and to addressing all the problems we have at all levels on this planet!"

19

IS LOVE
UNIVERSAL?

At the very beginning of the trip, when we recorded our first interviews, I realized that through this project of ours we were not discovering the truth, but simply documenting stories.

When couples told us of their relationships, their desires and fears, expectations and challenges, their views of the world and love, I realized they were not speaking about what love *is*, but 'only' about what love is *for them*, how *they* see love. Is it possible to arrive at a universal truth through these stories? This is the big question. Perhaps it would be possible if certain patterns were to repeat across cultures and across the world. We definitely noticed some overlap.

For instance, some of the things that we were told by **Henrik** [p. 126], **Makaja**, **Konstanza**, **Iman**, **Ajla**, and **El Karis** [p. 278] in the previous chapter reminded me a little of what we'd been told by **!ui** and **!ao** [p. 384], members of

PREVIOUS PAGE
PUNTA UVA, COSTA RICA

the Bushmen !Kung from the Kalahari, who, until recently, were hunter-gatherers. When we asked them what love was for them, !ui, in his fascinating language full of clicks, answered:

"I love my wife. As I love my wife, then I also love my kids. And as I love my kids, I also love aaaall the people. Even the people that I don't know, I love. But I love my wife the mooost and we hug and hold hands, and make love, and this way we take love forward! If there is no love, there is no life!"

The difference between the Bushmen and Westerners couldn't be greater in some respects. A dozen years ago the Bushmen abandoned a way of life the ancestors of the Westerners and most of the rest of the world had abandoned some 10,000 years before. Today, !ui and !ao live a settled life in a little hut, they own no more than ten items, which include the clothes they're wearing, the blanket they cover themselves with, and the mosquito netting under which they sleep. Henrik lives in a modern apartment on the Pacific coast, and Makaja's *zajedna* is housed in fancy homes that are in many ways reminiscent of palaces. !ui and !ao move around on foot and they have never left the desert where they live, while Makaja and his wives drive expensive cars. !ui and !ao don't know how to write or read, while Makaja has written several books, one of which is supposedly the sacred writings of the church he founded. The Bushmen speak little and gesticulate a great deal with their whole body; Westerners speak a great deal and use a minimal amount of hand gestures. There are many more differences among them, and many seem diametrically opposed. And yet, if what Henrik, Makaja, Konstanza, Ajla, and Iman said were translated into Anna Wierzbicka's meta-language that we mentioned in Chapter Two, some of the sentences would sound exactly like what !ui and !ao said.

We also interviewed hunter-gatherers from the tribe of the Matis in the heart of the Amazon, whom we met in Chapters Three and Six. When we asked them what love is, they told us they don't know because in their culture there is no such thing.

"We hear white people say *mi amor, mi amor*, but we don't say that; we call one another husband or wife," we were told by 60-year-old **Tume** [p. 268].

When we delved more deeply into talking about relationships and emotions, however, we began to have the impression that though there is no word for love, they feel something similar. Perhaps the person best at expressing this was **Baritsica**, 40, when we asked him to describe his feelings for his spouse, **Shawa** [p. 272].

"I think about her a lot, both with my heart and my head. I feel a lot for her and I know she feels for me, that is why we are together. I am glad she likes me. I feel good because of that. In the morning I wake up in my hammock with an erection, I go to her hammock, I lie next to her, and then we have sex."

Most of the couples we spoke to all over the world were too embarrassed to speak about sex. And we were often too embarrassed to introduce the topic. Only a few couples mentioned sex on their own, describing it as an essential component of love. Aside from Baritisica, **Vander** and **Fernanda** [p. 248], also from Brazil, spoke without embarrassment about sex at the other end of the country from where the Matis live—in Rio De Janeiro, one of Latin America's most modern cities.

"It doesn't matter how much you love each other, if there is no sex, the relationship won't work!" Vander declared.

"This is the foundation, the primordial, without it there is nothing!" Fernanda agreed.

"Sex is the first and the last, and all the rest is secondary, otherwise over time you become like brothers. Love without sex is nothing!" concluded Vander, his tone a little irritated but also confident.

We didn't just find similarities and patterns that repeated in the stories people from the most different cultures told us, we also found them in the non-verbal communication that often exposes what verbal communication tries to hide. With speech, it is easy to be manipulative. Often we do not verbally say what we really think and feel, but rather what we want to show we think and feel. Non-verbal communication is far more difficult to manipulate, and it often exposes what we truly think and feel even if this is not what we're saying.

Although in our interview **Fahad** from Saudi Arabia said that he and his wife **Tamadur** [p. 6] hadn't spoken until recently about love or emotions, nor did they display affection in public in any way, when I asked them to pose for a photograph at the end of the interview, Fahad took his wife Tamadur by the hand. This surprised us, because in Saudi Arabia we had often seen male friends holding hands, but almost never saw spouses do the same. Moreover, never in all the Arabic countries I have visited have I seen a woman who covers her whole body and face publicly before strangers express any sort of emotional intimacy with a physical sign.

As we were taking pictures after our interview with **Duddley** and **Juliane** [p. 133] from the Solomon Islands, they also held hands. They stood in front of their house, she only wearing her grass skirt, he only in his loincloth made of tree bark, as a dozen inquisitive people from the village watched on the side. Maybe there would have been nothing strange about it if Duddley hadn't told us moments before in their interview that in their culture all touching, hugging, kissing, and holding hands outside the house were strictly banned. Nobody would think of doing such a thing outside the house, because their neighbors could tease them about it, gossip about them, or even, we were told, kill them.

If men and women don't engage in public displays of affection in their cultures, why then did Duddley and Juliane as well as Fahad and Tamadur hold hands when I took their picture? Was this a spontaneous non-verbal reaction that disclosed the universality of love and its signs, or was it perhaps evidence of the influence of Western values even in some of the most traditional corners of the planet?

We noticed and recorded non-verbal signs of public displays of attachment and affection, small gestures of tenderness, warm gazes, sparking eyes, and sighs of emotion in many of the interviews regardless of whether the protagonists were part of traditional or modern cultures or the partners had chosen each other or their relationship had been arranged by parents or other matchmakers, even in some of the marriages that were categorized as forced. But, by the same token, in some of the arranged marriages as well as in some of the autonomous ones, in both traditional and modern cultures, we spoke with people who showed no signs of caring and attachment for their partners; their non-verbal communication showed cold and restrained relations without a lot of emotion.

How to conclude, then, on the question of whether love is universal or not?

We spoke about this with anthropologist Dr. **William Jankowiak**, who, globally, is one of the most competent scientists in this area. We mentioned earlier that his research into the universality of love shifted the ruling paradigm in the academic world. We asked him to explain what this ruling paradigm had been before his studies were introduced.

"When I began to ask whether love is universal in the 1980s, this was still a controversial subject," the famous anthropologist began the story at his home in Las Vegas. "At universities, they were teaching that love is a European contribution to world culture. That the French discovered it, and everyone else copied this from them. Through most of academic history, the opinion prevailed that Westerners have love, while the savages, meaning all those who are not Westerners, have only sex. It is very important to understand why love wasn't recognized more broadly: because this was our disease, we were culturally sophisticated, we suffered for love, while the savages lived in a natural state, they had good sex, but they weren't burdened by the moral concept we call love. I couldn't agree with this."

"But how is it possible that the paradigm lasted as long as it did?"

"This also fascinated me. In the 1920s, a psychologist by the name of John Watson claimed that love was not universal to the human race, and in saying that, he didn't have only romantic or passionate love in mind, but love in the broadest possible sense. He argued that even a child doesn't love its mother, but is only motivated by interest, because it needs nourishment from her. This slowly began to change in the 1950s when primatologist Harry Harlow ran a test with monkeys. He gave newborn monkeys monkey dolls instead of their biological mothers and they developed emotions toward them, though the dolls gave them nothing. If other primates are capable of developing emotional relationships, why wouldn't Homo sapiens? It is almost unbelievable that people even thought that way!"

He was a little agitated while he was saying this and then, all of a sudden, burst out laughing.

"And not only that. Academics are the most cynical of people. Men dominated academia at that time, and they thought that anything having to do with emotions did not merit study, that these are childish matters, that real men must study economy or history. Also, since 'common people' suffer because of love, academic professors felt they were above all this, that they mustn't stoop so low and deal with something as fickle as emotions. Perhaps they were masking their own failures in love. My personal experience in love was also a total failure. This was precisely what drove me to study love."

"But it is such a broad topic—how is it even possible to study the universality of love?"

"In the early 1980s, I worked in China and at that point I didn't think that romantic love is universal. Some of the Chinese people I interviewed told me about love, but I thought this was just proof of the penetration of Western values, I was convinced that they were simply trying to present themselves as modern people. But working on my dissertation, I studied some ancient, thousand-year-old texts from the Tang dynasty and realized that they were not only speaking about love, but about love exactly the way the contemporary Chinese people I'd interviewed had spoken of it! I got on the phone and called up my good friend, anthropologist Barry Hewlett, who studied Aka Pygmies, hunters and gatherers in Central Africa. I asked him whether he saw any signs of romantic love among the Aka. His first response was 'absolutely not' and he stated that the Aka don't have romantic love. Then I asked him whether he ever saw an Aka suffer for a partner they had lost and that they were attached to. After a long pause, he said he knew a young man who was very close to a young woman, and when she left him, he climbed a forest canopy, put a vine around his neck, and hanged himself. To me, that was an unquestionable proof of romantic, passionate love. That caused me to start talking to ethnographers, working with a variety of people all around the world, and particularly people working with hunters and gatherers. If something is conditioned through biology, then it must be present in the societies of hunters and gatherers—their societies are the oldest, simplest, and least influenced by global culture. Little by little, I realized that people all around the world are more or less the same."

William Jankowiak told us how he personally contacted many anthropologists and ethnographers, and where he couldn't make personal contact with them, he studied their field notes as well as the Human Relations Area Files, an ethnographic database that includes detailed insights into 186 representative cultures, both contemporary and from the past, designed to meet the needs of intercultural research. And little by little, he found proof of existing romantic feelings in 100% of the hunter-gatherer societies and 93% of all societies. The fact that he found no proof for the remaining 7% of cultures, he explained, didn't mean there had been no romantic love there, but just that this hadn't been registered in those cultures. When Dr. Jankowiak's study was published in the early 1990s, it brought about a change in the way academia looks at love. Today, his is one of the most cited studies in the field of cross-cultural research into the study of love.

"In all these societies, we did find traces of the proof of love, but this doesn't mean that love happens to all members of a society," continued William Jankowiak. "We can't establish how many people in any given society fall in love, would this be only 2%, 50%, or all? We can't know this. But what matters is that we all have the capacity for it. When we conducted this study, neuroscience was still in its infancy. Today, thanks to the amazing advances in the neurobiology of the brain, we know precisely where in the brain is the center for romantic love. This is not a modern adaptation. It developed more than several hundred thousand years ago and is typical of humankind. Earlier, we thought we aren't built for love but learn it through culture. But we got everything wrong and backwards. We are built for love, but the society in which we live either supports this capacity of ours or suppresses it. And even in societies that try to completely control love they do not succeed in this entirely. Love is stronger than that."

"What we saw when we traveled around the world totally bears out your theory," I said. "But I'm interested to know—are the norms and rules of a society the only reason that love doesn't happen to everyone, or is something else at play here?"

"I don't know. I can't answer scientifically, but I can give my opinion based on my own experience."

"I am very interested to hear."

"I think that emotions are not sufficient for love. An ethical, moral decision is also needed. In the late 20th century, authors from various theoretical perspectives noticed this same thing. That we increasingly allow ourselves to be determined by states that are based on feelings, and as those states change, so we follow them. But long-term relationships cannot be sustained that way. There needs to be the *volition* to remain in a relationship and work on it, and not to allow our egocentric feelings to prevail. That is my opinion."

"So what, then, is love for you?"

"Oh, definitely—a decision!"

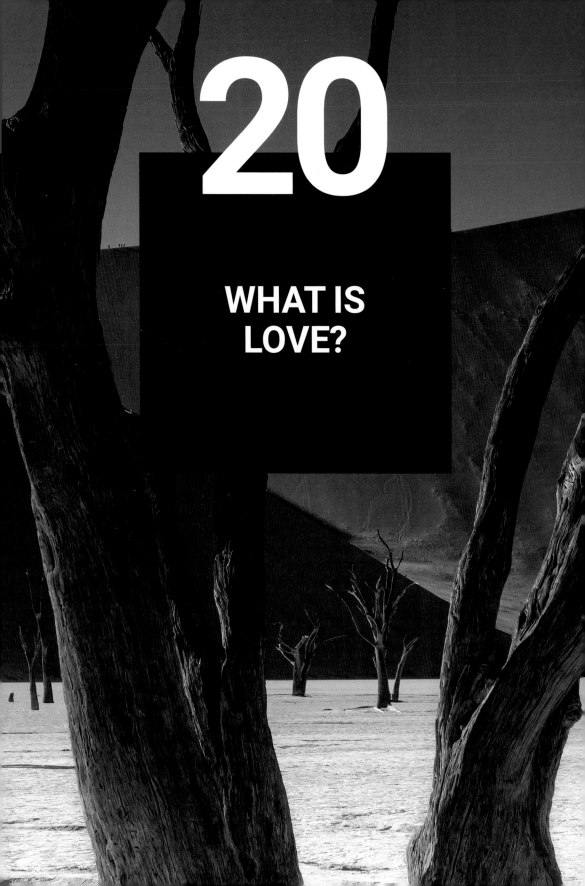

20

WHAT IS LOVE?

"Lacking in the definition of love is—decision, choice! Love is a choice!" Eva [p. 109], the Palestinian woman living in Costa Rica told us.

"Love is a combination of the psychological, physical, spiritual, and, more importantly—love is a choice! When I met Fabrice, I chose to love him. I chose to give this relationship a chance to grow. I could choose to love. The same way I can choose not to love. Love is a choice."

We asked everyone we interviewed what love is for them, and after they answered, we'd ask them to try to answer with a single word or brief phrase. When I analyzed the responses, I was surprised by how many different answers we were given; no one answer predominated. We spoke with 235 people in our 120 interviews, and there were more than 70 unique responses. No single answer was chosen by more than seven people. The most frequent responses were: respect, happiness, companionship, choice, commitment, sacrifice, life, everything, god, selflessness, acceptance, kindness, passion, trust, understanding…. This colorful assortment of answers is perhaps the best illustration of the likelihood that there is no single answer, that abstract concepts cannot be studied empirically, and that psychologist Dr. **Zoran Milivojević** was right when he concluded, with the vagueness of a horoscope, that love is "whatever people think love is."

There was great variety in the longer answers as well. **Djim** [p. 260] from Chad was very pragmatic when he answered that love is "a community of two people." For **Jenilyn** [p. 266] from New York, it is a "wavelength." **Richard** [p. 121] from Seattle said that love is the "action of building something that is constantly changing, you have no idea what it will look like in the end, but you're committed to building it." **Bernardo** [p. 138] from Colombia thinks that "nobody knows what love is, but it is something most similar to poetry." **Norkisaruni** [p. 106] from Kenya said that love "is what you feel for someone who understands you and doesn't beat you." **Tivo** [p. 380] from Zambia said that it is "unconditional acceptance above all expectation." And **Paolo** [p. 256] from Italy said that it is "that good feeling you can't have when you're alone."

Because we'd assumed that in our longer answers we'd find exceptional variety, we didn't just go around the world and survey people, but we worked to document their stories. Some answers don't mean much when taken out of context. Only within their story do the answers take on their full meaning. Let's have a look at this using the example of **Don** and **Sara** [p. 382], a lively couple in their 70s who live in the little town of Twisp amid the magnificent nature of the American Northwest. The first 20 of the 44 years they've been together they spent living in an Indian teepee in the wild where, on their own, they had five children and later went through two affairs, the serious, protracted illness of one of their children that ended in death, and many other challenges and stormy fights, teetering at times on the brink of violence.

"Love is a decision," said Sara. "A decision to be there for the other person whether you agree with them or not. Holding your tongue when you don't want to. Knowing that you can support the other person's decision or desire over your own. Not because you're selfless completely, but because you've made the decision to do so. I think it is when you're just hanging in there and going through the hard times and storms, even though you want to bail, even though there's a reason to bail."

The couples whose stories touched us most deeply, who brought us to tears, were always those who'd survived a difficult challenge. **Marcelo** and **Zulma** [p. 249] from Bolivia had been trying to have a child for years, but with no success. Zulma had been pregnant twice, but couldn't carry the pregnancy to term. After her second miscarriage, she thought she'd leave Marcelo so he'd have the chance to start a family with someone else, because that's what he'd dreamed of his whole life. But he wouldn't hear of it. He told her he wasn't with her so she could bear him children, but because he loved her.

On the Caribbean coast of Colombia, **Jorge** stayed with **Amalia** [p. 148] after she came down with a serious, incurable form of dementia. For years, she deteriorated gradually before his eyes, and by their 50th wedding anniversary she no longer recognized him. When we interviewed him, she was sitting there next to him, oblivious to everything, and he told us how sorry he was that she couldn't enjoy retirement and her grandchildren in the years that should have been their most wonderful, but how her condition was in no way an obstacle to his loving her madly and enjoying his happiness that he could be with her.

Sandra and **Patricia** [p. 246] from Germany met when they were still in school, when Patricia still hadn't outed herself as a trans woman and was going through life as Patrick, a man. For the first 20 years of their relationship they lived what appeared to be an ordinary, quiet life as man and woman in a heterosexual relationship, until Patricia could no longer bear the anxiety that came from suppressing the truth about her true nature—and out of fear that she might lose Sandra. She finally admitted to Sandra that she'd always been a woman and wanted to live as a woman. Heterosexual bookkeeper Sandra was suddenly faced with two major changes—that after their 20 years together her spouse would have all her sexual organs surgically altered and live publicly and sincerely as a woman, Patricia, and that she would suddenly be in a lesbian relationship. However, her first response was: "If you were hoping to get rid of me, you'll have to come up with a better excuse!"

I think these examples moved and inspired me because they speak of the heroes of our time who remained to fight for love when many would have given up. Is this a measure of true love? **Marcelo** [p. 111] from Chile told us that when he wants to see whether he loves someone, he wonders whether he'd stick around even if the other person ended up in a wheelchair. Perhaps this is a good criterion for evaluation. **Debora** and **Alexander** [p. 117] are the only couple we interviewed for whom we could say that they'd met Marcelo's standard of love, because on their first date they were in a traffic accident that left Alexander without one leg, but despite this they chose to stay together for life. They are also the only couple we interviewed whose love story passed this ultimate test of time. Alexander was killed a year after our interview.

Is death a measure of success? Must a relationship survive to the very end to be *true*? Death, the only certainty before us, threatening from all pores of life, sets and determines the measure and value of everything. When we march through the valley of death and *survive* together, only then can we speak of love. For love is not just a marvelous event, when our lives flow with milk and honey, love is also a terrifying process, full of horror and pain.

— — —

If this is love, if we dare to trust that we have perhaps succeeded in defining it, the next question that imposes itself is—*how* to love? If we presume that the most legitimate people to talk about this would be those who have been in their relationship the longest, then we'd have to look at what **Teruo**, 92, and **Michiko** [p. 147], 88, from Japan, had to tell us. They had been married 67 years, the longest of all the couples we interviewed. When we asked them what love was for them, Teruo rested his finger on his lower lip, slightly furrowed his brow, and said:

"Hmm, I've never thought about that."

"Nor have I," mused Michiko.

Does this mean that over-thinking it is not so wise? Perhaps.

Although I often envy people like Teruo and Michiko and think about whether it would be possible to *unlearn* all I have learned and live a simpler life, I can't help myself. I am curious. And I respond to the summons of my intuition that compels me to learn. So, I tend to agree with anthropologist Dr. **Helen Fisher**, who says that the more we know, the better equipped we are to face reality.

"Today, we have magnetic resonance imaging and with it we can scan brains!" exclaimed Helen Fisher. "And thanks to this we have discovered that there are couples who, after 20 and more years, succeed in keeping active all three cerebral systems for creating relationships—sex drive, feelings of intense romantic love, and feelings of a deep cosmic connection to the person. This is what I could call *real* love."

"So, what can we learn from these couples?" we asked her.

"In enduring happy relationships there are three cerebral systems that are especially active. The empathy system, the system that controls stress and emotions, and the system for what I call 'positive illusions'— the ability to overlook what you don't like about somebody and focus on what you do. So we need to express empathy, control our own stress and emotions, overlook the negative things and focus on the positive ones. And keep the sex drive alive! How can we do this? By having sex as frequently as possible! Sex is good for us. It triggers the dopamine system and sustains feelings of romantic love. Orgasm floods us with oxytocin, gives us the feeling of attachment. Sex is good for the body, good for the brain, for immunity, for the growth of brain cells, for the health of muscles, lungs, bladder, skin…. For maintaining romantic love, we need to do novel things together. Novelty, novelty, novelty! This is the main recipe—introduce novelty to our lives! That is why vacations are romantic, because we have new experiences. And for maintaining a sense of cosmic union and attachment: hold hands, touch each other as much as possible, kiss, hug—all these drive up the oxytocin system and develop feelings of attachment."

"You don't discover the good relationship, you create it!" said psychologist Dr. **Barry Schwartz**, author of the theory about the paradox of choice. "When a relationship isn't excellent, people have the tendency to think about all the other options they're missing out on, and then awkwardly conclude that some of these potential relationships might be better. But the key is to understand that a good relationship isn't found, it's created!"

Barry Schwartz advocates for modern stoicism, minimalism, and voluntary simplicity[1].

"Our culture tells us to make our lives more complicated, spend more, increase our options, work more…. This is being a good citizen. I think these should be resisted. If we simplify life, if we reduce the choices that aren't important and dedicate ourselves to those that matter, this will be better for us and for the planet. The secret to happiness is in lowering expectations. When we have a high level of expectation, even top-notch experiences can't match them. If we have realistic expectations, our realistic experiences can reach and outstrip them. Of course this doesn't mean that we need to do away with all expectations and tolerate everything bad. The secret, as always, lies in finding a balance. We need to adjust our expectations to reality. I believe that handling expectations is one of the most important and wisest things we can do—and the good news is—it is within our power!"

If we are to have realistic expectations, we need to know the world better. And ourselves. This is why I think that the ancient imperative of 'know thyself' is more relevant now than ever. Perhaps psychotherapist Zoran Milivojević showed me this the most clearly.

"We can imagine the human conceptual apparatus as a camera. When we're born, the world looks like a murky brightly colored image with low resolution, but the more we learn about the world, the greater the resolution and the image grows clearer and more detailed. The more we learn about the world, the more nuances we discern, the better we understand the emotions and processes that are happening inside us, the influences from without that shape us, the assumptions we have about the world around us and ourselves—the more we increase the resolution of the image. And an image with low resolution may be enough for us to move, for us even to find the right path, but the clearer the image we have, the more precisely we'll be able to move through life and accomplish what we truly need, to become what we want to be."

— — —

In closing, all I have left is to ask whether we've learned something through this process. I believe we have. When we embarked on the project, Anđela and I held certain assumptions about love that were not, perhaps, functional and possible to sustain—that love is the meaning of life, that love must last forever, or that happiness isn't possible without love. Both of us deconstructed certain shared illusions as well as some of our own. Although I was afraid that in doing so I'd lose a part of myself, now I feel that I've actually come a little closer to myself. And to us. I think that both of us can see each other more clearly and we now know each other a little better and love each other more deeply.

With each new shared victory, with each illusion unmasked, with each day we spent together, the chasm between us from the beginning of this story seemed a little smaller. Being in love gives us the illusion that there is no chasm. Reality shows us it does exist. Love teaches us how to bridge it.

We learned that modern society no longer guarantees emotional safety and certainty, that we cannot rely absolutely on one another, that we can no longer be sure that our partner will always be there for us, regardless. They won't. This must be earned. But that suits me. Because this way, I don't take our relationship for granted, I need to fight yet again for it each day. This is the more challenging path. But I always prefer the more challenging paths. Because they are the only place where I can use and practice the little freedom I have.

I have learned that our will is far less free than we'd like it to be or that our society tells us it is. We are slaves to an entire series of influences from nature and society that stand behind our thoughts, deeds, actions, and even behind many of our choices. Freedom, therefore, isn't something we do or don't have. We are free only up to a point. But our decisions and choices are the area where we can practice our freedom most. Choosing deliberately, choosing the harder paths, we conquer more and more freedom, inch by inch. I feel that freedom must be conquered. I believe that life evolves toward greater freedom. But this is a long journey to distant horizons through which, perhaps, the universe realizes its purpose. We still have a lot to learn. But I think we're on a good path.

This is, ultimately, all that matters. That we're on a good path. As always, there is nothing that delights me and fulfills me as much as a good journey, the *true* journey. And this journey is the best of all.

INTERMEZZO 3

PURGATORY

"Where do we go from here?" Anđela asks while we are in the bathroom getting ready for bed. We follow a practiced sequence that has come about spontaneously, which, in the crowded bathroom, looks like a grotesque dance as we take turns at the toilet, the sink, and negotiate our way around each other in passing…. Through the toothpaste foam we talk, our pace doesn't flag.

"Where can we go, we're still not done with this," I say, because she is still working on the movie, and I'm still working on the book. We have been at this for almost a year now since we returned from our trip around the world. Over the last ten days the coronavirus hit us, as well, luckily without serious consequences, but we retreated into self-isolation to my parents' cottage in the hills not far from Zagreb. I've already spent two winters here alone while I was writing some of my earlier books. I'm glad that we're here together now.

"That doesn't matter, come on, let's dream about something, so we have a goal to work toward…. Let's go somewhere warm, we should give ourselves a treat after all we've accomplished this year. And I'm missing travel, badly," she mumbles while brushing her teeth.

"But the world is being shaken by the pandemic, this isn't a time for traveling. If we buy tickets, there's a good chance we might not be able to use them. Can't we wait a few more months for things to hopefully get better?"

"Some countries are open. It's possible to travel to Cuba, the Dominican Republic, the Canary Islands, and I had a look at the Seychelles, Mauritius…."

"What about an exotic winter destination? A little house in the snow, in Switzerland, for instance, or Bosnia? I'd actually prefer a good round of skiing more than going to the sea."

"*You* would prefer *that*. See how different we are…" she spits the toothpaste into the sink and rinses her mouth with water. I spit too and reach for the towel.

"That isn't such a difference! After all, we could do both. Okay, let's go somewhere warm for New Year's…. Hey, what if we went somewhere we didn't go last year, we could keep going on the love around the world story—a sequel; we could find more people to interview…."

"Wait! Are you fucking with me?" she interrupts me, shocked, glares at me with a threatening, dark look full of disbelief and holds it frozen for a moment.

I feel as if I can hear the buzzing inside her head. I was not fucking with her, I didn't even know what I was saying, I was just letting ideas run through me, unfiltered…. But her reaction immediately reminds me of the chasm. I glare back at her chillingly in order to gain credibility for the move that is supposed to save the moment and… I burst out laughing. She rolls her eyes and smiles.

"Should we have a look at what our options are?" I ask her in a penitent, friendly tone. I am hiding my relief. One apocalypse has just been averted. We're waiting for the next one. "You decide, we can go anywhere, we will buy the tickets and go, without laptops, without the camera. Just a small backpack. A bathing suit, phone, and a book; we don't need more than ten things, and whatever happens, happens…."

As always when she gets her way, Anđela is happily quiet, she smiles, spins on her heels and heads to bed. I walk behind her and see she'd be wagging her tail if she had one.

In bed we lie on our sides, facing each other. We're cupping each other's faces. The only light is the bedside nightlight. Outside, heavy autumn fog has blanketed the countryside and for days it hasn't lifted. But the sun is shining in Anđela's smile.

"Shall we say our vows?" she asks.

We composed our vows for our wedding and then read them simultaneously, out loud, before a hundred of our nearest and dearest people. After the wedding, we said we'd recite them now and then to remind ourselves of what really matters in life. We do this most often in bed, before sleeping, like a prayer, to see us off into our dreams.

"Let's."

We breathe deeply in and out to bring ourselves into sync, and then start speaking in unison, sentence by sentence, looking into each other's eyes, smiling.

"You are my sun.
I am your moon.
You are my happiness
I am your peace
All my strength wells up from you

All my wisdom wells up from you
We'll count our love to the end
Me plus you
You plus me
And together we'll build our colorful world
Word by word
Deed by deed
I love you
I accept you
I belong to you
We are love
We are love
We are love
I want to spend my life with you
Because without you it's stupid."

We kiss tenderly and the moment before I'll close my eyes and turn off the light, I look into the deep blue of her eyes so this image will etch itself inside me, stay as long as possible in me, as darkness overtakes us all.

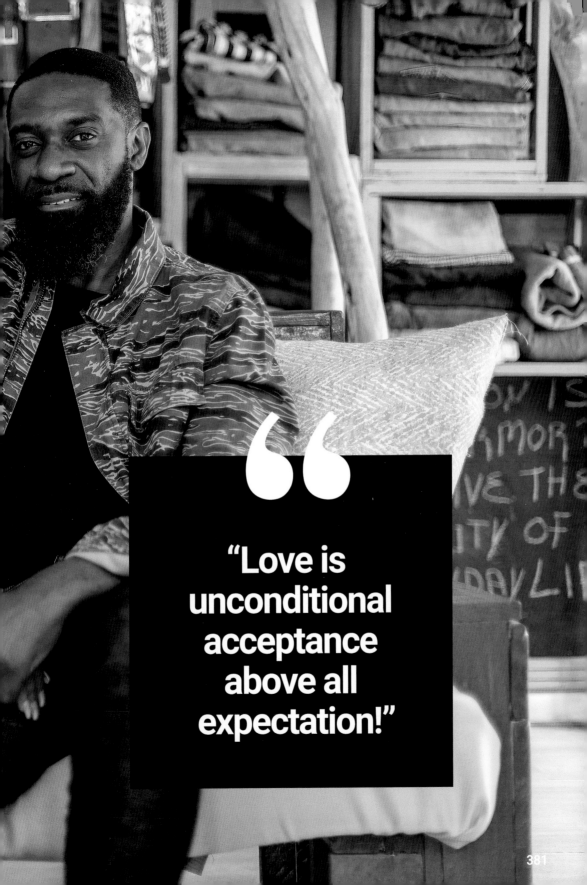

"Love is unconditional acceptance above all expectation!"

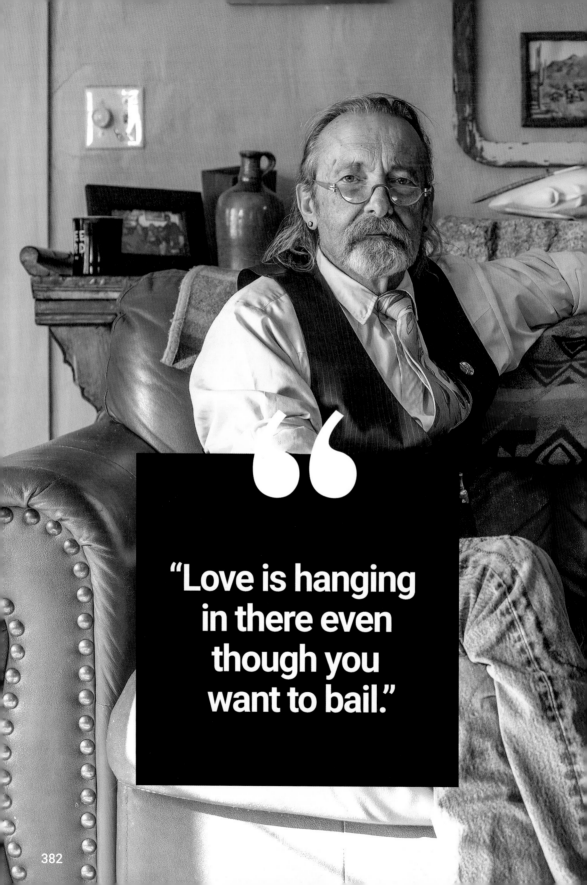

"Love is hanging
in there even
though you
want to bail."

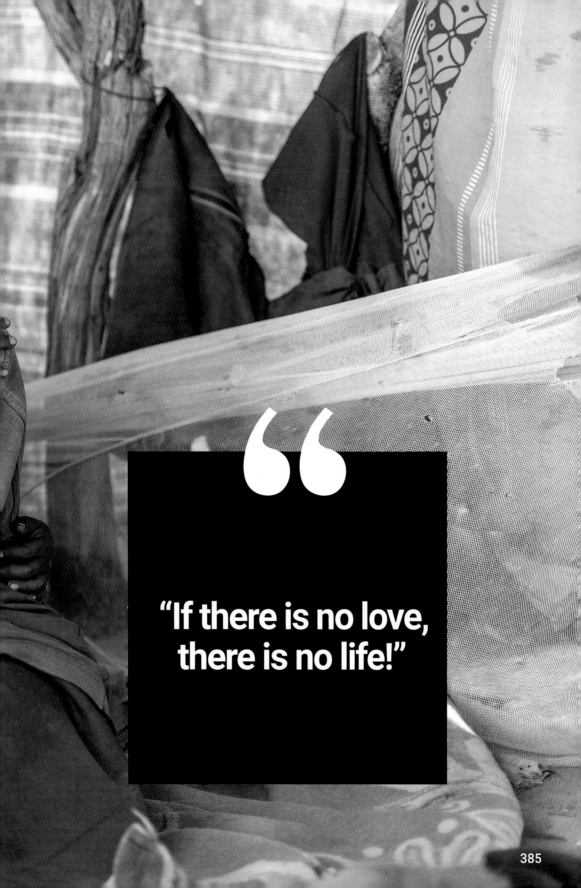

"If there is no love,
there is no life!"

P. 380

Salma (33) and Tivo (44) from Zambia knew each other in passing from the Zambian popular music scene, but their relationship only began after Tivo had left to work in the United States. For a year and a half, their relationship developed at a distance, and they then became engaged over the phone. "We got together in person only once when I'd flown out there so we could celebrate our engagement together," says Salma. "That's when we had our first kiss, our first dance, everything…. This is why I think our greatest strength is communication—for that was all we had when we started out. The first language we had to learn was the language of love."

P. 382

Don (69) and Sara (70) from the United States spent the first 20 years or so of their life together living in a teepee in the wild where, on their own, they had five children. "Sara was always more dedicated to our relationship than I was," says Don. "I was always holding the back door open a crack for other opportunities. However, when she learned of a second affair of mine, something changed. She changed. She realized she could manage without me, that she didn't need me anymore. She radiated self-confidence. She said, 'I am moving forward, you are free to destroy your own life.' Then I realized I would lose her and made the firm decision, if she'd give me another chance, to slam shut that back door forever."

P. 384

!ui (40) and !ao (36) from Namibia belong to one of the oldest peoples on earth—the !Kung Bushmen. Until ten years ago, they led a hunter-gatherer way of life in the Kalahari Desert. !ui had his eye on !ao for a long time and he thought about proposing to her. When he was ready, he crept up from behind her and shot a small arrow from his bow, which hit her on the buttocks. !ao pulled out the little arrow and returned it to him, which, according to Bushman customs, meant she was consenting to his proposal. "I love my wife," says !ui. "As I love my wife, I also love my kids. And as I love my kids, I also love aaaall the people. Even the people that I don't know, I love. But I love my wife the mooost. I hug her, we hold hands, make love, and this way our love grows! If there was no love, there would be no life!"

Behind the Scenes

30 countries   **365** days   **120** interviews

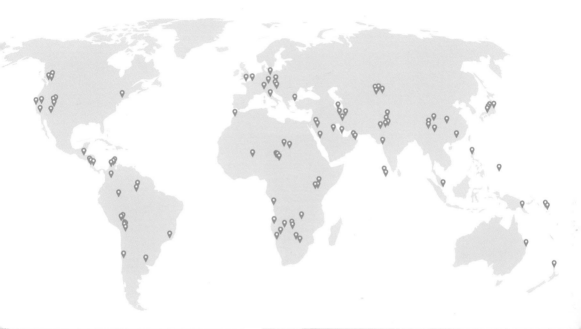

The Kalahari desert office

Sleeping in a train station in Japan

In the Amazon

Interview with Helen Fisher in New York

The first day in Saudi Arabia

Upon our arrival in Kyrgyzstan, Azamat gave us a warm welcome though we'd only met via couchsurfing

Our fixer and translator, Peter Marampei, at an interview in the Maasai Mara

On foot in the Himalayas

From the perspective of the people we interviewed

With Ghasiram and Kamla in Rajasthan

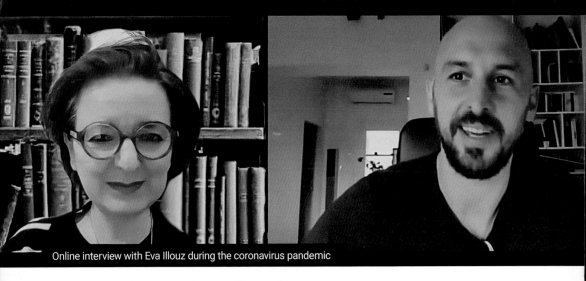
Online interview with Eva Illouz during the coronavirus pandemic

Interviewing Duddley and Juliane on the Solomon Islands

Sea kayaking in Micronesia

Camping in a bamboo grove in the middle of Kyoto

With the Bushmen in the Kalahari, Namibia

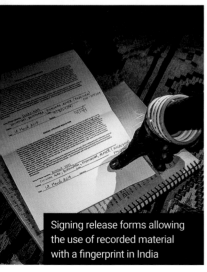
Signing release forms allowing the use of recorded material with a fingerprint in India

Celebrating in Palau

LOVE AROUND THE WORLD | DAVOR ROSTUHAR

NOTES

2. THE LANGUAGE OF LOVE

2.1. **Thobe [thawb]** — a long, loose men's garment, worn in the Arab world.

2.2. **Niqab** — a cloth covering that some women of the Muslim faith use to cover their hair and face, except their eyes. The veil that covers the whole face, hair and body is called a burka.

2.3. **Abaya** — a full-length, loose-fitting women's dress or robe which is worn over other clothes, and is often seen in the Arabic world. It is often combined with a hijab, a kerchief covering the hair and neck.

2.4. The theory of **linguistic determinism** claims that language and its structure entirely dictate the speaker's frame of mind and perception of reality, and therefore the organization of whole cultures. The theory was set out by Edward Sapir and Benjamin Whorf and was widely popular in the early 20th century. Contemporary linguists generally agree that this theory is erroneous, and instead the theory of **weak linguistic relativity** has been embraced, which states that language influences thinking and action, but does not determine them.

2.5. **Matrilineal** — handing down property through the mother's side of the family.

2.6. **Matrilocality** — a social system in which spouses live with the woman's family or tribe, or near them.

2.7. There are 56 ethnic groups in China, the most numerous of which are the Han Chinese, making up 92% of the population of China. The Mosuo people belong to the Nakhi ethnic group, numbering over 300,000 people, or about 0.02% of the population of China.

3. THE HISTORY OF LOVE

3.1. **The Neolithic or agrarian revolution** — the transition in human history from smaller, nomadic groups of hunter-gatherers to larger, settled societies, focused on agriculture. The agrarian revolution began in about 10,000 BC in the Middle East.

3.2. **The industrial revolution** — the period in the second half of the 18th century when the rural, agrarian communities of Europe and the United States developed into urban and industrial societies.

3.3. **The patriarchy** — a social system in which the men hold most of the power and leadership roles.

4. THE SOURCE OF LOVE

4.1. Ford, C. S., Beach, F. A. 1951. *Patterns of Sexual Behavior*. Manhattan, New York: Harper & Brothers.

Jones, D. et al. 1995. Sexual Selection, Physical Attractiveness, and Facial Neoteny: Cross-Cultural Evidence and Implications. *Current Anthropology*, 36(5), 723-748.

5. MARRIAGE

5.1. **Manyatta** — a fenced-in Maasai settlement consisting of several dwellings made of twigs, mud and cow dung, accommodating an extended family or clan.

5.2. **Female circumcision [female genital mutilation]** — a form of mutilation during which the woman's external genitalia are either partially or completely cut, removed or sewn. It is mainly practiced as a ritual in the traditional societies of Africa, Asia and the Middle East, most commonly among girls in their early childhood and up to the age of fifteen.

5.3. Gennep, A. V. 1960. *The Rites of Passage*. Chicago, Illinois: University of Chicago Press.

Arnold van Gennep formulates the **rite of passage** as a process that proceeds through three stages. 1) **separation** when the person withdraws away from their previous status; 2) **the liminal phase** when the person is briefly in a timeless and socially unstructured interval; 3) **reaggregation** when the person steps into a new phase of their life and acquires new and changed social status.

5.4. Turner, V. W. 1969. *The Ritual Process: Structure and Anti-Structure*. Ithaca, New York: Cornell University Press.

5.5. Arranged / Forced Marriage Statistics. https://www.statisticbrain.com/arranged-marriage-statistics/ (Retrieved January 1, 2021).

5.6. Bano, S. 2014. Personal Experiences of Marriage. *Muslim Women and Shari'ah Councils: Transcending the Boundaries of Community and Law* (142-180). London: Palgrave Macmillan.

Lee, G. R., Stone, L. H. 1980. Mate-Selection Systems and Criteria: Variation According to Family Structure. *Journal of Marriage and Family*, 42(2), 319-326.

5.7. India, National Commission for Protection of Children's Rights. 2018. *India Child Marriage and Teenage Pregnancy – Based on NFHS-4 (2015-16)*. New Delhi: Young Lives India.

Burns, J. Though Illegal, Child Marriage Is Popular in Part of India. *New York Times*. https://www.nytimes.com/1998/05/11/world/though-illegal-child-marriage-is-popular-in-part-of-india.html (Retrieved January 1, 2021).

5.8. Fisher, H. E. 2017. Future Sex: Slow Love and Forward to the Past. *Anatomy of Love: A Natural History of Mating, Marriage, and Why We Stray*. New York: W.W. Norton & Company.

5.9. Ortiz-Ospina, E., Roser, M. Marriages and Divorces. https://ourworldindata.org/marriages-and-divorces (Retrieved January 1, 2021).

Arranged / Forced Marriage Statistics. https://www.statisticbrain.com/arranged-marriage-statistics/ (Retrieved January 1, 2021).

Lee, J. Modern Lessons from Arranged Marriages. New York Times. https://www.nytimes.com/2013/01/20/fashion/weddings/parental-involvement-can-help-in-choosing-marriage-partners-experts-say.html (accessed on 1 January 2021).

6. POLYGAMY

6.1. Fisher, H. E. 2017. Is Monogamy Natural? Of Human Bonding ... and Cheating. *Anatomy of Love: A Natural History of Mating, Marriage, and Why We Stray*. New York: W.W. Norton & Company.

7.   THE PSYCHOLOGY OF LOVE

7.1.   Hazan, C., Shaver, P. 1987. Romantic Love Conceptualized as an Attachment Process. *Journal of Personality and Social Psychology,* 52(3), 511-524 (doi:10.1037/0022-3514.52.3.511).

Fletcher, G. J., Simpson, J. A., Campbell, L. 2015. Pair-Bonding, Romantic Love, and Evolution: The Curious Case of Homo Sapiens. *Perspectives on Psychological Science,* 10(1), 20-36.

7.2.   Zang, B. Is the Oedipus Complex Real? Encyclopedia Britannica. https://www.britannica.com/story/is-the-oedipus-complex-real (Retrieved January 1, 2021).

7.3.   Drescher, J. 2015. Out of DSM: Depathologizing Homosexuality. *Behavioral Sciences,* 5(4), 565-575.

Horton, K. 1937. *The Neurotic Personality of Our Time.* New York: Norton.

Millett, K. 1970. *Sexual Politics.* New York: Doubleday and Co.

8.   ASSUMPTIONS ABOUT LOVE

8.1.   Money, J. 1986. *Lovemaps: Clinical Concepts of Sexual/Erotic Health and Pathology, Paraphilia, and Gender Transposition of Childhood, Adolescence, and Maturity.* New York: Irvington.

Love maps — a concept introduced by US psychologist John Money; he defines them as assumptions we acquire as we mature and develop. These assumptions paint for us an idealized lover and an idealized template for sexual and erotic activity.

9.   LOVE AND IDENTITY

9.1.   Precht, R. D. 2017. *Ljubav: Dekonstrukcija jednog osjećaja* (189). Zagreb: V.B.Z.

9.2.   Precht, R. D. 2017. *Ljubav: Dekonstrukcija jednog osjećaja* (173). Zagreb: V.B.Z.

10.   THE SOCIOLOGY OF LOVE

10.1.   Kleinbach, R., Salimjanova, L. 2007. Kyz ala kachuuandadat: Non-Consensual Bride Kidnapping and Tradition in Kyrgyzstan. *Central Asian Survey,* 26(2), 217-233.

10.2.   OECD. 2019. *Society at a Glance 2019: OECD Social Indicators* (15-21). Paris: OECD Publishing.

Newport, F. In U.S., Estimate of LGBT Population Rises to 4.5%. Gallup. https://news.gallup.com/poll/234863/estimate-lgbt-population-rises.aspx (Retrieved January 1, 2021).

Deveaux, F. Counting the LGBT population: 6% of Europeans Identify as LGBT. Dalia Research. https://daliaresearch.com/blog/counting-the-lgbt-population-6-of-europeans-identify-as-lgbt/ (Retrieved January 1, 2021).

10.3.   **LGBTIQ+** — an acronym referring to lesbians, gay men, bisexual persons, transgender and transsexual persons, intersex and queer persons; the + serves as an umbrella marker for the inclusion of all people who function outside the framework of heternormativity, heterosexuality and cisgender.

11. ROMANTIC LOVE

11.1. Schnell, T. 2007. I Believe in Love. *Implicit Religion,* 3(2), 111-122.

12. FORBIDDEN LOVE

12.1. Goli, S., Singh, D., Sekher, T. 2013. Exploring the Myth of Mixed Marriages in India: Evidence from a Nation-Wide Survey. *Journal of Comparative Family Studies,* 44(2), 193-206.

12.2. Dhillon, A. India Expands Payment Scheme for Hindus to Marry Person of Dalit Caste. *Guardian.* https://www.theguardian.com/world/2017/dec/06/india-expands-payment-scheme-for-hindus-marry-person-dalit-caste (Retrieved January 1, 2021).

13. THE END OF LOVE

13.1. Betzig, L. 1989. Causes of Conjugal Dissolution: A Cross-Cultural Study. *Current Anthropology,* 30(5), 654-676.

13.2. Kreider, T. The Referendum. *New York Times.* http://happydays.blogs.nytimes.com/2009/09/17/the-referendum/?scp=3-b&sq=Light+Years&st=nyt (Retrieved October 11, 2021)

13.3. Dawkins, R. 2016. *The Selfish Gene.* Oxford: Oxford University Press.

13.4. Vedantam, S. If It Feels Good to Be Good, It Might Be Only Natural. *Washington Post.* https://www.washingtonpost.com/wp-dyn/content/article/2007/05/27/AR2007052701056.html (Retrieved January 1, 2021).

14. MODERN LOVE

14.1. Precht, R. D. 2017. *Ljubav: Dekonstrukcija jednog osjećaja.* Zagreb: V.B.Z.

14.2. Rosenfeld, M. J., Thomas, R. J., Hausen, S. 2019. Disintermediating Your Friends: How Online Dating in the United States Displaces Other Ways of Meeting. *PNAS,* 116(36), 17753-17758.

15. POLYAMORY

15.1. Moors, A. 2016. Has the American Public's Interest in Information Related to Relationships Beyond "The Couple" Increased Over Time?. *Journal of Sex Research.* 54(6), 677-684.

15.2. Langdridge, D., Butt, T. 2005. The Erotic Construction of Power Exchange. *Journal of Constructivist Psychology,* 18(1), 65-73.

16. THE LIMITS OF LOVE

16.1. **Pansexuality** is a sexual orientation based on emotional and sexual attraction to people regardless of their sex and gender identity.

16.2. Aunos, M., Feldman, M. 2002. Attitudes toward Sexuality, Sterilization and Parenting Rights of Persons with Intellectual Disabilities. *Journal of Applied Research in Intellectual Abilities,* 15(4), 285-296.

17. THE FUTURE OF LOVE

17.1. Schuldt, C. U: Precht, R. D. 2017. *Ljubav: Dekonstrukcija jednog osjećaja* (273). Zagreb: V.B.Z.

17.2. Precht, R. D. 2017. *Ljubav: Dekonstrukcija jednog osjećaja* (274). Zagreb: V.B.Z.

17.3. India, National Council of Applied Economic Research. 2005. *India Human Development Survey 2005*. New Delhi: Inter-University Consortium for Political and Social Research.

Drey, P. India's Arranged Marriage Traditions Live on in U.S. *New York Times*. https://archive.nytimes.com/www.nytimes.com/uwire/uwire_APLJ050720039401343.html (Retrieved January 1, 2021).

17.4. Ortiz-Ospina, E., Roser, M. Marriages and Divorces. https://ourworldindata. org/marriages-and-divorces (Retrieved January 1, 2021).

20. WHAT IS LOVE?

20.1. **Voluntary simplicity** is a way of life guided by simplicity and minimalism; it abandons the race to acquire wealth, prestige and material goods and instead promotes an authentic life and the balance between the internal and the external worlds. This concept was introduced in 1936 by US philosopher Richard Gregg.

SCHOLARS

Anna Wierzbicka

Professor of linguistics at the Australian National University in Canberra, Australia. She was born in 1938 in Poland and earned her doctorate at the Institute for Literary Research, Polish Academy of Sciences. She is known for her contribution to intercultural linguistics and semantics.

• Wierzbicka, A. 1972. *Semantic Primitives*. Frankfurt am Main: Athenäum-Verlag.

• Wierzbicka, A. 1980. *Lingua Mentalis: The Semantics of Natural Language*. Sydney: Academic Press.

• Wierzbicka, A. 1985. A Semantic Metalanguage for a Crosscultural Comparison of Speech Acts and Speech Genres. *Language in Society,* 14(4), 491-514.

Helen E. Fisher

Biological anthropologist and researcher at the Kinsey Institute, Indiana University in Bloomington, Indiana, United States. Her work focuses on the evolution, biology, and psychology of human sexuality. She is considered a world authority in her field.

• Fisher, H. E. 2000. Lust, Attraction, Attachment: Biology and Evolution of the Three Primary Emotion Systems for Mating, Reproduction, and Parenting. *Journal of Sex Education and Therapy,* 25(1), 96-104.

• Fisher, H. E. 2004. *Why We Love: The Nature and Chemistry of Romantic Love*. New York, Henry Holt & co.

• Fisher, H. E. 2017. *Anatomy of Love: A Natural History of Mating, Marriage, and Why We Stray*. New York: W.W. Norton & Company.

Eva Illouz

Sociologist whose scholarship is focused on capitalism, emotion, gender and culture. She researches topics such as the impact of capitalism on emotions, commodification of romance, and the meaning of freedom, choice, and individualism in the modern world. She teaches at the Department of Sociology of Hebrew University of Jerusalem, Israel.

- Illouz, E. 1998. The Lost Innocence of Love: Romance as a Postmodern Condition. *Theory, Culture & Society,* 15(3-4), 161–86.
- Illouz, E. 2007. *Cold Intimacies: The Making of Emotional Capitalism.* Cambridge, UK: Polity Press.
- Illouz, E. 2012. *Why Love Hurts: A Sociological Explanation.* Cambridge: Polity Press.
- Illouz, E. 2014. *Hard-Core Romance: Fifty Shades of Grey, Best-Sellers, and Society.* Chicago: University of Chicago Press.
- Illouz, E. 2019. *The End of Love. A Sociology of Negative Relations.* Oxford: Oxford University Press.

William R. Jankowiak

Professor of anthropology at the University of Nevada in Las Vegas, Nevada, United States. He is internationally known as one of the leading scientists in the fields of urban Chinese studies, urban Mongolian studies, polygyny among Mormon fundamentalists, and love around the world.

- Jankowiak, W. R. 1992. *A Cross-Cultural Perspective on Romantic Love.* Pittsburgh, University of Pittsburgh.
- Jankowiak, W. R. 1997. *Romantic Passion: A Universal Experience?* New York, Columbia University Press.
- Jankowiak, W.R. 2008. *Intimacies: Love and Sex across Cultures.* New York, Columbia University Press.

Zoran Milivojević

Psychotherapist with many years of experience in individual, partner, and group therapy. Works on developing transactional analysis in Serbia, Croatia, Bosnia and Herzegovina, Slovenia, and Montenegro. He is the author of the theory of emotions, the "model of circular emotional reactions." He lives and works in Novi Sad, Serbia and Ljubljana, Slovenia.

- Milivojević, Z. 2007. *Formule ljubavi: Kako ne upropastiti sopstveni život tražeći pravu ljubav.* Novi Sad: Psihopolis Institut.

Barry Schwartz

American psychologist studying the correlation between economics and psychology in modernity and capitalism. He teaches social theory and social action at Swarthmore College in Swarthmore, Pennsylvania, United States.

- Schwartz, B. 2004. *The Paradox of Choice.* New York: ECCO.

KEK
Klub za ekspedicionizam i kulturu

ABOUT THE PUBLISHER – THE CLUB FOR EXPEDITION AND CULTURE

We founded **The Club for Expedition and Culture (KEK)** in 2003 with the goal of exploring the world, documenting its natural and cultural wonders, and presenting our results to the public in books, reports, films, multimedia talks, exhibitions, and public appearances. The goal of all of our projects is to get to know and better understand the world in which we live while educating and promoting a greater tolerance for differences. KEK has already produced a series of culturally innovative interdisciplinary projects that have been greeted with enthusiasm and popularity by domestic and international publics alike. We have organized over 20 expeditions and trips to the most remote corners of our planet, collaborated with prestigious organizations such as *National Geographic*, and held more than 500 talks throughout Croatia and the region; during our projects we have also worked with over 250 schools.

Our biggest projects have produced the following books, which are available in English:

POLAR DREAM (2015-2018) – The project begins with Davor preparing for the first Croatian expedition to the South Pole and follows him as he undertakes the journey. He was the 26th person to have walked from the coast of Antarctica to the South Pole solo, unsupported, and unassisted. But this is not only the story of Davor's 48-day trek through one of the most extreme environments on Earth. It is also about what it takes to make your dreams come true. Davor explores questions such as: How to make a fleeting aspiration real? How to keep going when faced with impossible odds? And what do we learn about ourselves when we're faced with extreme conditions? *Polar Dream* is an inspirational story about passion, endurance, and what it takes to believe in yourself.

CROATIA FROM ABOVE (2007-2014) – In collaboration with *National Geographic*, this is the biggest photography project in Croatian history. For seven years, Davor took bird's eye view pictures of Croatia. The book of photographs, entitled *National Geographic: Croatia from Above*, is the bestselling book of its kind in Croatia. Over three years, an exhibition by the same name was seen by two million people in 20 countries.

THE JOURNEY'S MAGIC (2012) – In the year in which the number of people traveling long distance exceeded one billion for the first time in history, *The Journey's Magic* searches for answers to several important questions: Why do we like to travel? How do our journeys change us? What impact does travel have on our planet? Though the narrative is, in essence, non-fictional, replete with references to scientific literature, *The Journey's Magic* is also rich in engaging anecdotes from the author's first decade of globe-trotting as a professional photographer and travel writer and takes readers on a journey from tourism's historical roots all the way to contemporary responsible travel/tourism. Today, in the age of 'liquid modernity'—an era in which we have all become nomads and when, as a civilization, we have thoroughly explored most of Earth's former terra incognita—*The Journey's Magic* guides us on a voyage to new horizons and offers us fresh insights and approaches to travel.

Follow us on social media:
www.facebook.com/DavorRostuharPAGE
www.instagram.com/DavorRostuhar

AROUND THE WORLD

ON THE PROJECT — LOVE AROUND THE WORLD

Love Around the World was created during 2019 and 2020 when Anđela and Davor Rostuhar traveled through 30 countries and held 120 interviews with both couples and individuals on the subject of love and relationships and exploring what love is, how it differs from one society and culture to another, and whether it is universal.

All the protagonists were asked a similar set of questions: how did they meet, how did they feel at the beginning of the relationship, how would they describe their emotions now, what expectations do they have for their partners, what are their strengths and weaknesses, how do they meet challenges, what do they think about adultery and divorce, what does love mean for them, where do their ideas about love come from, what do they expect from the future, and so forth.

Aside from the couples and individuals, preeminent scientists Helen Fischer, William R. Jankowiak, Eva Illouz, Barry Schwartz, Anna Wierbicka, and Zoran Milivojević were interviewed about their work in the disciplines of anthropology, psychology, sociology, neuroscience, and linguistics.

The project has produced a book, a 75-minute movie, and a series of two 52-minute episodes, which were made in collaboration with the production companies Drugi Plan in Croatia and Autentic in Germany. After the world premiere—Valentine's Day 2021—on German-French Arte TV, the documentary film and the book set out on their own journey around the world.

Visit our digital platform at www.lovearoundtheworldproject.com, where you'll find in-depth multimedia stories about the couples and scientists who were interviewed, the schedule of film showings and lectures, more about the project, and details from Anđela and Davor's trip around the world. Share your own love story with us, because *Love Around the World* goes on!

ABOUT THE PROJECT CREATORS

Anđela and Davor met in 2013 when she applied for a job at
the organization he'd founded: The Club for Expedition and
Culture. Their connection was immediate and, not long after
they'd started working together, they fell in love. So far, they
have worked together on three projects: the *Croatia from Above*
photography project, the *Polar Dream* expedition—the first Croatian
expedition to the South Pole—and the multidisciplinary *Love
Around the World* project. They traveled through 30 countries
around the world and filmed and interviewed 120 couples so
they could form a fuller picture of what it is that connects people
everywhere—love. After they came back home, Davor worked on
the book and Anđela made the movie *Love Around the World*.

THE JOURNEY'S MAGIC
Why we travel and how traveling changes us and our world
KEK, 2012

In an era when tourism has become one of the biggest industries in the world, and when each year more than a billion people journey beyond the borders of their native countries, Davor Rostuhar searches for answers to several important questions: Why do we like to travel so much? How do our journeys change us? What impact, both positive and negative, does traveling have on our vulnerable planet?

The answers, the author finds, lie at the intersection of history, science, and lessons learned during a decade of globe-trotting. This book is in the realm of popular science as it is permeated by the perspectives on the phenomenon of travel offered by sociologists, anthropologists, psychologists, and other scholars. 'The Journey's Magic' is so deeply intimate and inspiring that a strong desire to set out to the Journey will overcome the reader. Nevertheless, the reader will stay in the comfort of their home and continue reading, realizing that the book itself – as the author says – is a big and unrepeatable journey. It is an adventure that will tell you how to travel more reasonably, more responsibly, and more sustainably. It will teach you to believe in miracles and the magic of the Journey, as well as how to join a quiet revolution of those who already travel in order to make the world a better place.

208 pages.

POLAR DREAM
KEK, 2018

Outside the windchill is -40°C. There isn't another soul within 200 kilometers. And the goal, the South Pole, is still over a thousand kilometers away. All Davor has to do to give up is make a call on his satellite phone, then he can be rescued and returned to civilization, but if he does that, his dream of walking to the South Pole solo, unassisted and unsupported will be over.

This is the story of Davor Rostuhar's 48 day trek to the South Pole. It is also a story about what it takes to make your dreams come true. In this book Davor explores how we can turn a vague aspiration into reality? How we can keep going when faced with impossible odds? And what we learn about ourselves when placed in extreme conditions? Polar Dream is an inspirational story about passion, endurance, and what it takes to believe in yourself.

288 pages. 96 photographs.